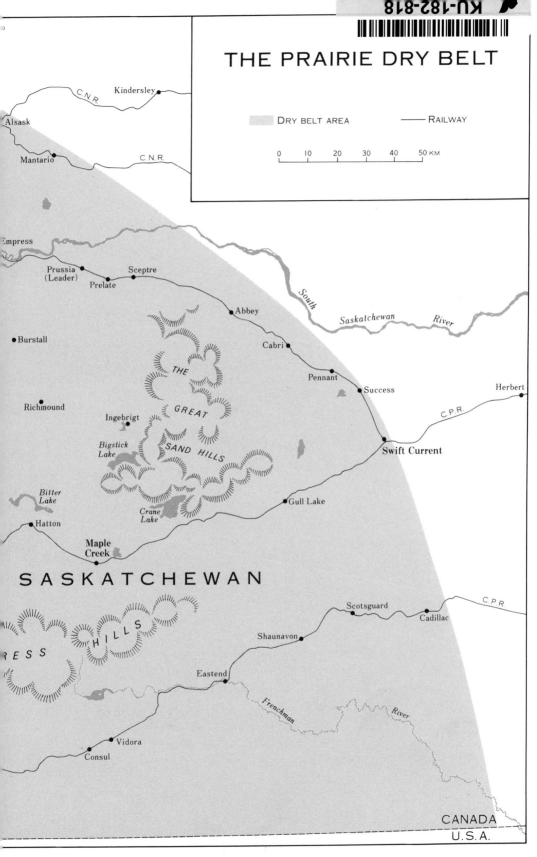

THE PRAIRIE DRY BELT

Dry belt area ——— Railway

0 10 20 30 40 50 KM

Kindersley

C.N.R.

Alsask

Mantario

C.N.R.

Empress

Prussia
(Leader)
Prelate   Sceptre

Burstall   Abbey

Cabri

Richmound   Pennant   Success   Herbert

Ingebrigt   THE

Bigstick   GREAT   C.P.R.
Lake
          SAND HILLS   Swift Current

Bitter
Lake   Gull Lake

Hatton   Crane
           Lake
Maple
Creek

SASKATCHEWAN

RESS   HILLS   Scotsguard   Cadillac   C.P.R.

                        Shaunavon

           Eastend
                        Frenchman   River

Vidora

Consul

South   Saskatchewan   River

CANADA
U.S.A.

Empire of Dust

EMPIRE

DAVID C. JONES

OF DUST

Settling and Abandoning the Prairie Dry Belt

UNIVERSITY OF
CALGARY
PRESS

University of Calgary Press
2500 University Drive NW
Calgary, Alberta
Canada T2N 1N4
www.uofcpress.com

Fifth printing 2002

National Library of Canada Cataloguing in Publication Data

Jones, David C., 1943-
    Empire of dust

Includes bibliographical references and index.
    ISBN 1-55238-085-8

    1. Alderson (Alta.)—History. 2. Medicine Hat Region (Alta.)—History.
    3. Droughts—Alberta—Medicine Hat Region—History.
    4. Agriculture—Alberta—Medicine Hat Region—History. I. Title.

FC3695.S65J65 2002   971.23'4   C2002-910853-5   F1079.S65J65 2002

1008130329

 Canada

We acknowledge the financial support of the Government of Canada
through the Book Publishing Industry Development Program (BPIDP)
for our publishing activities.

The Canada Council for the Arts
Le Conseil des Arts du Canada

Printed and bound in Canada by AGMV Marquis.
∞This book is printed on acid-free paper.

Typesetting by The Typeworks, Vancouver, British Columbia, Canada.

To the People of
Carlstadt/Alderson

CONTENTS

MAPS

ACKNOWLEDGEMENTS

I AM DEEPLY INDEBTED to three overlapping traditions in the writing of history—the one scholarly in which I took my training, the second popular, which holds the lessons of mass appeal, and the third literary, which harbors the secrets of art and expression. The academics I owe appear below and in the essay on sources; of the popularists, I thank the likes of Pierre Berton and James Gray for the sense of what reaches the common man; of the literary historians, I acclaim especially Donald Creighton and A. R. M. Lower for the mastery of their prose. Doubtless my mix of the three strains will disappoint some. For better or worse, however, this book is a modest attempt to inject pace, interest and literary values into academic history, without losing its rigor, completeness, respect for sources and insight.

Many people helped me write this book. For sharing their past, I acknowledge the late Nels Anderson, the late Orland Carlson, the late George Davison, the late Bertha (Swanby) Hostland, the late Neil Rutherford, May Carlson, Carl Anderson, Frank Cole, Bob White, Leonard O'Toole, Stein Gleddie, Vernon Gleddie, Sanford Gleddie, Howard Brigham, Jr., R. H. Thornton, Bud Starr, Thelma Starr, Olive Starr, Edna Lakie, Carol Poynton, Edythe Turnbull, Marie Parkkari, Inga (Carlson) Parkkari, Aune Parkkari, Doug Parkkari, Alice Loughlin, George Wagner, Alberta (Wagner) Pinsen, Florence Swanby, Jim Sharp, H. R. Metz, Edna Russell, Merv Nelson, Nellie McDougall, Ray McDougall, Ruth Collins,

Dale Cox, Ira Lapp, Buck Valli, Lois Valli, Margaret Holcek, Marjorie Gerhart, and Lilly Askew.

For their help beyond the call of duty, I am particularly grateful to Maren Burns, Ruth Daw, Pat Earl, Hazel Carlson, R. H. Cooper, Trygve Gleddie, Rolly Jardine, and Anita Jones.

For their comments, advice and other aid, I thank historians Alex Johnston, Paul Voisey, Ian MacPherson, David Breen, Andy den Otter, Roy Wilson, Rod Macleod, Doug Owram, Doug Francis, Nancy Sheehan, Bill Brennan, Howard Palmer, J. Donald Wilson and Gerald Friesen; archivists and librarians, Doug Cass, Georgeen Klassen, Tanya Yakimowich, Erik Gormley, Janet Kennedy, Susan Kooyman, Lindsay Moir, Catherine Myhr, Doug Bocking, Lloyd Rodwell, Ruth Wilson, Trevor Powell, Jean Goldie, David Leonard, Keith Stotyn, Merrily Aubrey, Cecil Halsey, Bill Curran, Trude MacLaren, Donny White, Greg Ellis, Michael Dawe, Rolly MacKenzie, and Tom Nesmith; agriculturists, the late Asael Palmer, Tracy Anderson, Doug Smith, and Wayne Lindwall. I also thank Hallvard and Betty Dahlie.

Half the photos were gratefully received from private citizens and were later deposited in the Glenbow Archives, along with relevant information on subjects and donors. They are cited in the text with their Glenbow catalogue numbers. Most of the professional photographs up to 1916 are the work of Chester Coffey.

For drafting the maps for the text and reproducing them, I acknowledge Marta Styk and Roger Wheate. Inge Wilson of the Cartography Section, Department of Geography, University of Alberta, prepared the endpaper map. For typing the manuscript, I recognize especially Shaun Penfold, as well as Lynda Krochenski, Lori Hadnagy, and Jeanne Keech. For funding the research, I credit the University of Calgary Research Grants Committee, the Alberta Advisory Committee for Educational Studies, and the Social Sciences and Humanities Research Council. Finally, for subventing the publication, I salute the Alberta Foundation for Literary Arts.

PREFACE   *Different Degrees of Nothing*

I REVISITED THE RUINS of Alderson in October 2001, contemplating a preface to a new printing of *Empire of Dust*. The ghost town sits south of Highway 1, half way between Brooks and Medicine Hat, in southeast Alberta.

Down a winding dirt road, I drove, past an abandoned field I had seen a farmer cultivating ten or twelve years earlier. The field was deathly grey, with dark clumps of thistle and burrs, pockmarking a peppery, ashened earth, utterly disfigured and disabled. Normally the prairie, even amid drought, is somewhat attractive, as the grasses appear to be mowed to a surface that resembles a beige-brown carpet. But this recently forsaken field was positively leprous.

In the townsite, the wind was howling from the southwest as ever, and the sun was out as usual. Here a drop of water vaporizes in seconds. Perhaps by instinct, I trudged first to the school, or its former site, where the hardy carragana bushes are now the sole pupils. They were spreading inside the cement and basementless foundation, and in the blowing they clung to their mooring like cables—for it did take determination to live here. Weathered, grey, wooden slats from the walls lay strewn about, mixed with ancient red bricks, stamped with "Redcliff," from the old Redcliff brick factory west of Medicine Hat.

Further south, in a basement, was the shell of an old Fargo truck, and elsewhere, a rusted bedspring and a derelict baby carriage. Walking was tricky, as the ground was colonized everywhere with cactus. The spines latch onto your shoes, and the shoes flick whole families, two and three at once, into your calves and thighs.

I trekked up Broadway Street, which ran north-south, perpendicular to the CPR tracks and Railway Avenue. Broadway was well-named for its width, a virtue that prevented the destruction of the whole town when the west side of Railway Avenue went up in flames in 1914, followed by the entire west block of Broadway in 1919. On east Broadway, at the demolished site of the Union Bank, a latter day dance hall, there were still piles of bricks, almost all broken, the good ones having been salvaged so long ago. Further east, the lone tree that had housed ferrugenous hawks in the 1980s was now down.

On the day I first saw Alderson in May 1984, I sensed but faintly the farm calamity brewing again in North America. In Canada a bonanza of agricultural credit in the 1970s had accompanied the expansion of overseas grain markets, but by the early 1980s the outreach stalled, surpluses appeared, and grain prices slipped. In 1983-84, number one, hard red, spring wheat sold for $194 a tonne; by 1987-88, it was $110 a tonne.[1] In southeastern Alberta, another dry cycle set in, and 1984 ended in drought reminiscent of the 1917-39 period.[2] The next year, conditions worsened, grasshoppers struck a million acres, and federal and provincial funding poured in $130 million for starving livestock.[3]

1. Terry Pugh, "The Invisible Crisis," in Terry Pugh, ed., *Fighting the Farm Crisis* (Saskatoon: Fifth House, 1987), p. 5.
2. Alberta, *Annual Report, Department of Agriculture*, hereafter *ARA*, 1984-85, p. 55.
3. *ARA* 1985-86, pp. 38, 59.

By 1986-87, financial distress, aggravated by years of sky-high interest rates, squeezed Alberta farmers relentlessly. In one huge region of the south, stretching to Saskatchewan, lenders reported 2 percent of farmers as bankrupt, 25 percent in arrears on their accounts, and 10 percent in serious default.[4] Simultaneously, land prices fell fast. Around Coronation, turf sold for $200 to $300 per acre, down 50 percent from 1979-80 values, on which many were still repaying insupportable loans.[5]

Meanwhile, city folk were often oblivious to the crisis. In July 1984, Vance Rodewalt, sketched an editorial cartoon for the *Calgary Herald*, featuring the desert in southern Alberta—the land searing, vultures soaring, skulls of steers lying about, and a thirst-crazed farmer crawling in the dust, eyes blank, tongue out, his hand up begging for help. Speeding to Calgary from the south-east is a car, licensed "Siddy." The driver spots the expiring farmer, races past him, and tells his wife, "You see that Midge, *that's* what I like about farmers, never too busy to wave!"[6]

Sometimes even prostrate tillers could laugh at their fate. Someone interviewed Neil Rutherford of Bowell in the 1960s about the harvest that year near Medicine Hat. "I put a crop in in '42," he said, "and it hasn't come up yet, and I'm not putting another one in till it *does* come up!"[7]

After *Empire of Dust* appeared in 1987, I sought relief from my long preoccupation with deprivation and disaster. *A Funny Bone That Was—Humor between the Wars* (1992), followed, perhaps naturally, founded on a humor column in the *Medicine Hat News* that caricatured all the strains and stupidities of the time.[8] Then I noticed that some "victims" of the long catastrophe from 1917 to 1939 had developed an immunity to dark events, a resistance, built on the reinterpretation of experience that a sense of humor always

---

4. *ARA* 1986-87, p. 66.
5. Ibid.
6. Vance Rodewalt, *RODEWALT—A Brush with Irreverence* (Calgary: Calgary Herald, 1988), p. 66.
7. Neil Rutherford, interview by David C. Jones, Bowell, AB, May 2, 1984.
8. David C. Jones, *A Funny Bone That Was—Humor Between the Wars* (Calgary: Detselig, 1992).

provides. Based on *Empire*, I penned a docudrama for the "Ideas" program of CBC Radio, and I began another book to answer questions I now deemed at least as primal as the disaster itself. *Feasting on Misfortune—Journeys of the Human Spirit in Alberta's Past* (1998) dealt with other crises too, but it also asked what the survivors of the dry belt disaster did with their misery, what kind of people it made of them, how they took in their misfortune, and how they invigorated amid grief.[9] Important matters these, for they plumb the depths of the psyche, and they begin to reveal the inner core of a Self so calm, so indestructible, that it is literally despair-proof, calamity-proof.

In 1999, Alberta Agriculture Minister Ty Lund lamented several hard blows—low market prices for grain and livestock, the Asian financial crisis, American trade action against Alberta agricultural products, and the spectre of drought again.[10] By 2000 some farmers had experienced five dry seasons running, and farm income support payments topped $300 million.[11]

In the southeast, the growing season of 2001 did not exist. Tens of thousands of acres supported no cattle at all, and herds were shipped to Saskatchewan for feed.[12] At Medicine Hat, by October, the previous twenty-four month period was the driest in recorded history. Average precipitation from April 1 to September 30 is 237 mm., but this year just 63 mm. fell. Seventy-year-old streams were drying up.[13]

No sooner did farmers turn their cattle into the drought ravaged crops than Bjorn Berg, an agricultural specialist, warned that even this solution might prove fatal. Stunted crops were potent in nitrates, which were richest at the base of the crop, and cattle were ingesting such high concentrations that nitrate *poisoning* was

9. David C. Jones, *Feasting on Misfortune—Journeys of the Human Spirit in Alberta's Past* (Edmonton: University of Alberta Press, 1998).
10. *ARA* 1998-99, p. 3.
11. *ARA* 1999-2000, p. 3.
12. Ric Swihart, "Summer Drought Effects Will Remain Over Winter," *Medicine Hat News*, Oct. 6, 2001, p. A4.
13. "Solberg Calls for Help for Area Farmers," *Medicine Hat News*, Oct. 2, 2001, np.

occurring. Stomach bacteria convert nitrates into nitrites which are then absorbed into the bloodstream, reducing the oxygen carrying capacity of the system. Plant nitrate levels of over .5 percent are dangerous, but in southern Alberta the year before, levels three times as bad appeared.[14] The blood of the afflicted bovine turns almost chocolate in color, eyelid capillaries turn brown, and the animal staggers and suffocates in the open air.

When provincial Agriculture Minister Shirley McClellan toured the farming communities around Medicine Hat after mid-August 2001, she saw an endless repetition field after field. "It's all the same," she said. "It's nothing. How many different degrees of nothing are there?"[15]

Next year, freakish rains moistened the Hat and southwest Saskatchewan, but drought was now everywhere else—in central and northern Alberta, central and northern Saskatchewan, and in two-thirds of the dry belt, where precipitation ranged from low to record low.[16] Near Hanna, Youngstown and Castor, Alberta, flights of grasshoppers chewed withered plants to the ground. One farmer lost 20 percent of his crop in twenty-four hours; he and a friend stood in a field and wept openly.[17]

Over thirty municipalities declared disaster, and on July 17, 2002, Alberta pledged $324 million in aid.[18]

It was all part of a massive North American tragedy—the unrelenting farmer exodus from the central core of the continent—from Oklahoma, Kansas, Missouri, Iowa, Nebraska, Wyoming, the Dakotas, Montana, and north into Alberta and Saskatchewan.[19]

---

14. Leah Prestayko, "Exercise Caution When Feeling Cattle Failed Crops," *Medicine Hat News*, July 25, 2001, np.
15. Jana G. Pruden, "Nothing to See on Drought Tour," *Medicine Hat News*, Aug. 18, 2001, np.
16. "Drought," *Calgary Herald*, July 16, 2002, p. A1.
17. "Farmers Battle 'Hoppers to No Avail," *Calgary Herald*, July 18, 2002, p. A10.
18. "Province Pledges $324 M to Help Farmers," *Calgary Herald*, July 18, 2002, p. 1.
19. For striking population losses in the American Great Plains states, from 1980 to 1990, see E.B. Espenshade, Jr., ed., *Goode's World Atlas* (New York: Rand McNally, 1995), p. 75; see also, Donald Worster, *Dust Bowl:*

But for all the Great Plains and all the Prairies, the quintessential sample and symbol of the overexpansion remained—Alderson.

Empire of Dust, the whole story, was meant to occur from the hour before dusk, when I first entered the townsite, until darkness fell. Much can be revealed in two hours of acute observation, and we often see so little. To stand in a silent, abandoned place where vibrancy once was, you cannot help but hear the voices and see the movement of shadows. You cannot help but become part of what you feel. And you cannot but feel the majesty of each soul facing its great adventure, as it steps into the unknown it has chosen for itself.

Yes, these are hallowed grounds, soul-testing grounds. In the late, hot summer of 2001, David Bly of the *Calgary Herald* stood, moved, amid the rubble of Alderson.[20] Yes, it ought to be made an historic site, thought he. There is much to tell here.

David C. Jones
August 1, 2002

The Southern Plains in the 1930s (New York: Oxford University Press, 1979); R. Douglas Hurt, *The Dust Bowl: An Agricultural and Social History* (Chicago: Nelson-Hall, 1981); Deborah Epstein Popper and Frank J. Popper, "The Great Plains: From Dust to Dust," *Planning* (December 1987): 12-18; James N. Gregory, *American Exodus: The Dust Bowl Migration and Okie Culture in California* (New York: Oxford University Press, 1989); Mary W.M. Hargreaves, *Dry Farming in the Northern Great Plains: Years of Adjustment, 1920-1990* (Lawrence, Kansas: University of Kansas Press, 1993); John R. Wunder, Frances W. Kaye and Vernon Carstensen, eds., *Dust Bowl: Americans View Their Experience* (Niwot, Co.: University Press of Colorado, 1999); Mary Nemeth, "Disappearing Saskatchewan," *Maclean's*, July 15, 2002, pp. 18-25.

20. David Bly, "Alberta's Disappearing Towns," and "Where Dreams Turn into Dust," *Calgary Herald*, Oct. 21, 2001, pp. A14-A15.

PROLOGUE   *The Untold Sorrow*

I CAME UPON THE RUINS of Alderson at May-end one hot afternoon in the hour before dusk. From the dark, oily CPR right-of-way thirty-five miles west of Medicine Hat, little at first distinguished itself from the pastel prairie of this barren expanse of short grass, cactus and low-lying burrs. But the sun, setting red, revealed with slanting rays the shadows of the hummocks and excavations of a departed race. In a land that Rudyard Kipling himself had once puffed up as the new Nineveh, there was hardly a board left block upon block, just the faintest impression of the criss-cross of streets and avenues.

It was half a lifetime since anyone had lived here and more than a lifetime since the village had been born in 1910 as Carlstadt, "Star of the Prairie." In those happier days of the land rush into the dry belt, the last great agricultural frontier of the southern prairies, Carlstadt was platted as a major distributing hub along two main business thoroughfares in the form of a "T"—the crosspiece, Railway Avenue running east-west, parallel with the tracks to the north, and the vertical stroke, Broadway Street, heading south.

I strained to see how it must have been. As the light faded, I moved swiftly westward, down overgrown Railway Avenue, stopping at the corner of Broadway where the Woollven store, the first business house south of the tracks, had stood facing the smart England and England Block, the gem of the first promoters. All the way to Tilley Street that block had burned to the ground in the inferno of the summer of 1914. Most of it had never been rebuilt, and so the prairie had reclaimed it.

At the west end of Railway was the mouldering foundation of the Carlstadt Hotel, once a three-storey edifice of elegance, the finest hotel of five in town. Now it was little more than a great pit, a mortared and stone-walled basement filled with rubble and refuse and rimmed with thistles and thorns.

As I made my uneasy way around the perimeter, the excavation resembled a barge sunken in the sands, its larder strewn across the hold in talus-cone shapes, as if the sinking had toppled columns of cargo. Halfway down the starboard side, I stumbled into the ill-wind of the sickening stench of carrion.

So choking was the smell in the warmth, that it must have come from this foul pit. Yet I saw nothing, until I looked back toward the bow—a calf had fallen into the hold, had struggled for God knows how long, and had died part way up the crumbling wall. It had been there for some time and was now plastered on the rubble like a lumpy brown blanket, trimmed with white and almost completely dehydrated by the hot, dry, sucking winds of this baked land.

My eyes moved slowly down the bowels of this strange barge and stopped near my feet at a mound of tarry substance with what seemed like pieces of rope and twine laid over it. I looked more closely and discovered the pieces were snakes, dozens, dead, lying belly up, curled and shriveled, young and old lying together in a grotesque tangle of seared tissue. I could not be sure of the species, though the country was full of garters and rattlers; nor could I bring myself to probe the ghastly heap for telltale rattles. How so many had come to this end was a mystery. It was as if some sadistic incendiary had somehow lured them from the crevices and crannies in these basements and roasted them en masse.

I shrank from the mound and stepped gingerly in the failing light down Broadway, past what had been the finest lots in town, until I came to the southernmost part. How immense the setting seemed, how distant the tracks, how broad the reach of the crosspiece of Railway Avenue. This had not been a tiny hamlet.

But what had caused such a fall, such total destruction? And what of the vast environs of this derelict town—what had happened to them and to the people who once lived here? What catastrophe had overtaken them?

The story of this ghost town and of the enormous surrounding tracts is a life-sized saga of frothy boosterism, lightning expansion, and utter miscalculation—of drought, destitution, and depopulation. It is a journey that begins with man at the pinnacle of his spiritual powers and ends with him cloaked in the darkness of the long night of the soul. It is the tale of the disaster that befell the prairie dry belt after the Great War, the untold sorrow of southwestern Saskatchewan and especially southeastern Alberta, an empire of dust.

Alderson, Alberta
May 26, 1984

1   The Wiles of the Desert

"O God, Help Me"

IN THE FALL OF 1876, Constable Mahoney of the North-West Mounted Police and a French half-breed freighter, en route to Fort Walsh with provisions, were near the forks of the Red Deer River where it joins the South Saskatchewan. More than a generation before the settlement of these arid plains, the land was barren and the route unpopulated. Mahoney's thoughts may have turned toward the harvest back home, for he had been a farmer two years earlier in Manitoba.

As the two men crossed the Saskatchewan, their boat capsized about forty feet from the far shore. The second they touched the shallows the half-breed instinctively sensed danger in the spongy softness of the river bottom scarcely two and a half feet below. Throwing himself forward, he half crawled, half swam ashore.

Mahoney, however, righted his huge six foot two inch, two hundred pound frame and proceeded to wade out. It was a mistake.

A long time resident of the region southward later described Mahoney's terror: "The bottom of the river was no longer sand; it was like muddy glue. Suddenly he sinks in. His feet have disappeared! He pulls his foot out and throws himself to the left. The sand comes up over his ankles! He pulls himself out and plunges to the right. Worse! The sand is up to the calf of the Mounted Police boot. Then Mahoney recognizes, with unspeakable terror, that he is caught in quicksands and that he has beneath him the fearful medium in which a man can no more walk than a fish can swim. Quicksand to the right and left. Quicksand all round him. He throws off his load, belt and revolver, and like a ship in distress tries to lighten himself. It is already too late. The sand has climbed above his knees. Meanwhile the breed, like a crazy thing, is running around hunting for a lariat or rope. No use; they are on the other side. Poor Mahoney is condemned to that appalling burial, long, infallible, implacable, impossible to avoid or to hasten, which endures for an hour or two, which seizes a man erect, free, in full health and strength, by the feet and, at every attempt he makes, at every shout he utters, drags him a little deeper, sinking slowly but surely in the bottom of the river bed, while he looks up on the blue sky above, the willows on the bank, the meadow lark singing on the knoll and an antelope gazing down spell-bound from a cut-bank on the left. Twenty minutes pass by; he is now up to the middle in water. Half an hour later he is only a bust floating—no, anchored—in the Saskatchewan. Realizing the end is near, he utters a prayer; calls the breed; makes a verbal will leaving the farm in Manitoba to his wife and children. He raises his hands and clutches at his hair! The water is now level with his shoulders! He says goodbye to the breed! Then he throws his head back like a man in a barber's chair. No use! The water keeps climbing. It laps around his throat. The horror-stricken face and wildly rolling eyes alone are visible. The mouth utters a hoarse cry, 'O God, help me!' The water puts its smothering hand over mouth and nostrils. Head bobs from right to left! Forehead decreases! No look! A little tuft of hair flutters! A hand comes to the surface, moves, shakes, disappears, then the current of the Saskatchewan rolls on as silently and relentlessly as before. . . ."[1]

The grisly tale was more than the sad end of a mountie. It was a revelation of things to come, a foretaste of the cold intransigence of nature, a parable of the relationship between man and water in the arid wastes. Again and again the great river and its tributaries, the Red Deer, the Bow and the Belly, would sweep away the interlopers, swallowing them up, sometimes snagging them on the bottom, other times spitting their carcasses out on sharp turns or sand bars. Always the river would be a force to reckon with, one with ability to give life and take it. Over the next half century, the pity lay in its seeming propensity to do more of the latter than the former, to offer through irrigation the wealth of Ophir and to deliver the poverty of the Sahara.

There was never any doubt in the mind of John Palliser, when he surveyed the same area earlier, that he was traversing the dark side of the moon. He saw the great river jutting through its deep, narrow valley of baked marls and clays, a jagged rent across an endless, parched plain of sage and sand and cactus. Everywhere what had been previously called the Great American Desert stretched to infinity. One night in southern Alberta the expedition camped on the remnant of a swamp where they butchered an infestation of rattlesnakes.[2]

Guided by Palliser's sketchy maps, Commissioner G. A. French and 275 troopers of the newly organized North-West Mounted Police force set out from Dufferin, Manitoba in July 1874 on an epic march to the Rockies. Their somewhat paradoxical purpose was to form peaceful relations with the Indians and to set the scene for the occupation of their country.

The march was most onerous and left an abiding impression on the minds of the mounties. By the time the troop crossed the midpoint of present-day Saskatchewan, French began to see what Palliser had seen—land of the "same hungry description." Sometimes "salt water or the refuse of a mud hole was the only liquid available," he wrote, "and I have seen this whole Force obliged to drink liquid, which passed through a filter was still the color of ink."

At Old Wives Creek French encountered a party of Sioux who had just skirmished with some Blackfoot near the Cypress Hills. "I impressed upon them the fact that we did not want their land," said he, who despite the intentions of his journey to link the country through show of force or force of arms, did not speak altogether deceptively. Just how the arid wastelands would ever be intensively settled baffled him. As he put it, "I think civilization will be hard pushed for room when it requires the coteau of the Missouri, at least for agricultural purposes."

Somewhat west of modern-day Medicine Hat, the weather turned cold, reminding French of the previous September when the ground was swept with a foot of snow and several men and horses froze to death. Already his mounts were wracked by hunger. Raked by cold rain and heavy winds, he camped on the edge of a deep coulee and directed his horses into a ravine for water and shelter. When the bone chilling sleet halted by mid-morning, he broke camp, there being absolutely no feed in the vicinity. So paralyzed from the cold and hunger were the horses that five could not climb from the ravine and perished in a few hours. Four more died later.

At the forks of the Belly and the Bow, the chief officers hoped for a week of rest and sustenance. Instead, they held a council of despair. With an unconscionable liar for a guide, his own scouts getting lost, his map egregiously misleading, and his animals starving, French waited for news from a trooper scouring the countryside thirty miles west. The mountie returned having seen "no signs of a road, not a blade of grass . . . buffalo moving south in thousands." Fearing impending doom, French shifted the camp to change the feeding site, adding mordantly, "if nibbling on bare plain can be called feeding." Horses, he noted, could at least pick up the strand or two of grass left by the bison, but the poor oxen could not. Consequently they were suffering far more than the mounts.

French had no sooner ordered Inspector Walsh with seventy men to Edmonton than a scout who had been seventy or eighty miles up the Bow River reported neither grass nor wood the whole distance. Clearly the country was a death trap. Countermanding his order to Walsh, French directed him to follow the main force toward Fort Benton to the south. One by one the oxen played out and were left behind. Not until close to the international boundary did the livestock come upon excellent feed. French and ten others then left the troop and headed speedily with empty wagons to Benton. They arrived in two days and returned with provisions and new horses to rendezvous with the troopers at a lake northeast of the Milk River crossing. Five weeks later the main contingent, tattered and scarred, arrived back in Winnipeg, having narrowly escaped the wiles of the desert.[3]

Ranchers and Would-be Settlers   SUCH EXPERIENCES CAPTURED the dominant view of the dry areas for many years. Yet, no matter how hot the summers, nor how frigid the winters, a single fact rose above all others—the land had supported thousands of buffalo for hundreds of years until the wanton killing time and their virtual disappearance in 1879. It did not take much grey matter to realize that the ground had inherent qualities as a grazing kingdom. The short grass was nutritious, the chinook winds melted the snow, the coulees gave shelter. In late 1881 John A. Macdonald's regime in Ottawa introduced a gilded grazing lease policy that allowed leases of up to 100,000 acres for twenty-one years. Huge cattle conglomerates were assembled, led by the Cochrane, Walrond, Oxley and North-West Ranche Companies. By 1884 Senator William F. Cochrane alone controlled over 330,000 acres.[4]

The cattle barons also had the blessing of a man who understood the dry belt as well as anyone. A former longtime surveyor for the Department of the Interior, and as of 1884 the department's superintendent of Mines, the ranchmen's benefactor was William Pearce. His job description was scarcely apt, for he performed a dozen functions—troubleshooting, advising, boosting, and so much of

The ranchers' benefactor—
William Pearce. NA 339-1,
Glenbow-Alberta Archives.

this and that, that he did much of everything. He soon became the central figure in the administration of the region—the czar of the department, as a colleague later put it.[5]

To Pearce southern Alberta and western Assiniboia were arid expanses, too dry for farming but ideal for ranching. The desert was real, requiring specific, responsible treatment of its natural resources. Cattlemen were the chosen people, and settlers the unwanted; grazing was in and cultivation was out. Under no circumstances were the sodbusters to interfere with the riders of the plain. It was not that there was no room for settlers, but the accommodation of their breed in the south would take place slowly, with the gradual development of irrigation.

Pearce was as much an apostle of irrigation—some called him a "nut" on the subject—as he was a defender of cattlemen. From the mid-1880s until 1894 when the federal North-West Irrigation Act was passed, he reported on irrigation, praised Mormon expertise in the art, assisted the drafting of legislation, and concocted his own personal project. Behind the scenes and in the spotlight, he promoted artificial watering, convinced it was the only means by which large tracts of the Territories could ever be settled at all.[6]

Of course, ranching was less expensive and rudimentary and was almost tried and true. From the beginning, therefore, Pearce entered into an iron-bound covenant with the stockmen, pampering and cosseting their industry at every turn. Pressured by settlers, he devised stock watering and shelter reservations so that the ranchers might monopolize access to water. As early as 1884, squatters were evicted from closed leases around Fort Macleod. When range war threatened in the next few years, the howling of the interlopers reached Ottawa, forcing the government to reassert its support for the ranchers, with modifications, and aligning the Liberal opposition with the sodbusters' cause.[7]

After the ranchers were obliged to provide homesteading provisions in their leases in 1892 (they could also *buy* 10 percent of the lease), Pearce vastly expanded the stock watering reserves. When squatters camped on the waterholes, he summoned the police on raid after raid to evict the miscreants. His reasoning was simple. When the squatters "stole" the waterways, the cattle naturally enough rubbed down the farm fences, and the squatters and their yowling dogs then ran off the cattle. Often the dogs would chase the stock without provocation. "In one run of a mile or two more flesh is lost than can be put on in two weeks," wrote Pearce. "Frequently cattle are absolutely ruined from the effects of dogging them."[8]

Pearce also resisted settler demands to scale down the reservations because the herds of a hundred to several thousand needed much grazing room, especially in summer when they would not wander far from water. At one point on the Belly River, the fencing of bottom-land homesteaders blocked access to water for thirty continuous miles, rendering useless 30,000 acres of grazing land.[9]

Such interference with the "natural" industry of the region was pernicious and irresponsible in Pearce's view. Even the small rancher came under his carping eye. The big men allowed their stock to run at large, and it was in their interests to keep all parts of the range accessible and in condition. The small rancher, on the other hand, generally kept his growing herd in winter close by in a narrow valley near a water hole, thus hogging and overgrazing an important area necessary for winter feed. "It has been asserted by those who probably best understand the situation," said Pearce, referring partly to himself, "that if settlement had been absolutely prohibited in all those portions valuable for winter pasture the country would have gained by such a policy."[10]

Deputy Minister of the Interior A. M. Burgess never shared Pearce's conviction about the desert and the uselessness of the region for farming. It was not that he disagreed, but that he was more open to experimentation on the subject. For years he suppressed Pearce's enthusiasm for irrigation, fearing it would discourage settlement because of the implication that the land would produce only with water.[11] "When the wave of settlement reaches the confines of the grazing country," he wrote ominously, "if that country be found fit for the purposes of actual settlement, it will in my humble opinion be impossible to maintain it for purely grazing purposes."[12]

Burgess knew that the West would some day step into the world's spotlight. And he was acutely aware of dissenting views concerning the desert. In particular, he had heard the sweet songs of a new, self-proclaimed maestro intent on piping the two tribes of the chosen people, Americans and Britons, into the heart of the dryness which to the maestro seemed more like some falsely maligned flood plain. The man was John Macoun. A botanist from Albert University, Belleville, Ontario, Macoun spent half his life in the self-imposed and oft misguided mission of debunking Palliser's warnings of deficient moisture.

Macoun's early opinion of the agricultural potential of the Northwest never changed. As he told the federal committee on agriculture and colonization in 1876, "the greater part of it is just as well suited for settlement as Ontario. . . ."[13] A year later, he recorded that save for a limited area the desert was a myth. True, Palliser's triangle for most years was overlarge—extending from modern day Brandon, 100 degrees west longitude, to the Rockies, 114 degrees west longitude. But the dry belt which was to succumb to disaster after the First War—the area roughly between 107 degrees west longitude and 113 degrees west longitude, sitting as the head of a bullet on the international boundary and curving northward to virtually 52 degrees north latitude—was scarcely limited. Nor was the broader expanse, nearly the whole of the original triangle, which fell during the Great Depression.

While Macoun's later, personal descriptions of the dry belt were by no means blanket approvals, he still saw glitter where Palliser had seen dust. With each succeeding observation in the next few years his rosy optimism grew. On one journey near present-day Maple Creek, Macoun's party visited a farm. "All the land broken up was in the flats along the creek and consisted almost wholly of soil which in my former reports I had pronounced worthless," said Macoun, deeply impressed. Apparently the farmer had located in April and had sown a little wheat before drought had set in, lasting all through June and leaving the seed dormant on the ground for three weeks. Nonetheless, on August 14 Macoun gathered heads of ripe wheat, and later he learned that most of the crop had ripened. "When I was there everything was growing finely but was generally very late," he concluded, adding with great significance, *"but the problem was solved that the apparently arid lands were only so in appearance, and that all the land where not covered with sand or gravel would yet 'blossom like the rose.'"*

The transformation seemed to occur at the touch of a plow. "Close to where [the farmer] had ploughed I could not penetrate the sun-baked clay," Macoun noticed with astonishment, "but not a yard away where he had done so I could dig to any depth. . . . On the one hand was luxuriance and life, while on the other the grass, artemesia and cactus gave evidence of, if not death, profound slumber. . . ."

Even on the worst ground Macoun saw promise. North of the

Cypress Hills, he passed through very difficult country and was warned that he would likely lose his horses. Encountering the sand dune country, he saw isolated patches of blown sand bereft of all vegetation. Water was very scarce, and at one salty lake in the Many Island chain the liquid stank so foully the horses, already fourteen hours without fluids, refused to drink. As the land appeared more and more like that which God gave to Cain, Macoun saw something.

Spying what seemed to be bushes amid moving hills of pure sand, Macoun walked five miles toward them and discovered to his amazement a stand of very large cottonwoods, all over two feet in diameter and more than fifty feet high "surrounded by blown sand on every side, and not a blade of grass within half a mile of them." Peering further into this sandy wonderland, he beheld a "perfect oasis" of more than a square mile, covered with ponds, meadows and large trees. Completely girded by dunes, the oasis had never been touched by fire. For Macoun, moved by the desire to dispell another "myth" about the West, the spectacle was "a testimony against the assertion that this country is too dry to support trees"![14]

An incorrigible optimist, Macoun believed fervently in his own teachings and their manifold significance. His revelations were recorded in numerous reports and speeches and in his book, *Manitoba and the Great North West* (1883). Quite likely a few settlers in the dry areas in the late 1880s were fleeting converts of this man of glad tidings. Moreover, when the Canadian Pacific Railway diverted its mainline through the desert, he was convinced, probably foolishly, that it was his own doing.[15] When the settlement of the land of Cain began in 1907, he believed vainly that he had been the prophet who had "set the people on fire."[16] However, the generation which elapsed between Macoun's pulpiteering and the rush of fools into the dry belt was eloquent testimony to the impotence of his message.

Not surprisingly, another early debunker of the desert image was the Canadian Pacific Railway. In 1884 the line published a pamphlet defending "The Wise Policy of Selecting the Southern Route. . . ." The tract began with what it considered the old lie—

that the territory between Moose Jaw and Calgary was completely unfit for settlement, being arid and alkaline, a projection of the Great American Desert—and it offered the truth. Establishing a system of ten experimental farms in the region from Secretan in the east to Gleichen in the west, the railway set out to *prove* the fertility of the region. After the first crop year, the results tumbled in—the land would provide crop yields as heavy as the gumbo of Manitoba; a fine crop could be expected the first year; and cereals, roots and garden products could be successfully grown at an altitude of 3000 feet. Putting the finishing touches on the matter, the railway added testimonials from eminent personages.

Former Prime Minister Alexander Mackenzie visited most of the farms and reinforced Macoun's observation that the aridity was a chimera which vanished with the application of a plow. Across the expanse, he was struck by the number of stalks of grain from single kernels, noting in one case forty-six heads from one root. Addressing the alleged problem of alkali deposits, he reminded readers that alkali existed in Manitoba too, but that it could be worked out after a few croppings. "Some districts well north of the railway, described by Palliser as more or less arid and sandy," Mackenzie added honestly, "I did not see."

If Mackenzie's testimonial betrayed at least a trace of caution, Sir Hector Langevin's was unblushingly enthusiastic. In honor of Langevin the railway had named after him a desolate spot on the map west of Medicine Hat. Later it would be renamed Carlstadt, and then Alderson. In all his travels Sir Hector said he "had not found an acre of bad land." He had heard stories about a great desert, "but it did not exist." The experimental farms were "as good as the best in the country." Langevin's hyperbole was bested by Sir Richard Temple, prominent member of the British Association for the Advancement of Science, who claimed that from Winnipeg to the Rockies there was "hardly a foot" of useless turf.[17]

Such mischievous palavering in the railway's tainted propaganda doubtlessly induced a few more souls into the wasteland. So did the continued ranting of a nest of Canadian expansionists back East, ensconced in the Crown Lands Department, on the staff of the

Toronto *Globe,* and elsewhere, who coveted the West as an agrarian hinterland necessary to the fulfilment of the Dominion's destiny.[18] Likewise, the *Macleod Gazette* raved for years about "this very El Dorado of the Canadian or American west" and pressed the federal government again and again to throw open "the settlers' paradise."[19] But until the mid-1890s the time was not ripe, not for the occupation west of Manitoba in general, let alone of the parched margins. Except for stockmen and a few embryo communities, the land remained vacant, and as far as the dry belt was concerned, a generation of farmers was spared the sacrifice another would make.

The Conspiring Elements

HISTORIANS HAVE OFTEN wondered why the growth of the Northwest between 1887 and 1896 languished so. Most have seen the subsequent settlement as an explosion set off by elaborate triggering devices—the filling of the American midwest and of better lands of Manitoba and Eastern Assiniboia, the abating of the power of the cattle compact, the receding of the memory of the stock crash of 1893, the escalation of wheat prices, the drop in interest rates and oceanic freight rates, the improvements in milling and grain storage technology, and the coming to power of the pro-settler Liberal Party of Canada. All were important, as were the stimulants of migrants to leave their homelands.[20] But in the heart of the dry belt, the Medicine Hat area, the king of explanations for the stunted growth was that farming, limited as it was, was a failure.

In August 1887, a writer informed *The Toronto Mail* that he had learned from three farmer friends in the Territories west of Moosomin that the crops were "a failure, as they have always been, and I fear ever will be, from lack of rain." Apparently there was a tendency every year for the cereals to do well early before "failing rapidly under the hot, scorching sun"—a phenomenon which would appear again and again, like a cruel trick, years later in the farmers' time of agony. In the Medicine Hat area for a radius of two

The trickle begins—American settlers enter southern Alberta, mid-1890s. NA 237-9, Glenbow-Alberta Archives.

hundred miles, there was not a hundred rods of wheat. In all the Northwest in the past five years, it had not rained ten times. There had been sprinkles, of course, mere teasing showers, but these "did more harm than good as they brought the roots of the grain to the surface to be killed by the heat of the burning sun." In winter the desiccating winds sucked up the snow, denying the moisture to the soil. Settlers who had entered the dubious region since 1882 with money and clothing and hope now had nothing. "I ask, in the name of humanity," said the writer waxing indignant, "is it not time for this sort of thing to stop?" The government knew of the desert; why did it stand by silently, sending sacrifices to the wilderness.[21]

While the besmirching of "the Hat" drew an irascible reply from an itinerant surveyor,[22] it was remarkable over the next decade how the young city's newspapers shilly-shallied on the region's agrarian potential. At first *The Times* attacked the farmers for refusing to release information which would promote settlement. "To the contrary they prefer to circulate reports that the country is worthless, that a man needs a national bank at his back to exist on a farm three years anywhere in the vicinity," snapped editor D. G. Holt who preferred to believe that the farmers were pursy misers content with prevailing high prices and antagonistic to more of their kind who would surely depress the market. "The farmers at Medicine Hat don't want any more settlers," concluded Holt.[23]

After a partial crop failure in 1889 and a complete failure in 1890, *The Times* changed its tune. If the region was "the finest ranching district in America," it could never hope to be the same for farmers until the return of the wet seasons oldtimers recalled a decade and more earlier. With the nemesis, drought, loose on the land summer upon summer, the paper swore, "it would be almost criminal to bring settlers here to try to make a living out of straight farming."[24]

Then the journal bit its tongue, as if it could not believe the blasphemy it had uttered. Recanting its pessimism, the deadliest of sins to news organs of the age, it drafted another directive to intending immigrants. The class of incomers the country could expect were agriculturists, and these were to consider the quality of the climate, the soil, and the water. "That we have them as nearly perfect in the Medicine Hat district as in any other portion of Canada or the United States, has been fully demonstrated by the experience of the past eight years," the paper now stated. In dilating on the climate, *The Times* admitted to past aridity. "However, a dry season does not necessarily mean a complete failure of crops," it said, underscoring a line that would be repeated *ad infinitum* during the boom years, "as under good cultivation fair crops can be raised every season."[25]

Even as the editor spoke, the elements were conspiring again, and the grain crops that season of 1892 were once more a disaster. So disheartened were the farmers by the succession of bad years that the next spring they despaired of putting in any crop at all.[26] A whole colony of Germans south at St. Josephburg were so chastened that the government lifted them from their predicament and landed them near Edmonton.[27]

Not until 1897 did the rain revisit. By then the truth of the land was known to the veterans. As the editor of the *Medicine Hat News* stood in a field of oats five feet high with the top of the headed oats ten or twelve inches long, he remembered with gratitude that he was viewing an exceptional year. "Occasionally there comes a season here when it is possible to grow such grain crops as it would be impossible to beat anywhere," he exulted in one of the abiding truths of the region. Regretting that the wait was often too long and the interval too rending, he admitted glumly that "the *News* would be committing a grievous error if it undertook to boom this district as a farming country. . . ." The year, alas, was a freak.[28]

No sooner had he spoken of this mutable land than the exception became the norm. Beguiling nature donned a cloak of vibrant green, smiled at lads with high spirits afar and an instinct to roam, and lured them one by one into the desert. In the twelve years before 1897 only four registered precipitation over ten inches, and the average was 8.92 inches. In the ensuing five years the precipitation ranged from 15.9 inches to a whopping 22.28, and the average was 19.51 inches.[29]

Despite the torrents from heaven, the *News* was wary. Sounding a warning to the rush of farm investors into ranching lands, the editor predicted that "these farmers in the ranching country, outside of the irrigated districts, will wish some kind friend had told them that the seasons are not all like the past two or three with plenty of rainfall." Straight farming was hazardous from township 22 to the international boundary, from range 10 east of the 3rd meridian to within thirty or forty miles of the Rockies. The neophytes did not understand the country, the paper implored, like some Cassandra who spoke the truth that none would heed. Falsely trusting that the incomers would hearken to the voice of experience, the editor intoned—"do not depend wholly upon the products of the soil."[30]

It was already too late.

2 The Planning of Nineveh

The Moment Has Come

N OT ONLY HAD NATURE smiled, but also the government had changed. The domineering Clifford Sifton, dubbed the Napoleon of the West, the Interior minister since the Liberal triumph of 1896 was at the height of his powers. In his hands, the department dumped its senior satrap, A. M. Burgess, architect of the old order. And when Calgary czar William Pearce was also stripped of his influence and accepted a post with the CPR, the wariness of the department about the wisdom of inhabiting the dry areas departed. The new orthodoxy was reflected in a Sifton promotional cartoon which said plainly—"There is no desert country. . . ."[1]

In early 1905 Frank Oliver, the vituperative editor of the *Edmonton Bulletin* succeeded Sifton, and the last ingredient in the potion which was to poison a generation of homesteaders dropped into the bubbling cauldron. Much more than Sifton, Oliver was the great facilitator of the monumental blunder of western settlement, for it was under his aegis that the dry belt came under the plow. Since the early 1880s, Oliver had cultivated a distaste for the confinements the Interior Department laid on the settlement process. To his chagrin, vast acreages had been reserved for the Hudson's Bay Company, the schools, the CPR, and the ranchers. In every township of thirty-six square miles, he wrote in 1896, sections 8 and 26 were held by the Bay, 11 and 29 were school lands, and the remaining odd sections were kept for the railroads—totalling twenty reserved sections of thirty-six. Thus in the northeast and southwest corners of every township, a solid block of five sections was withheld, hamstringing cooperative improvements. In the irrigable districts, every second section was withheld, thereby thwarting the introduction of large scale projects.[2]

As the mantle of power passed to Oliver, his favored people, the teeming settlers, were already in the outer courtyards of the citadel of the drylands. Speedily he moved to withdraw the stock watering reserves, to champion squatters' rights, and to halt the dispensation of closed leases puzzlingly reinstituted by his predecessor. He also revamped the Dominion Lands Act in 1908 to allow the pre-emption of the odd numbered sections between Moose Jaw and Calgary, a ploy which simultaneously doubled the size of dry belt farms to 320 acres and wreaked havoc with existing ranch leases.[3] Then he instructed eulogizers in the department to join the host of speculators, promoters and boosters to praise the region to the skies.

"Magician's wand never produced more striking effect than did the placing of a pair of steel rails over the stretch of prairies southwest from Saskatoon . . .," the dutiful pamphleteers responded in *Canada West: The Last Best West* in 1910. In 1908 there were no towns, no elevators, and few wheat fields. A year later there were seven villages, three incorporated, and dozens of elevators. "Nearly all of the wheat," the pamphlet said, "went No. 1 Northern, bringing 80 cents or more a bushel. . . ." Thousands of acres yielded thirty or more bushels each, and everyone made money.[4]

The selling of Alberta, 1910.
NA 789-21, Glenbow-Alberta
Archives.

I am The Great

ALBERTA

¶ The Empire of Fulfillment.

¶ The land where the opportunities are unlimited and the climate ideal.

¶ I am prosperity to him who would enter my gates.

¶ My storehouses are full and overflowing.

¶ Write to my friends

JOE LIMITED CALGARY (REAL ESTATE), and let them tell you all about me.

¶ They represent many of my best subjects.

Yours Intensively
Alberta
Canada

Leaping in, other interests too puffed up the region, expecting an orgy of wheeling and dealing and a bonanza of speculative profit. The Canadian Pacific Railway, beneficiary of unprecedented government largess, gifted with twenty-five million acres, mostly in Alberta and Saskatchewan where the Dominion retained control over lands and other natural resources, quickly laid out townsites and prepared for the sale of thousands of homesteads in the so-called irrigation districts. Large property owners including the Southern Alberta Land Company and the Canadian Wheatlands laid out their projects and readied their lands for sale. Speculators of every mark poured in, determined to benefit from the boom.

Many were purely parasitic, always feeding on the unearned in-

None was grander than the farmer in the promotion of the West. NA 789-25, Glenbow-Alberta Archives and *The Grain Growers' Guide*, August 3, 1910.

crement, sitting on properties, pumping up prices, never contributing to the new society, never interested. Others played the capitalist game of providing operating funds for expansion and improvement, and while that did not necessarily place their hearts in the communities they supported, at least it placed their pocketbooks there. Crucially important to the new West and to the dry areas was the interest of mortgagemen.

In time to come, one of the dominant investors in Alberta lands would be the Associated Mortgage Investors of Rochester, New York. The firm began in 1908 and soon established a central office at Calgary. Its treasurer, Kingman Nott Robins, had inspected booming Alberta as a potential field for farm mortgage investment, and though he had been an investment counsellor for farm mortgages in Texas, Iowa, Kansas, and North Dakota, he concluded that here was the safest site for the nesting of the mortgage birds.

Swiftly Robins drafted a report to attract mortgage capital to Alberta. Focusing overlong on the fabled drylands, he stressed that the fertility of the semi-arid regions was better maintained than that of humid lands because of the leeching of the latter. "The farmer can protect himself against loss from little rainfall," he quoted the famous dry farming Professor H. W. Campbell, "but not from too much rainfall." Should this assurance appear slim, Robins added another of similar girth: "It is a matter of common observation that rainfall in a newly settled prairie country increases with settlement, cultivation and tree planting." For proof he wheeled in the mysterious pedant, Professor Agassiz, who theorized that the building of railroads and settlements would invariably disturb the electrical currents in the winds, bringing on the inevitable—rain.

"As the area of cultivated land is increased," Robins ranted on, "the danger from early frosts diminishes." Hail storms were at best a minor irritation in Alberta, and wind storms were never violent enough to do serious damage. In fact, Alberta "never suffered from the hot winds which [had] blighted the Central States for many years."

Average wheat yields in Alberta were double those of the Dakotas and Nebraska; the irrigated area of Southern Alberta was more than double that of California. According to F. H. Newell, chief of the United States Reclamation Service, the Bow River Valley alone was destined to have a *rural* population of over 300,000 people. "Hard times will never affect Southern Alberta," Robins quoted Canadian paladin of the soil, Professor James W. Robertson. "The interests of this district are now so diversified that there is no possibility of a pronounced depression."

Transportation and marketing facilities were first rate and were constantly being improved. From the hub city of Calgary radiated eleven railways, constructed or projected; no fewer than seven lines stretched across the dry tracts.

Even so, Alberta farm lands were the cheapest in the country, said Robins, selling for $18.20 an acre in January 1909, compared to $47.30 in Ontario and $76.10 in British Columbia. Since the value of the land vastly exceeded the price, loaning on such properties, escalating by the day toward their intrinsic value, was hardly risky.

Beaming, Robins then reviewed the laws of western Canada. "In its application to farm mortgages," he noted, "the Canadian law is the most advantageous in the world. . . ." Under the Torrens system of land titles registration, titles were beyond dispute. "Mortgages are founded upon such titles," he explained, "and are accompanied by official certificates that no taxes remain unpaid, that no executions, judgments or orders stand against the property. . . ." There were no irksome usury laws to limit the dictates of the lender, no messy dower rights to confuse the title, no irritating exemptions or prior liens to impair the sanctity of the first mortgage, no maddening hitches or delays in foreclosure proceedings, should the borrower submerge.

Finally, Robins came to the essence of his pitch—the demand for loans. The division of large ranch holdings into smaller farms, the purchase of costly farm equipment, the expansion of cropped land and the improvement of homes—all intensified the demand for capital in the pioneer province. Canadian chartered banks, however, could not loan on real estate security. "There is no capital in the country for that purpose," declared Robins, "so the funds must be secured from non-resident investors, who are in a position to dictate terms. . . ." Even with twenty trust and mortgage companies in the field, from Canada, England and France, the demand for money could not be met. The happy result was "liberal interest rates" and an absence of "dangerous competition" among lenders. Conditions were ripe for the orderly flow of capital into the new parts of the West in preparation for harvests certain to come.[5]

There was just one other matter—a misconception that needed to be cleared up—and the invasion of the dry belt could proceed.

The Weather Factory
═══════════════════

ONE DAY IN EARLY 1908, Elliott Flower of the *Chicago Tribune* went in search of the mythical apparition of Medicine Hat.

As he said, he was unsure if it was "a place, an article of apparel, a physician's prescription or a summer drink." After asking some strangers, he came upon a Great Lakes captain who told him what he knew.

"Medicine Hat," said the captain, "is a place—a breeding place for trouble. It sends us, among other things, the close of navigation every year, and sometimes it sends this without warning. It is the most cantankerous place in the world; you can't be sure what it will do next, even when it tells you, for very likely it won't do it. If called upon to classify it, I should say it was the one worst bet."

"But where is it?" Elliott and a friend asked.

"Somewhere between the northern boundary of the United States and the Arctic circle," he responded.

"Such general directions, as you give," the two persisted, "will not assist us materially in getting there."

The mariner was stupefied. "You want to go there?"

The two said yes.

"You'll excuse me," he said, "but somehow it doesn't seem just human to want to go to Medicine Hat. I never heard of anybody that wanted to go there, and I never met anybody that had been there. I shouldn't believe really there was such a place, if it wasn't branded on the weather. But you ought to be able to get there easy."

"How?"

"Catch the head of a blizzard, follow it back to the tail, and you'll be there."[6]

The story captured the predominant American impression of Medicine Hat, nurtured since the 1880s. "It is a common belief in these United States," said the *Chicago Record-Herald,* "that Medicine Hat is about a mile and a half the other side of the north pole, and so cold that the inhabitants look upon ice cream as a consomme."[7] A dubious reputation it was, but one with an explanation. Because the first meteorological station in the Northwest was at the Hat, all reports of storms in the whole region bore a Medicine Hat byline—hence the impression of the city as the great weather factory, the home of the blizzard.

After a visit to "the Canadian Banana Belt," as the Hat *News* editor dubbed it, Elliott Flower was subtly, though impressively re-educated. Accepted on this occasion as a Yankee's confession and redemption, tales about the weather factory were really a sorespot for the band of Hatters gearing up for the greatest promotion in the history of the drylands.

To counteract the myth, the boosters not only invited Chicago newspaper representatives to see for themselves, but they also released pamphlets as correctives. The Board of Trade's aptly titled *Hot Stuff* thus highlighted the Hat's production of roses and cut flowers for the Prairies.[8] The *News* also jocularly offered three prizes to any "damphool," uninformed American poets prepared to versify their slanderous musings about the Hat weather. First prize would be a framed photograph of the bucking and roping competition at the Medicine Hat athletic grounds held December 24 to 26. Second prize was a photo of a baseball game played in shirt sleeves at the Hat on Christmas Day. And third prize was another photo showing a basket of ripe tomatoes picked from the vine, also on Christmas Day. "Get in now, ye bighouse maligners of a fair and beautiful climate," exhorted the editor, "hurry in and see who can make the most consummate ass of himself. . . ."[9]

Sometime before this sardonic publicity stunt, Medicine Hat had hired her own industrial and publicity commissioner. A former Hamilton alderman who had answered the call of the West, John T. Hall was the ultimate booster. For three years in the Hat, a year in Brandon and a short span in Lethbridge in 1911, Hall directed city publicity. Secretary of the Associated Boards of Trade in Western Canada and the Western Canada Irrigation Association, he was struck down at the height of his powers, in Lethbridge, by erysipelas, a loathsome inflammatory disease of skin and sub-cutaneous tissues caused by a streptococcus.[10]

Hall exemplified many of the positive features of the booster mentality—showing attention to strangers, extending the hand of friendship to visitors, cultivating a feeling of mission, of belonging, of personal worth in the grand, cooperative enterprise of building a community. At its finest, there was an element of God and of the mystical power of the new land in boosting. It sought to galvanize a spirit of good will, of social and economic responsibility. Some of the most fervent beliefs of the boosters were couched in religious terms. As one line ran, "You can never tell at what hour the seed is being sown which will come back to us in the harvest." The best boosters, like Hall, were usually credited with dispelling the mood of apathetic indifference toward a community's future. Boosterism and its agents, like Hall or James Richardson, the publicity commissioner of Macleod, were part of the new society that wanted to set off on the right foot, to experience the fullness of the joy of progress. Sensing that they were at a pivotal time in their own existence and that of the new frontier, many citizens sought the ecstasy of this moment with utter possessiveness, as if it were part of their birthright. To miss it or to experience it imperfectly was to pass by a stage in life without knowing it, to surrender a very special time of exultation. That is why knockers and cavillers were given such short shrift. Knockers were the crepe-hangers, the purveyors of gloom who were forever mistaking the happy celebration of baptism for the solemn sacrament of the last rites. As David Elton, editor of *The Magrath Pioneer,* said, "The Knocker is an offspring of failure and envy. When you meet a Knocker, hit him where his brains ought to be and kick where they are."[11]

One of Hall's operatives was the Reverend John Sillak, an Estonian preacher from the Hat. In late 1909, Sillak slipped across the border on a long mission through Montana and the Dakotas. He carried with him Hall's literature to seed amongst Yankee tillers whose roots were shallow. In South Dakota he was accused of being a common agent of the Canadian government, seeking to coax Russians from the state. The charge, said the indignant but guilty Sillak, was absurd. "I am no agent to anybody except to my Lord, Jesus Christ. I may not be innocent that these people are going to Canada," he allowed, "but I don't consider it a big crime that my countrymen follow me to Canada." "Nearly all Estonians" in South

Dakota, he claimed, had left for Alberta. Bringing $5,000 with them, a colony was starting a new settlement west of Lake Pakowki. The basic reason for the migration, concluded the preacher, was the comparative richness of southern Alberta land.[12]

It was all very pleasing to John Hall who smiled, as usual. In his three years as publicity commissioner, Hall paraded the Hat's virtues back East, he ferried the Hat's exhibits to the 1908 Dominion Exhibition at Calgary, and he was a prominent fixture at every civic triumph, no matter how modest. A man of many arts and strategems, he even sang tolerably well "The Death of Nelson" at the banquet celebrating the opening of the Finlay Bridge by Premier Rutherford.[13]

Aided by the *Medicine Hat News,* Hall pumped out several promotional pamphlets, the most notable of which related the observations of Rudyard Kipling after his famous visit to the gas city "with all hell for a basement." Kipling was the poet of the empire, and on his trip through Western Canada in 1907, he was the master of hyperbole. Scarcely was there a centre he passed that he did not praise as the most enterprising and prosperous under heaven.[14]

Waxing evocative, Kipling described his tour of a show farm near the Hat one warm Sunday. The owner, M. A. Zahnizer, had taken his fold to church, but the visitors nonetheless "slipped through the gates and reached the silent spic and span house, with its trim barn, and a vast mound of copper-colored wheat, piled in the sun between two mounds of golden chaff." "Everyone thumbed a sample of it and passed judgment," said Kipling, "—it must have been worth a few hundred golden sovereigns as it lay out on the veldt—and we sat around on the farm machinery, and in the hush that a shut up house always imposes, we seemed to hear the lavish earth getting ready for new harvests. There was no true wind, but a push, as it were, of the whole crystal atmosphere."

At a picnic the locals, perhaps elements of the "new enterprises" committee operating in John Hall's time, talked of the projects and the building in the town that was "born lucky." Deeply impressed, Kipling saw them as the strong arm of resolve which would refashion the countryside a hundred miles around. Together they talked of projects first in their own city and then in numerous tributary towns. Said Kipling, "I felt as though I were assisting at the planning of Nineveh. . . ."[15]

Blessed by the recent cycle of wet seasons, the farming environs of Nineveh grew apace. Incoming settlers from the northern states commented, "Your land is all right, your season is two months longer than that of the grain growing districts, we will take our chances on the rainfall."[16] Zahnizer, the show farmer, had arrived from Kansas in the summer of 1902. Two and a half years later, he put in his wheat on February 23, doubtlessly a record for the Territories.[17] Suffering no ill effects, the audacious husbandman also noted the success of apples in the next few years and fervently believed they would presently be produced by the bushel.[18]

The year after Zahnizer settled, another American from Souris, North Dakota, arrived. Amassing some 1,900 acres and possessing a traction engine, W. R. Babington speedily became one of the region's largest farm operators. He considered the district a paradise.[19] Naturally when John Hall came on the scene he sought out this progressive tiller and extracted a testimonial. In the wake of the season of 1907, the driest by far in twenty years, Babington started slowly. Poor farming gave poor crops almost everywhere, he said, but especially in Medicine Hat. Success was a matter of method, and the method was "the Campbell System of Soil Culture." "In ten years from now," Babington prophesied ironically, "Medicine Hat will be the ideal all round farming district of Canada."[20]

The Bread of the Future
——————————

THE SAVIOR TO WHOM Babington referred—Professor H. W. Campbell—was trumpeted the length and breadth of the dry areas between 1908 and 1910. Plastered with his pronouncements, the papers ran his columns, week after week, like sermons. Promoters everywhere were converted, even the hierarchy of the Department of Agriculture in the fledgling province. Through Campbell and like prophets, a new interpretation of the failures of the early 1890s emerged. As George Harcourt, Alberta deputy minister of Agriculture said, "Much of the discouragement met with in the early settlement of the country was due to the ignorance of the settler concerning soil moisture and the relation it bore to successful crop raising."[21] To dispel such ignorance, Harcourt invited Professor Campbell to conduct a lecture tour through the south and to establish a demonstration station at the Hat.

That Campbell was a false messiah, only a few suspected, for in 1909 he was at the peak of popularity. Theorizing hazily, he believed that significant amounts of water escaped dryland soil by capillary action. He thus urged subsoil packing to bring the water to the plant roots as well as surface mulching to disrupt the upward flow of moisture into the air. In time the dust mulch would take to the winds, and the Northwest would again be the home of blizzards, black blizzards.[22]

It would be unfair to blame Campbell for the evil that was to befall the drylands in a few years, for a bevy of dry farming "specialists" had sprung up, preaching a very similar doctrine. All believed in the triumph of man over nature and in the dawning epoch of progress. All taught that recurrent cycles of crop failures were past.

At the Indian Head Experimental Farm Angus McKay had so developed the summerfallow that he firmly believed that leaving some land idle one year in two or three, plowing deeply and cultivating during the growing season would ensure a crop every year.[23] Concurring, W. R. Motherwell, minister of Agriculture in Saskatchewan, became such a water conservation fanatic that he was nicknamed "the moisture minister." A few years later, the *Carlstadt Progress* printed the "Ten Commandments of the Dry Farmer" by Professor W. C. Palmer of North Dakota Agricultural College. The message was very similar—plow deep to let in rain without run off; keep the surface loose to stop evaporation and to let in rain; compact the lower soil to bring moisture to the plant roots; summerfallow to save two years' moisture for a single crop; keep down the weeds; plant trees, and so on.[24]

The basic assumption of most dry farm mentors was that one had only to know how to conserve moisture and no crop would fail. When George Harcourt, former commissioner of Agriculture at Regina and later Alberta deputy minister, commented on the crop disaster of 1910, he did not mention the 6.45 inches of rain for the year at Medicine Hat, nor the claims of settlers around Lomond and other centres that the wheat never came up till September.[25] What impressed him was the alleged fact that he could see on opposite sides of a road or fence one crop a disgrace and the other a godsend. "The difference," he declared, "lay in the intelligence with which the cultivation of the land had been done."[26]

A supporting assumption of the moisture clique was that a crop could be assured if enough moisture resided in the soil at seeding. The corollary was stated by the aptly named Professor H. A. Surface, a botanist from Philadelphia, whose pronouncements reached the ear of many drybelters through the *Medicine Hat News*. "Summer rain is not an essential to the raising of good crops," he said, "nor is drought necessarily fatal to high productiveness of the soil." Moisture naturally moved from earth to air; hence all that was required was the cutting of the escape channels, like slicing the wick of an oil lamp.[27] As advice for drylanders, it was midway between hyperbole and poppycock, but that revelation was yet to come.

For the moment, the generation of farm practice intellectuals believed as fervently as any other that it knew what its predecessors did not. Professor J. W. Worst, president of North Dakota Agricultural College and of the International Dry Farming Congress at Lethbridge in 1911, captured the state of mind when he reminded listeners at Lethbridge that the world population was increasing while the sustaining land base was limited. For thousands of settlers who had rushed into the dry areas, here was their contribution. "The bread of the future," he intoned, "will come largely from the desert of the past."[28]

Even as the dry areas were being thrown open, itinerating potentates and pundits passed their benediction on the new promised land. "No more startling change has taken place anywhere in Canada than has taken place in the dry part of Alberta," declared

Sydney Fisher, Canadian minister of Agriculture. "We can all re-member when it was considered that the country was useless from an agricultural standpoint and the ranchers were supposed to have full sway and possession for all time."[29] In the summer of 1908, a reporter for the *Calgary Herald* predicted that Taber would double its wheat yield that year. "The one thing about Alberta," he smiled, "is that the rain falls when it is needed."[30] "'The Hat' expects to have a population of half a million by the time its young men are middle-aged," another enthusiast wrote. "The South Saskatchewan gives it the purest drinking water and in the summer the prairie will be making gold for the farmers...."[31] Southern Alberta, said a writer for the *Canada West Magazine,* was "a land blessed of the Gods—a land over which bending nature ever smiles and into whose cradle she emptied her golden horn...."[32]

The Rush of Fools

GIVEN SUCH SUPERLATIVES, it was little wonder that as the caretakers of the dry areas changed from ranchers to farmers there was a remarkable series of land rushes. In September 1909, the news that eight townships south of Seven Persons, Winnifred and Whitla would be available brought trainloads of settlers to the Dominion Lands Office at Lethbridge. Locomotives Saturday and Sunday were still applying the brakes when the coach doors flung open and hordes of settlers, with the smell of gold in their nostrils, tore across to the land office.

A chute was constructed to funnel the mob to the land agent, dis-penser of paradise. At the appointed moment, the crowd stormed the chute, and Paul Meister from Ohio popped through first to the cheers of onlookers. To relieve the pressure, the gatekeeper moved to let more in, but the rush collapsed the chute. Crushed in the log jam, J. McCuaig who had waited four days in line was squeezed out, and two ladies went through the pulverizer only to faint at the door from the pushing, the shoving and the bad air. The women were carried upstairs where the sight of the land agent, like that of

Gabriel, quickly revived them. As the dazed and winded settlers stumbled down the stairs and through the basement, the Lethbridge reporter noted, they finally reached the outside "where they had room to stretch themselves and regain their normal shape and size."[33]

In December 1909, an announcement was made that a single valuable homestead worth $5,000 would be opened eight miles from Medicine Hat. For two days and nights two men camped out on the steps of the land office at the Hat. At 6 A.M. a dozen others arrived, and by 9 A.M. twenty were in line. Ten minutes before the doors opened, T. Spencer whisked in, accompanied by several friends, including real estate promoter F. M. Ginther. As the early-birds chatted with the newcomers, Spencer wheeled to the front of the line somehow unnoticed. All in the same moment the men were told that tickets for places could be had upstairs, the fire whistle blew, Spencer grabbed the door knob, and the heavy swinging doors were ripped off their hinges. The two early-birds and Spencer raced to the second floor. One of the men was checked into the bannister, and the other, hanging onto Spencer's coat, was given a free ride to the top. In a final, deft manoeuvre, Spencer shook the gent free, along with his coat and vest, and was awarded the number 1 ticket.[34]

When 747 quarters of school land around the Hat were put up for auction at city hall a few months later, some five hundred bidders from all over the West swarmed into the city. At the request of the Board of Trade, scores of citizens threw their homes open to take billets. Most of the land went for $7 to $10 an acre, though as the auctioneer offered a half section in 29-12-5 on the bench near Dunmore Hill, east of the Hat, the apex was reached. Hugh Smith of Castor who had made a fortune in Saskatoon and Castor land deals paid $60 an acre for one quarter, and an incredible $165 an acre for the other.[35]

One of the greatest land rushes of all occurred at Lethbridge in January 1910, when twenty-one townships south of Bow Island to the International boundary were listed. In the line of a thousand

On the stationery of a Medicine Hat realtor was this picture of the Lockrem farm near Carlstadt, 1911 c. NA 4711-8, Glenbow-Alberta Archives.

Awaiting a piece of paradise—settlers at Medicine Hat, 1912 c. P 3493.3, Medicine Hat Archives.

Land rush at Lethbridge, 1909 c. P 19738609000, Sir Alexander Galt Archives.

was Perren Baker, aged thirty-three, an unordained minister from Illinois who was to make his mark on the new province.

Baker had spied out the land several weeks previously. Between the Chin and Etzikom coulees squatters had taken almost every available section. A pile of lumber or three boards nailed at one end and set upright as a tripod were symbols of their claims which were honored by others and which gave them priority in filing.[36] Further south, near Lucky Strike, Baker had been caught in a snow storm. Chancing on a shack, he and his partner were welcomed and fed. Before long, no fewer than six transients were holed up in the place; two would soon be Baker's neighbors. On the second morning the storm let up, and Baker headed north for Burdett, forty or fifty miles away. After many hours of tough slogging, his team was exhausted. By night they were nearly finished, and Baker was uncertain of his direction. Without shelter or signpost, he lashed the team into an agonizing trot, praying that he was still moving north. At last in the blackness he perceived a dim row of lights, and the team, near collapse, was whipped on. Between nine and ten o'clock they staggered into Burdett, utterly spent.

As Monday, January 10, the day for filing, approached, a long queue began to form; so Baker, his brother and a friend, fearful of falling too far behind, stepped in line about ten o'clock Saturday evening. The temperature in the long night fortunately stayed well above 0 degrees Fahrenheit. Throughout the next day the motley crew of exuberant young men, stooped old gents, and a scattering of women, from several countries in Europe, from all provinces of Canada and from as far south as Texas, bantered with the amused locals. When night fell again, rumors became rife. An organized gang of riffraff was said to be preparing an onslaught to break into the line. Some trouble-pedlar was said to be orchestrating a cattle stampede to disrupt the sequence. Baker and company were prepared to rip up a picket fence to fend off any ruffians, but they wondered what effect these primitive weapons might have on a stampede. In the end, city police and redcoats, some under cover, thwarted the numerous attempts at claim jumping, and the cattle rush never materialized.

Everyone in line had an opportunity to acquire a quarter section by paying a $10 registration, breaking eighty acres, building a home worth at least $300, and living there six months each year for three years. After "proving up," settlers in the dry areas could pre-empt another quarter section by breaking thirty acres thereon and paying $3 an acre. In addition, an intending settler could procure two kinds of scrip, each entitling him to another half section. Half-breed scrip had been given to Metis after the Riel Rebellion and could be purchased outright. South African scrip had been given to the veterans of the Boer War but could only be used by a vet, though after he had filed his claim he was free to transfer it. Baker had purchased a veteran's scrip in Calgary for $600–$800.

Under terms of the contract, the Calgary agent had to produce the veteran at the filing wicket. The ex-serviceman, whom Baker later called Riley, had been a veterinary surgeon from a good family, but now was little more than a troublesome, tumbledown sot. Baker took pains to pay a stand-in since the vet could not be expected to wait in line for days, but he neglected to pay several watchdogs to keep track of Riley. No sooner was Baker disappointed to find that his number would not be called the first day than the agent reported that he had lost Riley. Frantically he searched the taprooms of Lethbridge, but to no avail. Touring the dens of forbidden pleasures, he finally found Riley in the capable palms of two voluptuaries. Confident that their handling would absorb Riley for the evening, the agent left.

Tuesday morning Baker learned early that his number would not come up till next day; then he heard that Riley was leaving town. Moonstruck, the amorous toper was set on following the strumpets to Spokane. Riley informed the agent that he had agreed to be present January 10th only, and that had passed. When the agent returned empty-handed, Baker threatened legal action, reminding him that the contract was with him, not Riley. Off went the agent again, and how he returned with the veteran is unclear—perhaps in the interim the trollops had taken advantage of Riley once more, and temporarily sated, he had lost his resolve to board the train for more of the same; perhaps his bank roll had so slimmed that the ladies had lost their motivation to be pleasing. At any rate, Riley was now directed to his other love, the bar. There Perren Baker took his side, brother Archie stayed in line, and the friend acted as communicator when the number approached. At the friend's urgent call, Baker began trundling bleary-eyed Riley to the gate. The number was announced when both were still two hundred yards distant and in grave danger of losing their place. At the last second, the two arrived, one in a state of terror and the other in a state of torpor.

At the wicket Baker claimed the area he had chosen, the NW quarter of section 21-5-10, and the SW quarter as his pre-emption. Riley took the adjacent piece and then signed the transfer to Perren's wife, Blanche. Said Baker, "It was a very shaky hand that grasped the pen and I watched with some misgiving as he executed certain strange marks more resembling a Persian inscription than a Christian signature. However it proved to be valid enough and Riley's work was done. We parted without regret."[37]

Perhaps a thousand homeseekers poured through the turnstiles that same week in Lethbridge. The year ending March 31, 1910, was the most hectic on record for the Lethbridge land office. Over 52,000 letters were received, 8,273 homestead and pre-emption entries were granted, and the office revenue topped $243,000.[38] As the lands tributary to Lethbridge filled up, attention turned to the new office in the Hat. In April and May that agency worked night and day processing 2,899 entries for 371,160 acres. As well, 76,000 acres of school lands were sold. Considering that the total cultivated acreage in the Hat region in 1909 was only 30,000 acres, the increase was absolutely astonishing.[39]

By 1911 the Medicine Hat census district was the most populous in the province and boasted 70,606 citizens. Only 15 percent had been born in Alberta or Saskatchewan, and roughly the same proportions came from the British Isles and Ontario. The new plurality were American-born, comprising over a third of the budding society.[40]

The first phase of the creation of a strange new heartland was nearly complete. A heartland is a region of dominance. As such a region goes, so goes a province or state; when it flourishes, all flourish; when it hurts, all hurt; when it demands, all answer. Touted now as the great new breadbasket, the dry belt was a heartland in the making, genuine it seemed, but odd in its locale, filling all right, but on curious terrain. As a region of great import, it drew settlers to itself like a magnet, and to it they transferred their loyalties, their affections, their hopes, their purses, their very beings.

Amid the hoopla the new metropolis of the vanquished desert grew as never before. Between 1904 and 1909 Medicine Hat's assessment multiplied almost seven fold.[41] By the end of 1911, the city led all others in the Dominion in percentage of building permits increase over 1910.[42] More miles of steel were laid in Alberta in 1912 than in all other provinces combined, and several new lines were projected through the Hat region.[43] In early 1913, the western manager of the *Financial Post of Canada* reported, "Everywhere things are moving fast but Medicine Hat is beating them all. Down east more is heard of this city than any other. . . ."[44] In the past fourteen months, local real estate agent F. M. Ginther reported that the population had almost doubled again, and was hovering around 12,000.[45]

Ginther was born in Ohio in 1879 and later moved to Cando, North Dakota where he resided till 1906. Then, according to *The Medicine Hat Manufacturer,* he began to appreciate "the magnificent possibilities of the Canadian northwest." After reconnoitering infant Alberta, he chose Medicine Hat "as the spot that above all others would grow to be a great and important centre." Immediately he became one of the great builders of the city. President of the Medicine Hat Pump and Brass Manufacturing Company, he was also a member of the Industrial Bureau of the Board of Trade and president of the Medicine Hat baseball club of the Western Canada League.[46]

Ginther's major interest was his land company, capitalized by early 1913 at $250,000.[47] Specializing in farm lands and representing the CPR and the Hudson's Bay Company land offices in the region, Ginther advertised plainly, "We Sell the Earth." Always exaggeration-prone, he asserted that Sunny Southern Alberta around the Hat had a rainfall of "about 15 inches," a flagrant lie, for only 1911 of the ten previous years exceeded fifteen inches, the average of the others being 9.2.[48] Winter, he added, undeterred, set in during the latter part of December and broke up in the latter part of February.[49] And one acre of average soil in Alberta was worth more than twenty acres of average soil on the eastern seaboard.[50]

Ginther's company was the leading farm land dealer in the district. In the great settlement year of 1911 the business sold ten thousand acres of farm land, an expansion that rebounded on the Hat itself.[51] By late 1913, twenty-one industries had been established, another eight were building, and another six were located.[52] When the boom peaked early in 1913 Ginther's promotion extended halfway across the globe. His letters to clients and to prospective clients disclosed a Midas touch, a boundless optimism, and all the persuasion of a seasoned speculator.

To an American investor he estimated that with all industries working there would be a population of at least 25,000 in the factory district alone, and with the great flour mills, Medicine Hat would rival Minneapolis.[53] One Jamaican he assured that the Hat was "destined to be the manufacturing city of the Western Prairie Provinces." The asset beyond computation was the natural gas, available to manufacturers at a mere 5¢ per thousand cubic feet. No wonder, he crowed, that "during the past five years we have invested thousands of dollars for people in England, and in every instance we have made good."[54]

Delirious with success, Ginther confessed to one Scottish investor that recent developments had been "even beyond our fondest dreams." In the pell-mell rush for real estate, the people had overlooked the construction of apartment houses, stores, and offices. "There is an office famine in Medicine Hat," he told the Scot. "Almost fabulous prices are being paid for just simply desk room and store room—in offices, stores and restaurants and other places." A syndicate with the foresight to construct an office and store building would surely be rewarded handsomely. Ginther admitted to his prospective client, however, that doing business by mail was unsatisfactory because the properties might be sold, or come off the market, or increase in price. Windfalls came only to the resolute and unhesitating. Investors could help themselves by responding by cable, he suggested. Mindful of the canny race with whom he dealt, Ginther urged the Scot to consult the Medicine Hat banks for confirmation of the company's fine standing.[55]

To a confederate apparently charged with the task of convincing Prince Edward Islanders to buy Hat properties, Ginther wrote: "Try and persuade the people there are other GOOD investments besides 'Black Foxes,' these sometimes die, while it is pretty hard to kill a good pair of lots 50 x 130 in a live city like Medicine Hat."[56]

Fitting it was, when in October 1913 the cartoonist of the *Chicago Daily Tribune* resurrected the old joke about the Hat being the source of bad weather, Ginther lectured the editor forthwith. "The joke has passed rather beyond the point of amusement," he fumed, "and we now set it down as ignorance." To correct "such absolutely wrong impressions," he rushed off a copy of the truth—inscribed in a section on the weather in a board of trade booklet.[57]

Glimpses of the Shortfall

B EFORE THE FLASHING falseness of the promotional diatribe peaked, real life set in, and settlers encountered a habitat that had been eons in the making and that mystified them. Sixty million years before, the Prairies, once abounding in prehistoric creatures, had risen from a shallow sea, and the ancestral Rocky Mountains were created. For thirty million years primordial rivers and streams deposited thousands of feet of nonmarine sediments across the plains. Then the glaciers came, covering the land several times in the past million years, until the last ice age, the Wisconsin, receded about twelve thousand years ago, leaving the landscape very much as the settlers found it. As the ice retreated, glacial lakes appeared and gargantuan channels were formed to drain the water into the Milk and Missouri River systems. When the settlers first saw these channels they called them coulees and they wondered how they had come to be, for they were now dry. Stretching for many miles, these ancient rivers became known as the Etzikom, Chin, Forty Mile, Pakowki and other coulees, and they made travel difficult. In time, but too late for most first-comers, the lakes the coulees had drained became the heart of irrigation projects.[1]

The mountains cast a long rain shadow over the plains, extending well into Saskatchewan. The aridity, the elevation, and the winds combined to create a most volatile climate. Across the region from Lethbridge to Swift Current, the daily minimum and maximum temperatures could differ by over 80 degrees F; in two consecutive days they could vary by 75–85 degrees; and in a year, by 150 degrees. Generally the closer one got to the strange weather factory of Medicine Hat, the more erratic conditions became. There the difference between record minimum and maximum temperatures in each month from November through April varied from 112 degrees to 137 degrees F.—fluctuations unmatched anywhere else on the Prairies, or in Canada. Annual precipitation averaged 15–16 inches in Lethbridge and Swift Current, perhaps an inch more in Calgary, and two or three inches less in Medicine Hat. Again, the annual variability at the Hat was the greatest. From 1900 to 1936, not one year in Swift Current registered less than 11 inches of precipitation; there were two such years in Calgary, three in Lethbridge, and *sixteen* in the Hat.[2]

Knowing little of the past and less of the future, settlers stumbled out onto the arid lands after 1908 and encountered the most astonishing weather sequences (patterns is too strong a word) most had ever witnessed. Nowhere on earth, it seemed, could the weather change on such short notice. It could rain, hail and snow, and be clear, warm and sunny all on the same day and almost any time of the year. For two weeks on end in the depths of winter, children could go without jackets or mitts—they could even play baseball as the literature promised—but in two hours the temperature could drop out of sight to thirty or forty below. From horizon to horizon, the azure vault could be absolutely cloudless, and thirty minutes later it could be entirely overcast. Like mythical Proteus, the atmosphere seemed to assume a new form as soon as it was grasped.

Yet there were two elements that were constant—the intense summer sun and the interminable blowing. The sun could bake crops to a crisp in less than ten days, and it could knock a man out from heat stroke in a few hours. Abetted by Old Sol, the desiccating winds scorched and parched and burnt like nothing the homesteaders had ever seen before. Always there were the bone-dry southwesterly chinooks, demoisturized by the Rockies, gusting under their characteristic arches, soughing across the land, howling through the fences and telegraph lines, aligning small coulees in their direction, lifting the typical thin brown regional soils and piling vast sand dunes southeast of Brooks, northeast of Purple Springs, north of the Hat and into Saskatchewan. In the badlands the winds had stripped the vegetation almost entirely and were inexorably carving grotesque and barren formations called hoodoos. Relentless, the blowing was all-powerful. It could rain for days in spring, sometimes a quarter or a third of the year's allotment, filling the sloughs, turning roads into bogs and fields into lakes, with the whole prairie awash, but it always took the winds less time to dry it than the downpour to drench it.

It was as if King Aeolus, ruler of the winds, had hatched a foul plot high in the Rockies and had set the west wind and the south wind, those normally gentle and compliant breezes, against each other in a struggle of influence and dominion. It was as if the two had clashed in fury, creating a deviant southwester, almost vampirish in its appetite for moisture.

Years passed before the new settlers appreciated the power of the winds the way the old time ranchers had. And lies in the promotional blurbs did not help. Immigrants were told that it was so calm that surveyors could lay their papers on post tops without fear of them blowing away;[3] they were assured that there were "no wind storms or cyclones to scare people out of their wits, and no blizzards in the winter."[4] Seasons later, the sarcastic may well have nodded, "It is true. Most of the blizzards in southern Alberta occur in other seasons."

Settlers learned soon enough that there were indeed blizzards in the dry belt, and while tornados were scarce, the gales nearly scared some newcomers to death.[5] Winter storms blew up suddenly, catching people off guard, confounding them, blinding them, testing them, sometimes burying them.

One day in their first season near Richmound, Saskatchewan, the two eldest children of Tony Steigel, an ex-Minnesotan of Polish extraction who was temporarily away from home, were sent to school in the intense cold. When it was time to return the two miles home, a blizzard was blowing. For seeming hours the two slogged through the driving whiteout until at last they came upon a building which they recognized in shock as the school! Two non-anglophone Linacre homesteaders, taking English lessons, were still present, and they offered to guide the children partway home. The homesteaders bade them follow a fence line in the general area, but off their beaten path. After some reassuring moments, the guides veered toward their own refuges, and the children were again alone. Their despair climaxed when the fence ran out and they realized they were lost in the gloom. Their hearts sinking, their limbs quivering, terror seized them, imparting blurred images of an icy end. Suddenly from the swirls before them emerged a shadow. Driven by faint instinct, it was their mother—who had left the other children and the baby to search for them.[6]

Another time, a neighbor of two Finnish paupers, Jacob Ainas, aged sixty-seven and his wife aged forty-five, called at their ten by ten dugout south of Seven Persons after a heavy snowstorm. Seeing the drifts jammed against the door and hearing nothing, he shovelled the snow away and pried open the door. On the floor were the man, his wife, the dog and the cat—all dead. Without ventilation except through the door which the drifts had sealed, the couple had suffocated. The wind had blown over the stove pipe, and likely the burning coal had robbed them of oxygen. The man was near the door with a hatchet at his side, suggesting that he had tried to break out of the tomb but was overcome. So poor were the two that the community had to bear the funeral costs.[7]

Earlier that same winter of 1910–11, Constable Smith of the

North-West Mounties, patrolling the Red Deer River country, found the frozen body of W. S. Romine, a recent emigrant from Colorado, half-standing in a snow bank, grasping the top strand of a wire fence, bearing the vacant, betrayed look of utter exhaustion. Two others, both Englishmen, were lost without a trace. What especially appalled Smith was the lack of foresight among so many newcomers in not laying up fuel for their first winter and not recognizing the country for what it was. It was hoped, commented the *Medicine Hat News,* turning briefly from its prattle about baseball games in January, "that these fatalities will prove a warning to homesteaders who persist in wandering about."[8]

Again and again settlers were caught or almost caught in the grip of winter. Several froze to death or froze limbs, sometimes within a short distance of help. Disoriented, some just trudged into the wilderness and were never seen again. Occasionally howling, ravenous coyotes directed a search, and sometimes they cleaned the bones of star-crossed wayfarers before other interlopers could discover the remains. Once only a foot in a boot was found.[9]

Strange things could happen in a blizzard. Charlie Stokes and Tom Marks were returning to the Lomond district with two wagons of coal from Bow City when a blizzard blew in. After it became impossible to drive the teams further, they unhitched the loads, mounted the horses, and trusted the homing instinct of the animals. The horses saved them, as they did many others over the years. Apparently the storm lasted a long while, perhaps days, but when it was spent, the men returned for the coal. They discovered it beside a bachelor's shack where they might have sought refuge. The bachelor too had been caught unawares, and without enough fuel, or knowledge of the gift of coal at his doorstep, he had burned his furniture to keep from freezing.[10]

Had the drybelters known first hand the torments of the winter of 1906–7, perhaps they would have been more cautious. Ironically, the icy blasts of that season of execution prepared the way for the sodbusters, for it annihilated the rangers' stock by the thousands. Rather more snow that usual fell before Christmas. A chinook melted the top layer, forming a crust, followed by another snowfall, a second brief chinook and a second hard crust. The snow on the range was now twelve to eighteen inches deep, and the hungry animals, further hampered by the new fences of homesteaders, were immobilized. Without winter feed—for the winters, even the cattlemen said, were too mild to require it—and without the intelligence of horses to paw the snow for grass, the pitiful cattle drifted south before the frigid gales, searching the coulees, eating shrubs, sticks and manure. They even followed coyote trails seeking food. Swaying along in single file up the rivers, they left a trail of blood, their legs slashed to shreds by the sharp ice crusts. For weeks their moaning and bellowing carried across the frozen wastes.

In the new year, for weeks on end the temperature rose to 20 below zero in the day and dropped to 30 below at night. Driven more and more to water to assuage their hunger, the cattle were swallowed up by air holes in the rivers. Thousands died by the rivers or fell into coulees, never to rise. Amid a pile of seven hundred head perishing by the Little Bow River, one passing cowhand saw a big steer standing in the centre of the funereal heap, obviously unable to lie down and die in relative peace. The hand made his way to the steer and twitched the tail to get the animal to dislodge itself. The tail broke off in his hand—the steer was frozen solid.[11]

That winter half the herds were lost. Until July the effluvium of rotting carcasses tainted the winds.[12] When the settlers invaded shortly thereafter, the prairie was a literal boneyard. Most discovered later what had happened.

Landseekers also discovered after they arrived, often *immediately* after, the terror of grass fires. The phenomenon was not new to those from the northern great plains but the danger was magnified by the fact that this was virgin prairie without the breaks of plowed fields and roads.

As the wagons rolled out of the new towns of Kindersley, Burdett, Bassano, and Carlstadt, many riders were troubled by haze and smoke in the distance, wafted skyward by prairie fires. R. S. Tribe, his father and two brothers had shipped two carloads of effects to Carlstadt, west of the Hat, in spring 1910. The day after

Grassfire—the homesteaders' terror, Lethbridge area, 1911 c. NC 2-176, Glenbow-Alberta Archives.

they arrived at their homestead, northward near Tide Lake, they saw the smoke from an inferno about twenty miles to the southeast, moving slowly to the northwest. That night the distance closed to ten miles, and the fire was now due west. Fearing a wind shift before the flames reached the Red Deer River, Tribe insisted on building a fire guard to protect the men and wagons.

The others were dubious, and anyway they had not brought the plow with the first load. Assisted after a time by the doubting Thomases, Tribe shovelled a small guard before leaving for Carlstadt the next morning. He made two trips over the following days, always eyeing the fire. On his last return voyage, he recalled, "when I got within 10 or 12 miles of the camp, I could see a long way North and East and the prairie was black as far as I could see." Lashing like a scorpion, the fire had indeed turned and had swept over the entire region. With a sinking feeling, he urged his team over the char, speeding to a vantage point several miles further

Ready for the fray—Colorado settlers arrive at Bassano, 1914. NA 984-3, Glenbow-Alberta Archives.

where he could see the area of the camp. When he reached the point, he beheld the fluttering tent and was greatly relieved. An hour or more later, Tribe's father told him that the little guard had saved their lives by allowing them to back-fire just before the conflagration swooped down on them.[13]

A year earlier, Francis Hart and family arrived from Napanee, Ontario, at Bassano, the jumping-off point for the western portion of the dry areas. Their destination was first the Red Deer River, then across the wide and as yet empty Berry Creek region, north to a place that would be called Scotfield, a few miles east of where Hanna now lies.

Late that summer nineteen-year-old son George took the wagon back to Bassano for winter supplies. Returning, he suffered two mishaps. On the treacherous banks of the Red Deer one wagon overturned, mixing coal oil with the oatmeal, flour and sugar. That winter they ate the fortified vittles and even began to consider a meal without kerosene somewhat bland. George's second misfortune was to be trapped in the great prairie fire of 1909.

Creaking along with two full loads, he beheld to the northwest a whitish, yellow pall which turned red as the sun went down. Realizing it was smoke, he fell back on earlier advice—if a prairie fire approaches, ascend a rise, burn off the grass and let the monster pass. The closest hill was several miles distant, but he lumbered toward it with full despatch, racing the demon. On reaching the prominence, he tethered the horses at the bottom and torched the knoll. As the flames tore down the hill, they almost escaped his frantic, flailing, wet gunny sack. No sooner had he completed the task and run the horses and wagons to the top than the first gusts from the fire storm hit. Soaking the tarpaulins and wagons, he braced himself.

Bounding ahead of the devouring flames, pronghorned antelope, rabbits and coyotes joined him. Even an owl alighted, but none of the visitors paid any attention to him. All eyes were riveted on the enveloping flames, the flying sparks and the cloud of acrid smoke. So oppressive the smoke became that George wetted a bandana and knotted it over his stinging face. The horses plunged and whinneyed, and the wind howled. Flaming grass, swooping on the wings of the wind, fell on his clothing and on the wagon tarpaulin, scorching and singeing. When it grew dark with the gusts puffing like a bellows, the thick prairie wool glowed like a bed of coals. It was a weird sight, like a lake of crimson lava from the bowels of the earth.

Long after Hephaestus, the fire god, had passed, the stygian gloom remained, punctuated by flashing embers burning to a whiteness, then dying. Fearing the heat of the firmament, George bade his horses stay while the cool of the night slowly rendered walking across the waste bearable. The next day, after a sleepless night, the twenty remaining miles across the ashes turned the grey Percherons black with soot.

At the homestead, the family had circled a fire guard around their belongings. Mrs. Hart had made a swing from a rope and a board, and the eighty-year-old grandfather was lowered, protesting all the way, into the well. There he stayed, protecting his infirm lungs, as the others thought, until the blaze passed. When he was hauled to

The new town of Hanna nearly burnt down in its infancy. NA 3596-186, Glenbow-Alberta Archives.

Incomers at Cereal, 1911 c. NS 2056-2, Glenbow-Alberta Archives.

the surface in the aftermath, he declared indignantly that he was leaving this hellish land forthwith. And leave he did.[14]

Charles Seefeldt, one of the early settlers of the Berry Creek area, was not so lucky. When he got back from a coal trip to Sheerness he discovered the fire had jumped the guard and consumed his tent and goods. The fierce conflagration tore all the way from Lloydminster two hundred miles to Steveville when a wind shift turned it westward. One settler, Seeglestadt, almost a dwarf, and his daughter were caught in the fire. Frantically, they gathered household goods and dashed before the running flames toward Berry Creek. Relentlessly the inferno overtook them, ran past them, igniting the high grass, enveloping them in a swirl of smoke and flashing pain. Seeglestadt perished, and his daughter, her clothes burned off and her flesh terribly scorched, was taken to the Calgary hospital where she lived after a long ordeal.[15]

Year after year, in spring, summer, and fall, fires ravaged the shortgrass areas, often leaping from the stacks of passing locomotives, fearsome fire wagons, as the natives knew them, and spreading for miles at the whim of the winds. Soon every settler knew the terror of prairie fire. Even the rivers were no guarantee of safety, for the great Hutton fire of early settlement days leapt the Red Deer with ease, catapulting burning debris to the other side. Neither was winter safe. The frequent snowless periods, blown dry by desiccating chinooks, were very vulnerable to fire.

Just after Christmas Day 1912, a terrible conflagration bore down on the new town of Hanna. Called from supper, the townspeople hesitated to rush to the front of flame six miles away lest the flames should outflank them and wipe out the undefended town. In moments, the gap was narrowed to four miles, so the citizens rode out with sacks and brooms to confront the menace. When they arrived, they encountered a wall of flames five or six feet high, and they fell back in fear. Attention shifted to the Canadian Northern right-of-way, for the fire was south of it, and if it crossed the grade, the whole town would be lost. Backfires lit in the stubble spread so fast in the high wind that the men nearly burned down the town themselves before they could return to the two mile front across the main blaze. After several hours of frantic flailing, the grimy, blackened workers ran the blaze into a big backfire where it soon sputtered from want of fuel and died.[16]

Dry Wells

THE BAPTISM BY FIRE was only one of the first experiences of homesteaders. The object of the trek from the jumping off points was the search for the township stake, about 1¼ inches in diameter and left by surveyors. Within each township the thirty-six sections were marked off with smaller stakes. Sometimes the markers were impossible to find, and it was widely believed that cross-grained ranchers seeing their hegemony disintegrating, had torn them from the earth and cast them away. Emmanual and Theresa Hagel and their nine children, recent immigrants to the Schuler area from Russia, could not find the stakes because of the high virgin grass. They erected a dwelling half a mile off course and were forced to move when the legitimate homesteader discovered his tenants.[17]

Some settlers, though not as many as legend suggests, sculpted sod huts from the matted prairie, and a few in the southeast of German-Russian origin even built adobe houses from sun-dried mud and straw bricks.[18] Despite the complete absence of wood in the region, however, most houses in the dry belt were wood frame abodes.

This fact explained the great importance and number of lumber yards in the burgeoning towns. Carlstadt, for example, had three. The cost of high quality B.C. lumber, according to R. S. Tribe, was roughly $38 per thousand board feet for shiplap and two-by-fours—prohibitive enough, especially when the buyer had to stay overnight in town and pay livery and hotel bills. A three thousand pound load for a two-horse team, plodding thirty-five miles into the hinterland, was also a long, arduous trek.[19]

To the horror of many incomers, the dry areas, especially southward, were infested with rattlesnakes. These sidewinders crawled into bedrolls, into boots, into tents; they were in heaps of brush, in the stooks, and beneath the steps. They were even more numerous near water, in the coolness of the river beds, where they lurked along the ledges and in rocks and crannies. Wherever they were, they spooked the horses and terrified the women. On the first day that P. O. Warner broke the sod on his homestead near Winnifred, he killed eighteen of them.[20] When Marjory Gow killed her first rattler near Bindloss, she cleaved it in half with an axe, and the part with the head wriggled away. Like others she soon learned to destroy the head.[21]

The serpents were a nuisance. What was worse was the scarcity of water. Finding good water in the dry belt was like looking for gold. The largest lakes in the region—Sullivan, north of Hanna,

Pakowki, southwest of the Hat, and Bigstick, north of Maple Creek—were all foul. The first water R. S. Tribe sipped from a slough north of Carlstadt, he said, tasted "like turpentine." A day later, his party passed a homestead of two bachelors who had just struck a gusher at sixty feet. The water was so alkaline no one would touch it.[22]

Sometimes, as with Len Armstrong's well south of Youngstown, Glauber salt fouled the water. For the stock, there was nothing else, and they eventually got used to it. For the family, soap would not make suds, and the liquid had to be "broken" with lye on wash day. Except in winter, when the snow could be melted, all water for cooking and drinking had to be hauled.[23] Under such circumstances, which prevailed over much of the dry belt, water was precious and was used over and over. In the Pendant d'Oreille country south of Medicine Hat, for example, they used the same water for cooking, for bathing, for washing clothes and for scrubbing the floors—in that order.[24]

After her young husband died of cancer, Martha Smith left Carmangay, Alberta, and homesteaded near Bindloss on the Saskatchewan border. Greatly handicapped by three tots, the oldest just three, she too had to haul water. This usually meant leaving the children alone while she went a mile and a half to the nearest well. Once when she returned, she discovered one of the children had been into the syrup pail, spilled it all over the floor, tracked it over the furniture and plastered it over herself. From then on, she tied the children to a chair when she left for water—a most hazardous remedy given the numerous dangers from fire to rattlesnakes.[25]

Sinking wells was a painful, precarious and often disappointing enterprise. Several settlers died digging their way to hell when the desert released an effluvium known as damp gas from the bowels of the earth. Joseph Tucker who very likely was in the long line at Lethbridge when the last major block of free land was thrown open, was eighty feet down in a well he was excavating south of Bow Island when he called to those above that he sensed foul air. A rope was thrown, he quickly tied it around himself, and friends began hoisting. They hauled him up fifty feet when the knot slipped and he plunged into the pit to his death.[26]

The great water shortage—irrigating gardens by hand, the ultimate futility, Pendant d'Oreille, 1913 c. NS 1546-12, Glenbow-Alberta Archives.

For many years Nels and Nikolai Sokvitne bored wells in the Lomond area. They knew the wiles of poison gas enough to lower a candle into the abyss to test the air for impurities. But they lacked principle. Sometimes they would substitute a cat for a candle. If the unfortunate feline were dragged to the surface limp and unconscious, it was time to bore another hole.[27] Once near Bowell another well-digger grabbed a rooster, sent it down, and a few minutes later brought it up dead. The fatality seemed inconsequential enough until the owner saw the corpse, then slumped in stupefaction and mumbled something about its being a champion bird.[28]

Even without noxious fumes, well-digging was treacherous. Hiram Beech, a pioneer near the Hat from Missouri, was laboriously deepening his excavation while above him towered sixty-five feet of cribbing resting on a post. Swinging away in the dimness with his pick and shovel, he accidentally knocked out the prop and the monstrous weight of the cribbing crashed down on him like a blunt guillotine. To the horror of his wife and son at the top, his life gurgled out in seconds.[29]

In the first winter north of brand new Carlstadt, Nels Anderson and his brother were determined to dig a well on the virgin land. By hand they dug down through the hard blue clay, with one manning a windlass on top and the other chipping and prying and filling a pail on the bottom. At the eighty foot level, the shaft was as dry as the air. The brothers thereupon rigged a wood auger to a ¾ inch pipe and continued boring another ten, twenty, thirty, forty feet. At the 120 foot level there was still no trace of moisture, so the two quit in disgust.

They wondered if a water diviner might help. An old Swedish witcher had passed by their mound of frustration and had offered them a literal fountain. When his magic stick pointed to a spot scarcely forty feet away, Nels and his brother were understandably hesitant. The witcher, however, saw nothing untoward in his prediction and proceeded to explain the mysteries of subterranean impermeability which included the clear possibility of a dry hole right next to a gusher. The argument sounded all right, thought Nels and his brother, and the two set to work. Anyway the diviner had forecast the strike at forty feet. Down again they went into their second mine—all the way to 120 feet again, with the same result. Nothing.

There was another man in the district said to be able to find water with a wire. After he marked the spot, the Andersons with a new two-foot auger promptly corkscrewed down a hundred feet. Then they hit a boulder which would not budge. With pry bar in hand and a foot on a stirrup attached to the winch, slim Nels was lowered into the narrow casing. At the bottom of a claustrophobe's nightmare, his body pressing against the sides of the earthen tube, his lungs straining in the bad air, Nels chipped away at the edge of the rock and eventually dislodged it. He attached a device to remove it and signalled his worried brother in the white spot above to inch him to the surface. They then set the auger in motion again. Ten feet later they hit another boulder. The brothers looked at each other, shook their heads and quit. It was not until years later that Nels Anderson had a well worthy of the name, and then his well driller had to go down 245 feet.[30]

The railways too suffered from the water famine. At smaller terminals, like Lethbridge, the CPR required for locomotives, coaches and roundhouse service 375,000 gallons daily. A larger point, like Moose Jaw, needed nearly twice that much. The average water station on the main line needed 150,000 gallons daily. Even a branch line water supply had to generate 20,000 gallons during the ten hour working day.

The first CPR well in the Lethbridge region was sunk at Foremost in 1914. Seven hundred twenty-four feet deep, it yielded just 7,000 gallons of "light" sodic water. Not only did this inadequate flow soon diminish, as was the case with several other artesian wells, but also it was adulterated with 7½ pounds of sodium salts per thousand gallons. The salts caused the water to foam badly in the boilers. At Burdett, the railway found water at only 230 feet, but it contained 5½ pounds of scale-producing salts, plus 13 pounds of sodium salts per thousand gallons, and therefore was very poor boiler water. The deep wells at Abbey and Sceptre in southwestern Saskatchewan were inferior too, being very hard and corrosive on boilers. The latter was even sulphuretted.[31]

In the new Canaan the search for good water, it soon became clear, would be the fundamental pursuit. Very early on, a story with veiled allusion to the water-poor town of Carlstadt and with general application to the entire dry belt circulated in a local newspaper:

A traveller driving across the country to a village near Brooks met a wagoner hauling water.

"Where do you get water?" the traveller asked.

"Up the road about seven miles," the settler replied.

"And do you haul water seven miles for your family and stock?"

"Yep."

"Why in the name of sense don't you dig a well?" inquired the traveller.

"Because it's just as far one way as the other, stranger."[32]

4

Carlstadt, Star of the Prairie

The "Cream de la Creame"

A T THE VERY MOMENT that pioneers were first learning the elemental truths of their chosen land, they and those immediately following were subjected to another round of intense boosterism centring this time on the mushrooming trade hubs which were the new towns. Unleashed and uninhibited, the Lethbridge and Medicine Hat newspapers promoted them with a vengeance. The boosting of Seven Persons, southwest of the Hat, was typical. In early 1911 the *Medicine Hat News* announced that the progressive citizens of the burg would "recognize no obstacles to growth until it attains the title of being the biggest town on the Crow line. . . ." Within a forty mile radius nary a homestead was left unclaimed. Already in the town thirty-three businesses had sprung up, capped by F. N.

Stubbs's stately three-storey hotel which was "the envy of every town along the line."

Stubbs, several businessmen and promoters had formed an energetic board of trade under President J. B. Murray, agent for the townsite company and manager of the Seven Persons Land Company. Consistent with the promotion of the West at every level, Murray stressed that "the country tributary to Seven Persons is generally acknowledged to be the richest agricultural district in Alberta." So fine was the chocolate loam and its clay subsoil, so "famous" was it "for holding moisture during the warm summer months," that in a record unequalled, but often claimed in the West, the first crop would pay for the farm. Murray himself was praised as an original resident—one who had always worked for the development of the country, and one who was "in a better position to give reliable information than any real estate man."[1]

The smaller promoters often played these tricks, attempting to distinguish themselves from parasitic, lucre-crazed speculators. Several times William Salvage of Grassy Lake ran a full page advertisement in the *Medicine Hat News* listing over thirty new business houses, three burgeoning coal mines, the nearby "Old Glory" gas well, greatest on the continent, the coming glass industry to tap the great sand deposits north of the city, "the finest agricultural land" and unexcelled climate, the "85 bushels of oats per the acre and 44 bushels of No. 1 hard wheat," the doubling of town lot prices in six months, and the absence of pauper farmers. "We have to have the cream de la creame," the ad exclaimed. At its climax, the advertisement divorced itself from scores of lesser promotions by asking thinking settlers everywhere, "Why Is Grassy Lake Going Right Ahead Without Boosting?"[2]

Of course, Salvage was anything but a nonbooster. Between him and Harry Driggs, owner of another Grassy Lake townsite company, the two had carved up roughly eighteen hundred lots.[3] In 1910 and 1911 the village literally erupted from the desert floor. Pushing for all they were worth, Driggs and Salvage engineered the incorporation of Grassy Lake as a village in February 1911. Still passing trains unloaded settlers at the bustling centre, and when the

The mecca of William Salvage and Harry Driggs—Grassy Lake, 1912 c. NC 2-376, Glenbow-Alberta Archives.

A familiar sight to first-arrivals—the general store, Burdett, 1910. NA 729-24, Glenbow-Alberta Archives.

Dominion census was completed later that year the population had reached a healthy 247.[4] The burgeoning continued, and even before spring 1912 the two speculators were plotting the upgrading of the village into a town. Commissioning a census to chart the growth of the fledging colossus, the two were elated to discover that the population stood abrimming at 460 souls by April 24.[5] Their dreams were only temporarily dispelled, they opined, when some crepe-hanging deputy minister of Municipal Affairs informed the village secretary that they needed 700 people to become an official town![6]

Everywhere in the dry belt this tale of unbelievable growth was repeated. On the eastern edge at Kindersley, Saskatchewan, within

The elegant Alamo, Suffield, 1911 c. P 1668.1, Medicine Hat Archives.

The smart England and England Block on the corner of Railway Avenue and Broadway, Carlstadt, 1912 c. P 3519.24, Medicine Hat Archives.

nine days of the sale of the first townsite lots, a board of trade popped up, and thirty days later there were 125 buildings in town.[7]

While in every quarter new construction reached for the sky, few structures in the new Eden could match Suffield's new hotel, the Alamo. Constructed at a cost of $30,000 in 1910 by W. R. Martin, superintendent of CPR oil and gas exploration, A. M. Grace, chief engineer of the Southern Alberta Land Company, and A. P. Phillips, the edifice was named and modelled after the historic Alamo in Texas, a favorite haunt of Martin's during his eight year stay in the far south.

Martin, the designer, highlighted severe lines and soft colorings, achieving a simple but striking elegance. A broad, open gallery stretched across the front, and inside, the walls were kalsomined "in soft brown tints and burlapped in a darker shade. . . ." The floors were maple, the appointments, oak, and the windows, plate glass. Of solid mahogany, the front bar was seemingly set in an imaginary forest of dark green walls offset by full mission oak appurtenances. At the rear bar petite windows and low mirrors let in subdued light. In the dining room was the same classy oak furniture with pale and burlapped walls. Upstairs, the impressed correspondent revealed, "the suites are fitted up with brush[ed] brass beds, mahogany furniture, Brussels rugs and ecru curtains, and supplied with hot and cold water." There were holland blinds, net curtains, felt mattresses, and eiderdown comforters. In the basement—a wine cellar, a refrigerator, a laundry, a steam heating plant, and a capacious, well-lit sample room.

The Alamo was lit by natural gas, courtesy of a productive well owned by the Southern Alberta Land Company. It had its own 230 foot well from which water was pumped to a hundred barrel tank on the third floor for distribution to the kitchen, suites and toilets.[8] Not surprisingly such opulence deserved more than a single grand opening. At one such celebration one hundred fifty guests were entertained to a lavish oyster dinner.[9]

Down the track westward from Suffield was the new town of Carlstadt, formerly called Langevin when it was merely a section house. For some years prior to the birth of Carlstadt, Charles and Elmer England had resided in the area as ranchers. Seeing the writing on the wall for the cattlemen, they moved into town early in 1909, established a real estate office, and began dispensing acreages in the new heartland. In short order they became selling agents for the Hudson's Bay Company, representatives of leading fire and life insurance companies, and exclusive agents for the townsite properties.[10]

Like J. B. Murray of Seven Persons, the Englands operated as locators for intending settlers, always stressing their longstanding connection with the land. Augmented by the enthusiasm, the frenzied occupation of the environs soon took place. Mammoth farm outfits, such as the New Dominion Farms, the Boston-Alberta Company, and the Carlstadt Development Company, rolled their

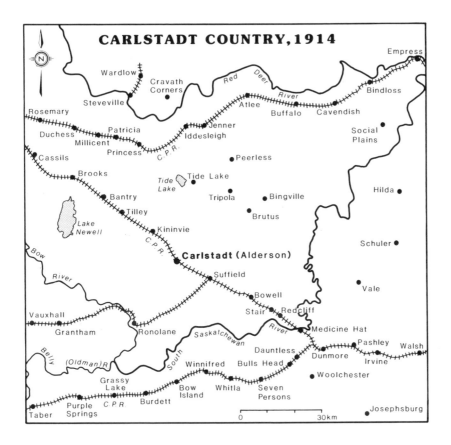

CARLSTADT COUNTRY, 1914

steam engines out onto the flats and began working some of the largest acreages, between twelve and twenty sections, in the history of the West.[11]

At first the village of Carlstadt was located north of the tracks on school land. As new businesses and new homes sprang from the prairie, spirits were light and overflowing with a joie de vivre, the fulfilment of hard work, the fatigue of the satisfied, and the tangible evidences of remarkable progress. If there was a feeling of grand destiny in the air, there was also a playfulness in the reports, an easiness. "The short order house of Hannum and Sobie," the Carlstadt correspondent reported in September 1909, "is serving everything the palate of the epicurean could desire, from quail on toast to nightingales' tongues."[12]

Many Carlstadt newcomers were met by Thom Swanby. NA 4756-1, Glenbow-Alberta Archives.

In the frenzied influx, Annie Swanby, wife of Thom, and daughter Lily, turned their home into a hotel. NA 5048-1, Glenbow-Alberta Archives.

The genial blacksmith, working like Vulcan amid the expansion, kept company with a pig, a bright one, it seemed, for the smithy spoke to him regularly, and wherever he went the pig was sure to follow. It was a sign of the times that the smithy grew so busy he had scarcely the time to talk to his confidant.[13] When the smithy visited the Hat, the Carlstadt correspondent wrote: "The pig, of course, being left behind, walked right up to the restaurant and ordered his meals, regardless of expense."[14]

That fall the rush began in earnest. As settlers tumbled off the trains they were met by locators like Thom Swanby and John Goehring who ferried them into the surrounding country estates. Day and night, Swanby's wife Annie labored in their impressive three-storey home cooking meals and keeping house for settlers who had no place to stay before journeying out, usually early next morning with Thom to the promised land.[15]

The townspeople spent their first Christmas in a sort of dreamland, entertaining and coming to know their neighbors more intimately. When Bertha Swanby, aged sixteen, had arrived a few months earlier and had seen that only the Woollven store and the station constituted the town, she broke down and cried.[16] Her father Thom, however, had no intentions of living in a community so modest and subdued. Norwegian-born and proud owner of the first hardware store, Thom, a handsome man in his mid-forties and always restless and venturesome, was a natural host and reveller who loved good company and a good time. In the Christmas season of 1909, Swanby staged a surprise party inviting more than fifty guests, including the Englands, the F. E. McDiarmids, implement dealers, and the Harry Wagners, a couple who managed the Finlay Lumber Company and who would soon endear themselves to so many and come to represent the finest elements of the town's spirit. To the tunes of mandolin, guitar, violins, flute and accordion, McDiarmid, temporarily lame, called off the dances. A whist party roared with hilarity in an adjoining room. The guests partook of refreshments regularly, for it was common knowledge, Lex the reporter wrote, that "Mr. Swanby is a connoisseur and keeps nothing 'under five years old.'"[17] This party, and others more modest, did much to knit the community in that first season.

This Year Is Carlstadt's   AFTER THE CPR TOWNSITE was surveyed in February 1910, the inhabitants moved lock, stock and barrel to the southside of the tracks. As the tempo picked up that month there were two restaurants in town open round the clock. When the midnight trains disgorged further homeseekers, the restaurant floors were already jammed with bodies, most lost in reverie and others too excited to catnap. Many who had detrained were given a few square inches of "board" room

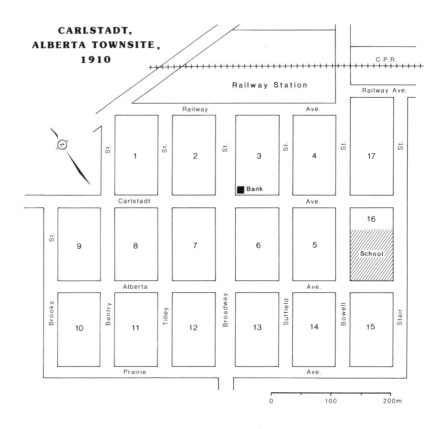

CARLSTADT, ALBERTA TOWNSITE, 1910

on which to sit and try to sleep.[18] By March-end Brussard's Great West Restaurant had erected a tent to take the overflow.[19] A month later H. D. Patterson, the station agent, suffered a near nervous breakdown from overwork. Two men took his place, and they were immediately run off their feet. Three or four would have been worked into a lather.[20]

The town layout comprised seventeen blocks varying generally from sixteen to twenty-eight lots to a block. In the first six weeks after February 17, fully 166 lots were sold. Almost everyone bought something, with Thom Swanby and F. E. McDiarmid latching onto seven each, Harry Wagner four, and the Englands, a dozen. Some employees of the Merchants' Bank at Calgary were tipped off and jumped in, and a crafty speculator from Nebraska, Harry

The west side of Railway Avenue at its height, Carlstadt, 1912 c. NA 4768-1, Glenbow-Alberta Archives.

Shedd, corralled no fewer than nineteen. The big winner was the railway which pocketed a cool $27,000 between mid-February and May.[21]

Newspapers began to appear, irregularly at first, until in 1911 when the weekly *Carlstadt Progress* began. The editor was Calvin Goss, a Liberal who also ran a Brooks paper.[22] Goss was a classic extension of the propaganda of the railways, the Interior Department, the mortgage interests, and the large regional papers. He reckoned fortunes would be made in real estate in the new towns between the Hat and Calgary. "Three years ago Bassano was nothing," he wrote in early 1912, "two years ago Brooks was nothing; but look at them today. This year is Carlstadt's."[23] Already local lots which had sold for $150 two years before were trading hands at $600.[24] "Watch Carlstadt, the Star of the Prairie," Goss intoned.[25]

Turning to the burgeoning essence of the new heartland, its agrarian potential, Goss preached, "Let us have faith in this Land of Opportunity, and make it the garden and granary of the world."[26] Farm values would never be lower. And yet they had leapt from $3 an acre a few years earlier to $35. Lands that produced $40 of grain an acre, he believed, were easily worth $50 an acre.[27] "There is a cause for their increasing value and it is in the fact that with proper farming methods there need be no crop failures and no farmers that are failures."[28]

A rhymester of sorts, Goss wrote poetry which captured his sense of the momentous changes affecting the new West. In "Valley of the Bow," his heart "Re-peoples the space with a race that has died," and the host of wild warriors stands ready to strike a death blow to recapture their heritage. In the hanging mists the warriors are lost, and in their place a caravan of the husbandman materializes, bound for "A land where the sower and reaper [are] king, and none is a vassal and all men are free."[29]

Despite a triteness, the poem revealed Goss's sensitivity for the past, a feeling even more pronounced in "The Rancher's Lament." Recently one of the season's many masters of hyperbole claimed he'd witnessed a battle royal between a seed of grain and ten thousand steers—and the seed had won.[30] Goss, however, felt for the rancher in the apparent death throes of his industry. In the beginning of his poem, the herd is being disturbed by passing homesteaders, and the cattlemen fear "they will oust us root and branch." As more wagons roll in, the rancher despairs. Then he thinks of the arctic winds short years ago which froze thousands of steers, leaving the bleaching bones shining among the turf and the rocks. Sensing the same fate for himself, he feels drawn into the vortex of "a new and faster time," puzzling and incomprehensible, "when the desert lands shall bloom [l]ike some southern tropic clime." Off to the west he goes, to the far-off mountains, cursing his fate, refusing to become one with the invaders. "Let them make their bloomin' farms," he says. Though he loved the boundless prairie, the round-up, and the life on the land, he "can never wear the chains of the farmer's slavery."[31]

Perhaps there was more to the lament than met the eye, for only days later Goss sold the *Progress* to Herbert S. Ketchum, a young man from Illinois who had worked the past month with the Bassano *News*.[32]

With Goss's retirement the paper became known as *The Carlstadt News*—a slight change, perhaps, but one which revealed a move in the West away from the unbounded exuberance of the settling in, toward a more workaday attitude of solving the problems of living. The boosting, of course, continued, but it gradually receded as the dominant motif.

By January 1911, there were thirty-five occupied dwelling houses in Carlstadt, and later that year the village was incorporated.[33] Though several merchants lived officially on nearby homesteads at night, the census revealed its population in 1911 to be 162.[34] Land values rose steadily at least until 1912 when Dr. McEwen, village secretary, reported the valuation of the village to be close to $200,000. The best lots which had originally sold for $150 could not be bought now, he said in March, for less than $800.[35] Charles England had picked up lots 5, 6, 9, and 10 running down the heart of Railway Avenue right across from the station and cornering on the west side of Broadway. Together these gems came into his hands on November 1, 1910, for $425.[36] When he transferred the title of twenty-four feet of the prestigious twenty-five foot corner lot to Carlstadt lawyer Virginius Lee Lloyd on May 30, 1913, it alone was worth $1,000.[37]

The Carlstadt News reported before Christmas 1912 that the readership of the paper had tripled since August 1.[38] Little more than a year later the town reached its peak and an impressive array of businesses greeted the visitor, including two dry goods and general merchandise stores, three lumber companies, three insurance, real estate and loans establishments, two implement dealers, two hardware stores, two pool halls, at least two churches, a drug store, a meat market, a bakery, a Union Bank, one of the finest two-room schools in the south country, and five hotels, including the elegant three-storey Carlstadt.[39] Proudly the citizens bought packets of postcards of the entrepot and its shining new structures produced by professional photographer and local jeweller, Chester M. Coffey.

Several social clubs operated including one of the first, the Adanac, originally for young men, housed above McEwen's pharmacy. During Fred Conn's stay as a teacher in Carlstadt in

1913 the Adanac Club hosted Professor Sachs of Berlin who played piano and violin selections. That year the club also sponsored political rallies, dances, and its own play, appropriately called "A Daughter of the Desert," which it performed "abroad" at Suffield and Redcliff as well as at home.[40]

In addition, there was another association called simply "the social club," a Methodist Ladies' Aid, a junior branch of the Women's Christian Temperance Union, several nearby United Farmer locals, and for wishful souls on these treeless plains, a lodge of the Modern Woodmen of America. During the war there was an active Knights of Pythias Lodge. Tennis enthusiasts played regularly next to the bank, up from the corner of Broadway Street and Carlstadt Avenue, a few dabbled at croquet in back yards, many stroked baseballs on the school grounds and vacant lots, and everyone attended the combined field and Dominion Days, the odd circus, and later a Chautauqua or two. As for local government, a village council existed, as well as a board of trade of sorts, and two councils of the adjacent municipalities, King and Sunny South.

Perhaps 70 percent of the newcomers were from the States, the Dakotas and Minnesota particularly, where many had gathered from Europe shortly before.[41] If the countryside attracted a plurality of Scandinavians, with colonies of Poles and Dutchmen northward, Carlstadt itself was staunchly Anglo Celtic. Even as late as 1921, fully two-thirds of the villagers were classified as part of the British races.[42] About 80 percent were Protestant, roughly half of whom were Methodist.[43] A unique blend of the sons of John Bull and Uncle Sam, the town's leading lights sought to secure what they considered the common elements of English-speaking cultures. Thus when the likeable Swede, Neils Andersen, applied for his citizenship, Judge Wagner induced him to render his name "less cumbersome" and more in keeping with orthographic patterns already established. And so Neils became Nels, and Andersen became Anderson.[44]

Given this flavoring, the town occasionally exhibited strains of racism. The Chinese of the community seem never to have been included in any census and were treated with all the contempt due to a species of subhumans. In October 1914, the paper reported that

Carlstadt's Chinatown had burned to the ground. The sector was a single building, the proverbial laundry, which was consumed in a flash. "The lone inhabitant of the district," the journalist wrote touchingly, "Long Pin or whatever his name was, escaped death . . . but as he had to make his exit through a broken window, his hands and feet were badly cut." Apparently the smoke was so dense he could not see the door. According to the reporter, "The excited Celestial was put to bed in the Carlstadt hotel where some of his compatriots work." With a smattering of English Long Pin blurted—"Some one play trick on me." That was all the interview the paper got, or cared to get.[45]

A month later the *News* exposed a bevy of "Celestials," three from Suffield and two from Strathmore, conspiring to start another laundry, or failing that, a restaurant. When they could find no building, a relieved reporter sighed appreciatively, "Carlstadt still has no yellow peril!"[46] Two years later a "progressive Celestial" spent several days in town seeking to reopen the laundry. "Finding that Chinks were about as welcome here as the Kaiser would be in London," the paper snapped, "he changed his mind and left."[47]

If the presence of Orientals injected a divisive element into the town, other factors did too. Occasionally a feeling of antagonism erupted between the town and country. Several attempts were made to generate an enthusiastic board of trade, but all were short-lived. While possessed of many admirable citizens, the town lacked a clear-cut leader. Sensing the softening of the real estate market and having reaped the bounty of the boom, Charles England soon sold out and headed for the lax life of Calgary.

There was, it was true, the progressive businessman Henry R. Bean. Born in Ontario in 1868, a graduate of Victoria University in Toronto in 1898, a high school principal and even a school superintendent in Indiana, he brought to Carstadt in 1911 a champion of virtue, a cultured intellect and an affable temperament. A staunch supporter of the Methodist Church, he was devoted to the Bible class and the choir which he directed. His home was always open, and many young men far from home sat at his table and were refreshed and encouraged. There was something uplifting about the man, a spiritual fineness. In so many respects he was a symbol of

Off the main thoroughfare—
looking north on Tilley Street,
rear of Carlstadt Hotel, far left,
1912. NA 4711-1, Glenbow-
Alberta Archives.

The first store south of the
tracks, Carlstadt, 1912. NA
4711-6, Glenbow-Alberta
Archives.

Doc McEwen's pharmacy,
Carlstadt, 1914. Lilly Askew,
employee, B. A. Barnes,
druggist. NA 5034-1,
Glenbow-Alberta Archives.

Henry Bean's store on Broadway, Carlstadt, 1912 c. NA 5082-2, Glenbow-Alberta Archives.

Inside Bean's General Store, Carlstadt, 1912, c. NA 5082-3, Glenbow-Alberta Archives.

The town newspaper office on Broadway, 1914 c. W. D. McKay, Delsey Askew, Herbert S. Ketchum, editor, left to right. NA 5034-2, Glenbow-Alberta Archives.

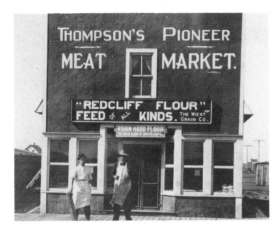

Butcher shop, Carlstadt, 1911, A. D. Thompson, Confederate veteran, proprietor. NA 2083-17, Glenbow-Alberta Archives.

Conley's Livery, Carlstadt, 1912. NA 4711-5, Glenbow-Alberta Archives.

Lumber for the treeless plains— C. F. Starr, proprietor, Carlstadt, 1911 c. NA 5081-2, Glenbow-Alberta Archives.

Implement dealers in Carlstadt —Mr. and Mrs. W. G. Scollard, left of child, and Mr. and Mrs. E. C. Hegy, right. NA 5034-5, Glenbow-Alberta Archives.

The interior of the Askew Machine Shop, Carlstadt, 1914 c. NA 5034-4, Glenbow-Alberta Archives.

Only the station and section houses had gas in Carlstadt, 1913 c. NA 4789-1, Glenbow-Alberta Archives.

the best of the age, a bellwether in education at a time when the fullness of its blessings was just being realized, driven by a faith in God, by a passion to experience the new West as fully as possible, and by a zeal to succor the weak and the uncertain. And he was at the prime of life—forty-three—when he came to Carlstadt.

Some time in mid-1913, Bean began feeling unwell. Possessing the funds, he travelled to the coast for a rest, but on his return he was stricken suddenly at Calgary. At the hospital that September he was diagnosed as having cancer, and was operated on. Able to return to Carlstadt, he ran his general store until January 1914 when he grew worse. Taken to hospital again, he was told that nothing could be done. This grim communication he received again at the Mayo Clinic in Rochester, Minnesota, the last refuge of the cancer-ridden and terminally ill with means.

Again he returned to Carlstadt where his long illness was borne with equanimity and Christian resignation; indeed, it was said that "his sick room was a benediction to all who visited him." One Sunday in June his suffering ended, and his remarkable spirit departed. He left behind a wife and two young daughters.

On the day of Bean's funeral it was a mark of the vast respect of the community that all businesses were closed and the school of which he had been trustee was let out. A stirring tribute was delivered before the grieving multitude by Rev. R. E. Clysdale, pastor of the Methodist Church. The cortege then proceeded to the morning train at the depot, and thence to Hillside Cemetery at Medicine Hat.[48]

Harry Wagner

IT WAS FITTING that at least two of the pall bearers were candidates for the leadership mantle which Bean so richly merited and wore for so short a time. One was S. F. McEwen, as a doctor the desideratum of small communities in the West. McEwen operated the drug store, the upstairs of which served as the Adanac Club, a centre of the town's social life. Serving under the first two mayors, Charles England and A. J.

Drummond, he was the town's first secretary-treasurer and health officer.[49] As such he helped superintend the first three years of the town's growth—the building of wooden sidewalks, the erection of more elevators, the grading of the streets, the setting of bylaws and the community's moral tone, and the procurement of a cemetery east of town.[50]

Another of Henry Bean's pall bearers was C. H. Wagner, in some ways not unlike the departed. Born in England, Harry Wagner had attended an elite Tunbridge Wells private school with his two brothers, Orland and Bert. Operated by Harry's father, the school attracted such personages as the son of the King of Siam whom Harry apparently knew.[51]

Wagner operated the Finlay lumber yard in town, a business extension of W. T. Finlay of the Hat. He had been present at that first grand Christmas party where minds had touched, friendships had been welded and the soul of the embryo community had been formed. Liked and respected, he later served as town councilman and warden of the Anglican Church. Long a Liberal supporter, he enquired through his employer Finlay in Medicine Hat if he might be considered for the job of Justice of the Peace in Carlstadt. After Charles England vouched for him, Liberal Attorney General C. R. Mitchell made the appointment.[52] Wagner's position as justice enhanced his stature as a man of fairness and honesty, but it likely also set him beyond the pale, more aloof than a leader could afford to be. Yet the fact that he arbitrated their own cases seems not to have impaired the residents' esteem and affection for him.

Wagner was always involved in matters that counted. As village councillor in 1913, he and W. G. Scollard, another of Bean's pall bearers, were encharged with solving the town's chronic water supply problem.[53] In the 1880s when the CPR was searching for water, workers had dug down and had struck gas—the first such well in Alberta. A generation later when the Englands began their promotion, they hauled water from outside the town. The arrangement was imperfect and impermanent, and it was not until late 1913 that a ninety-one foot well with seven feet of water and a windmill provided a measure of satisfaction.[54]

Just before Christmas 1913, the new Anglican St. Mary's Church with square tower and Gothic windows was dedicated. For the Wagners particularly, it was a crowning moment. Led by Mrs. Wagner, president of the Women's Auxiliary, the ladies ignored their Christmas cake and pudding and held bazaars and debt reduction sales in Suffield and Carlstadt just before the opening. All the church furnishings, it seemed, came from someone or some place special. The altar, prayer desk, lectern and pews were donated by St. Barnabas Church in the Hat; the brass altar cross was a gift of post mistress Mrs. W. M. Cotter and another lady; the brass alms dish, of Mrs. F. C. Woollven of the first general store; the brass altar vases, of the Wagners. Several large cash donations for site and building were also received from parties in England, including Mr. Henry Wagner, Sr. After the service, the judge and his wife hosted a reception for the Bishop and clergy in their home, the former house of worship, decorated now with mauve chrysanthemums and asparagus ferns.[55]

The erection of the church was one more very powerful influence which turned thoughts toward the preservation of the handsome new village. In March 1914, the council looked into the possibility of adding to the Broadway cistern several others. They bought a water tank belonging to Wagner's lumber yard.[56] And as if some spirit had nudged them, they began to worry about operating the new windmill and well which had been shut down by the worst of winter.[57]

On Saturday morning June 20, 1914, fire engulfed the Farmer's Hotel, obliterating it and threatening to destroy the entire business section of town. As the flames flew from the doomed building, the wind wafted fiery arrows blocks away, igniting a blaze near McEwen's pharmacy. For an hour the struggle raged between the townspeople and the flames, the balance tipping one way then the other. All the businessmen near the fire removed their wares to the street, and the ladies all the way to Broadway made preparations to leave at once. At a crucial moment sparks fell on the fire hose, burning through and necessitating the removal of a section. At last the hotel burned itself out, and adjacent structures, though badly charred, were saved.

Ruins of the fierce fire that razed Railway Avenue from the England and England Block to Tilley Street, Carlstadt, 1914. NA 2083-9, Glenbow-Alberta Archives.

Fortunately the always meagre water supply held, though CPR agent Brown wisely had a tank shipped up from Suffield. The fire-fighters were grateful for the Little Giant fire engine which the Council had bought in 1912. As for the Farmer's Hotel, it was owned by Thom Swanby, and was without insurance.[58]

The next council meeting discussed the creation of a fire chief and a fire brigade.[59] Dallying here, members at least moved to fill Lockrem's cistern, emptied during the fire, and to deepen the town well by ten feet. The fire hall was covered with roofing, and at Judge Wagner's request the village school board was asked to put a cistern on the school grounds.[60]

Scant weeks later, a conflagration ten times the magnitude, the worst in the brief history of Carlstadt, broke out in the Brassy Arms Hotel on the left side of the crosspiece formed by the intersection of Railway Avenue and Broadway. First noticed by the night tele-graph operator at the depot, the fire demon within ten minutes was devouring most of the structures from Tilley Street to Broadway—

a feed store, pool room, general store, real estate office, telephone office and two homes. Twenty minutes later the heat seized the clock in the telephone office, the last building on the block. So voracious were the flames that the townspeople immediately surrendered the block, concentrating a stream of water on Woollven's store, across Broadway to the east, and the Great West Hotel, south on Broadway. Two families with four little children escaped into the night with only their night clothes. While the wind was in his favor, John Leonard emptied his bakery; with another hose, he might have saved the building. A providential rainstorm, one of the first of a tinder dry season, saved the whole town from destruction. That and the heroic efforts of Harry Wagner who directed the defence and manned the nozzle through the smoky night.

The next day entrepreneurs from Calgary, including Charles England and Oscar Tweeten, destined to make his name as a Chicago industrialist, came to view through the smaze the tangled, blackened remnants of their business houses.[61]

To the residents it must have seemed that the four horsemen of the Apocalypse had thundered down on them that summer, for the infernos in the town were accompanied by parching famine on the land. Across the dry belt, the 1914 crop was a total disaster. Hundreds of men poured out of the regions tributary to Carlstadt, indeed out of all southern Alberta and southwestern Saskatchewan, to aid in the harvest to the north and further east. Broke, they desperately needed a grubstake for the coming winter. Without seed, they appealed to their governments for aid. Federal seed grain, fodder and relief advances in Alberta the next year reached $408,000 and in Saskatchewan $913,000—both figures hundreds of times greater than the total advanced in all the years since 1886.[62] Amid deliberations over what to do about the massive farm debt, war broke out.

For the dry belt as for the rest of the plains, the war was a pity of untold sacrifice to come; for Carlstadt, it was the third calamity in less than three months. Soon young men everywhere, the cream of their communities, came to the defense of the empire and stepped into hell. From Carlstadt several enlisted, they wrote letters to their parents and siblings, and some died. The conflict had not raged many months before the residents grew ashamed of the German sounding title of their town, even though some thought it derived from John Carlson, a Norwegian and one of the first pioneers. In May 1915, the town folk considered alternate names submitted by the ladies of the district and chose Alliance first, Sheldon second, and Alderson third. The last had been submitted by Charlotte Cotter, wife of postmaster Wemyss Cotter, a striking woman with a penchant for the spotlight. A petition was sent to Ottawa, and not long after, an answer arrived. The new name was Charlotte's choice—Alderson—after the British commander of that name.[63]

Soon after the outbreak of the war, Harry Wagner organized a Home Guard, said to be the country's first. The group regularly performed manoeuvres in the drill hall and kept the patriotic spirit of the town brimming. Moved by the mounting turbulence in Europe, Wagner nonetheless felt a malaise, a yearning for some greater part. In this respect he was little different from the many other Britishers who swarmed the departure depots and embarkation points seeking the speediest conveyance to the threatened homeland. For Harry there was another factor irresistibly drawing him away—his mother in England who was desperately ill.

In the Christmas season of 1914, Wagner and his wife made preparations to leave the town they had helped found. At the drill hall, the Home Guard, wheeling and about-facing with smart precision, performed a special parade before the departing friends and numerous guests. Mrs. Wagner was given a Persian ivory toilet set by the ladies, and Harry received a steam trunk "cram full of our best wishes," as postmaster Cotter said. On December 21 the social club staged a farewell dance with excellent music provided by the Bassano Orchestra. The next evening the entire town turned out at the station to wish the esteemed and well-loved couple Godspeed. The two planned to spend Christmas in Moose Jaw with her relatives before Harry left for England.[64]

Over the next eighteen months, Wagner served at Gallipoli, Lemnos, Africa, in Egypt, Greece and the Balkans. Once, as he passed through the mined waters of the Dardanelles on a submarine, he wrote his brother Bert with great foreboding, fearing for his life.[65] In May 1916, after a four day steamer trip and forty-eight hours on the train, he arrived out of the heat of the eastern Mediterranean at a little village in France. "From now on until the end whatever that may be," he said, "[we] shall remain in France." The loveliness of the village was spoiled only by the distant rumbling of cannon. At this idyllic spot the respite was to be brief, for they were refitting for the trenches, said Harry, "and we all understand what that spells for some of us."

Then Wagner fell to musing, imagining he was in Alderson again, for he had maintained his ties and had somehow managed to receive the town paper. In a long letter, he addressed one by one his old cronies—Wemyss Cotter of the postal service about a registered letter that never came, Bill Scollard about his new auto, Doc about the village pump, O. J. Wood of the Union Bank about loaning his new car. Stopping at the Great West Hotel, Wagner partook of a Lucullan feast, listening the while to H. Johnson puff up the Liberals. At last, he dropped into the stately Carlstadt Hotel for one last drink with Martin Stubbs, the proprietor. "... And then when I can almost see the beer in front of me," he wrote, "I realize that it is only a day dream and the bugle is calling the fall in, and my tongue is as dry as ever. . . ."[66]

A few months later, Harry Wagner was killed.[67]

5 Motoring on the Boulevard of Sunnynook

The War

ELSEWHERE ACROSS the drylands, other grim communications were received. Harry Blois had been one of the pioneers of Hanna. Loved as Harry Wagner was in Alderson, Blois had been a member of the Loyal Orange Lodge, the Masons and the Independent Order of Odd Fellows. A barrister and a booster of an unrugged build, he had passed the army medical, received a commission, and had left for the fray with a Calgary battalion. In spring 1917 news came of his death. As so often happened, the telegram was disbelieved, and anxious hours were spent awaiting the sad confirmation.[1] A few days later, a comrade in the same battalion fell. He was Lieutenant J. R. Sharp, formerly editor of the Calgary *Albertan* and the man largely responsible for the establishment of *The Hanna Herald* in 1912.[2]

Sometimes the hand of death lay heavily upon single families. It was not unusual for two brothers to be called, but it was the misfortune of W. H. Tindall of Lonebutte, south of Hanna, to lose four. The second died six days before Armistice and the third and fourth, some days after the truce, succumbing to wounds, pneumonia and influenza.[3]

While the conflict raged, patriotism flowered. Like sister communities elsewhere in the West, dry belt hamlets stumbled over each other competing in prisoners' relief drives, Red Cross Fund drives, soldiers' tobacco drives, and Victory Loan drives. Ingenuity was often the byword. At Etzikom, east of Foremost, one woman had a chicken with a broken leg. She nursed the hen along, and it soon laid eggs. When the eggs hatched, she sold the chicks and bought a young pig. When the pig fattened, she raffled it for $25, and the new owner raffled it again for $25. Thus the crippled hen added $50 to the Red Cross fund.[4]

For those who lacked motivation to contribute to the war effort, the local papers kept the letters and sacrifice of area youths, the alleged inhumanity of Germany, the prowling of suspected enemy spies and the war-related charities ever before the public. If subsequent generations sometimes wondered about the meaning of the conflict, middle-class newsmen at least of this generation rarely did. In November 1916, *The Hanna Herald* captured the significance of the war in a sardonic poem by J. W. Bengough entitled "The Triumph of Germany."

> When your Parliament's abolished, and your Legislature's
> gone,
> And your old accustomed liberties in Canada have flown;
> When throughout our wide Dominion there is not a man who
> dare
> Express a free opinion with the old Canadian air;
> When a little bunch of tyrants, in breast-plate made of tin,
> Sit at Ottawa to rule you on Orders from Berlin;
> When inspectors poke their noses into everything you do,
> And you're strictly regulated on a system through and through;

When you've got to eat and sleep and think as Government
    dictates,
And nothing is the citizen's, and all things are the State's;
When police officials tell you you can't do this or that,
And to every passing soldier you've got to touch your hat;
When civilians are nonentities, and have to knuckle down
To the martinets in uniform who lord it o'er the town!
When your wife must step off in the mud with all the common
    throng
When pigeon-breasted officers come swaggering along;
When every town and city has its military caste,
And the red tape of bureaucracy has tied you hard and fast;
When your autocratic bosses have three votes to your one,
And you have to bear a tax-load that weighs about a ton;
When your thoughts about the "War-Lord," you mustn't dare
    to speak,
And the gutt'ral German jargon is the language you must
    speak;
When the papers are all censored in the printing of the news,
And the editors forbidden to express their honest views;
When your schools are made "efficient" in dishonor, fraud and
    lies,
And your children are transmogrified to traitors, sneaks and
    spies—
When all these things have come to pass you'll know the War
    is done
The decision has been rendered—and Germany has won;
Great Britain and her allies have lost their gallant fight,
And Canada is Germanized, and henceforth Might is Right.
How do you like the prospect? By Those glorious Flanders
    graves,
Our mothers never reared us to be the Teuton slaves!
The day is here; the hour has struck; behold the Hun's mailed
    fist—
Arise, Canadian Freemen, enlist,
    ENLIST ENLIST![5]

When Edna D. Norton, New York journalist and poetess, toured the West in early 1917, staying a few days at Martin Stubbs's Alberta Hotel in Alderson, she penned another poem about the meaning of the war. Entitled "The Mother's Story," the ode featured a mother telling her little son of the struggle for "King and country [and] for Liberty and Justice." Impassioned, she told of a "desperate monarch" who had swept men and women to watery graves in the sea and who had "torn the crown from Belgium's brow . . . and laid in desolation the hearths and homes in France." All this "just to wear the Crown of England and to make her bow the knee." Tearfully, the son promised one day to be a soldier to fight for England. The mother nodded knowingly, solemnly, "for she knew he like his father would answer the call of his race." Then she asked the ultimate question—could she give this child, were he grown, "to be crushed by the heel of a tyrant and to die in a foreign land?" And as she cuddled him to her breast, the answer came—"Yes! . . . I could wish no nobler end for him than to die a Soldier's death."[6]

It was a mark of a degree of popular disenchantment with such chauvinism that settlers of the dry areas joined farmers elsewhere on the Prairies in opposing conscription. When the federal government announced that the draft would be invoked, it was understood that the farming classes would be exempted.[7] When the understanding proved false, many farmers waxed furious. Some wondered how the exhortation to increase production could be answered by decimating the already thinned agricultural work force. Stanmore farmers, east of Hanna, declared it would be impossible even to harvest the 1918 crop, if young twenty- to twenty-two-year-olds were drafted.[8]

In time, local tribunals were assembled to distinguish between desired labor and essential labor, but their work was never entirely satisfactory, and when government began to overrule their exemptions, discontent brewed. More than one plot was hatched by a father on behalf of his conscriptable son. Sometimes the strategem worked, other times not. Albert Hyndman of the Consort area cunningly turned his farm over to son Floyd, a palpable draft dodger, and then, lending authenticity to the ruse, he returned to the

United States. At war-end he reappeared, assuming matters to be much as they were before his self-imposed exile. Alas, son Floyd would not relinquish the farm, and even more infuriating for Albert was the fact that his own double-dealing wife supported the pretender. After a bitter quarrel, the father put in the crop himself. Realizing that he was a *persona non grata,* an unpaid hired hand, he fell into a fit of despondency, shot his son to death, then his wife, and finally himself.[9]

The war did strange things to people. It raised their expectations regarding public service to an unprecedented degree. Accentuating participation and dedication, it highlighted collective effort for group betterment. Stressing the triumph of democracy, it blighted the names of aristocracy and oligarchy. As C. W. Peterson, editor of *The Farm and Ranch Review* and author of the excellent period piece, *Wake Up, Canada! Reflections on Vital National Issues,* wrote in 1919: "the end of this bloody war is ushering in a new era. . . . We shall be taught to renounce many things that the present generation has most admired in men; wealth, power, position and fame, and to estimate men and things at their true worth."[10]

Focusing on Justice, Liberty and Freedom, the war precipitated an unmatched fit of national introspection. If these principles had prevailed overseas at such a cost, they must surely prevail at home too. What Canadians began to see was that the war had drawn attention to these precepts, especially in the way that the propaganda differentiated Britannic from Teutonic culture, and they sensed that the war and its ghastly sacrifice in blood could be made meaningful only by the implementation of the principles at home. Rarely have Canadians been as critical of the status quo as they were after 1918. Thus, particularly in the West, longstanding opposition mounted against the vested interests, the eastern bankers, the CPR, and the political party system.

The war also provided an atmosphere favorable to the last great effusion of country life propaganda. Federal Agriculture Minister Martin Burrell had set the scene when he introduced the Agricultural Instruction Bill in 1913. Worried about growing urbanization, the threat to national food production, and the evils of "squalor, hunger and crime" in the cities, Burrell urgently proclaimed the desirability of a rural civilization, enlightened and uplifted. That "solitary figure in the distant furrow, that stooped form tending the hearth of the isolated home," he said, was the symbol of "our national necessities, our national virtues, and our national strengths."[11] Burrell called for a healthy injection of federal money to enhance rural life by focusing on agricultural education.

Close on the heels of Burrell's exhortation came the mammoth crops of 1915 and 1916. Nothing else could have so invigorated the back to the land movement and the sense of an ever grander destiny. The growth of southwestern Saskatchewan and southeastern Alberta to that point had been astounding. The population in the former had leapt from 17,692 in 1901 to 178,200 in 1916; the number of farms jumped from 2,436 to 37,954; and the area in crop catapulted from 123,790 acres to 4,473,038.[12] The dry belt population in Alberta had bounded from 4,415 in 1901 to 101,679 in 1916; the number of farms increased from roughly 2,000 to 30,883;[13] and the area in crop spread from about 80,700 acres to 2,690,230 acres in 1915.[14]

On the Alberta side no less than 45 percent of all farms in the province in 1916 were in the dry areas, and the wheat crop there came to 75 percent of the provincial total.[15] In 1900 the southeastern Alberta wheat harvest had been a drop in the ocean and that in southwestern Saskatchewan hardly more, at just over a million bushels. By 1915 the respective figures stood at fifty million bushels and ninety-six million.[16]

Surely in this year the new heartland lived up to its advanced billing as "a land blessed of the Gods." Everywhere there was jubilation. "If the Garden of Eden looked as enticing as did Saskatchewan during the past summer," wrote one observer, "it is difficult to understand why the Garden was vacated so soon."[17] One southern Albertan had offered his farm for sale for $800 the season before. The farm had just yielded sixty-three bushels of wheat an acre, and it was now worth $8,000! A man who had changed his hired help double-seeded a piece of his land by mistake and took off eighty-four bushels an acre. Another had no time to spring plow, so he

Threshing on the 5000 acre Ginther-Finlay farm, Suffield, 1915. NA 2003-41, Glenbow-Alberta Archives.

disked the seed into the stubble. ". . . The gol-darn thing run 40 bushels to the acre all the same," he said.[18]

In late August real estate magnate F. M. Ginther led a contingent of Hatters, including Mayor Hawthorn, Aldermen Ireland and Cruikshank and others on an auto excursion to view the bounty. "If at the start there were any pessimists or any who doubted the value of the Medicine Hat district as a grain raising district, the thousands and thousands of acres of the finest wheat and oat crops imaginable proved a most effectual cure," hooted the paper. "No one could look unmoved upon the vast fields of waving golden grain, and the more practical and hardheaded they were the more it appealed to them." Crops were so thick and full that they choked the binders and forced farmers to cut narrower swaths.[19]

Hamlets tributary to Alderson chaffed each other with good natured banter. R. Huisman Jr. of Tide Lake told *The Alderson News* in spring 1916 that the claims of Brutus and Tripola of seventy-two

Manna from Heaven—the bumper crop at Alderson, 1915. Mrs. Dolly Scollard, Mrs. O'Brien, Mrs. Kate Cole, Franklin Cole, and his father, Al Cole, left to right. NA 4777-2, Glenbow-Alberta Archives.

One effect of the bounty of 1915 and 1916—renovations on Broadway Street, Alderson, 1917. NA 5081-5, Glenbow-Alberta Archives.

bushels of wheat and 102 bushels of oats an acre were "imaginative products." "But as for realities?" he asked. "There is only one place. TIDE LAKE."

Fixing on the vegetable crop, Huisman continued, "we grew beets [growers'] names sent on request, and by Golly they grew so big that parts above looked like new Towers of Babel. In fact one grew so big that the elements working at its growth got confused and quit at the 50th stor[e]y." Brutus bragged that its carrots were the size of cedar posts, but those, said the Tide Lake mountebank, "would look like regular toothpicks alongside the ones we grew." The beans grew so monstrous that several gardeners had to go to A. J. Drummond's hardware in Alderson for wash boilers to cook them "as the ordi[n]ary pots wouldn[']t hold one bean."[20]

In reality, the great harvest had reversed an alarming trend. Some reports indicated that there had not been a decent crop in the newly opened regions from 1910 to 1915. Differences of opinion existed concerning the years 1911 and 1912, but not about the un-mitigated disasters in 1910 and 1914. Scorching July temperatures in 1914 have probably never been exceeded in degree or duration.[21] That year many of the faint-hearted left, most of the gargantuan farm operations around Carlstadt terminated for good, and the rail-ways began to wonder about the future of their projected lines in the dry areas.[22]

New Railways

IT WAS TOO LATE to fret over the new Suffield-Lomond and Bassano-Empress branches of the CPR, for they were already in place. Anyway, their mere existence brought hope, despite the weather. Elated, local pamphleteers at Empress bragged that the conurbation would be a divisional point on no fewer than six railways. When George L. Brown, president of the Board of Trade, received a cablegram from the editor of *Canadian News* of London, England, in spring 1914, enquiring about the population, he wired, "—approximately five hundred. Rapidly rising." By mid-August, local census-takers tallied 841 inhabitants and began chanting for town status. If the numbers were right, it was the biggest Empress ever got. Six years later, Secretary M. A. Blodgett of the Board of Trade was still bab-bling the same figures, though by then promoters were obviously counting shadows too, for the official census returns of 1916 and 1921 were precisely half as grand.[23]

Sixty miles from Empress, halfway to Bassano, was the new vil-lage of Jenner. As 1917 dawned, A. D. Fidler, a servant of the De-partment of Municipal Affairs, inspected the burg and discovered twenty-eight businesses in place, including four general stores, four restaurants, three elevators, three liveries, two lumber yards, a bank and a drug store, as well as the NWMP barracks. Fidler noted the

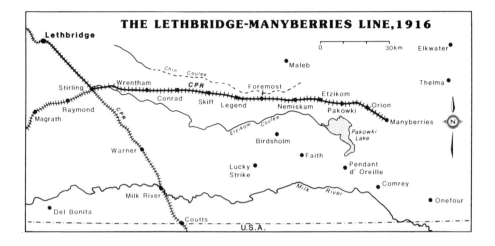

THE LETHBRIDGE-MANYBERRIES LINE, 1916

vast area—twenty-five miles north and twenty-five miles south—from which the town drew its trade, and he predicted prosperity.[24] What he did not know was that Jenner was near its short-lived peak, and what he did not mention was that its hinterland took virtually every foot of turf to the doorstep of Alderson, due south. Thus as the wind took Jenner's sails, Alderson fell gradually into the doldrums.[25]

The so-called Lethbridge-Weyburn line of the CPR, which never did get to Weyburn, had reached Foremost in 1913. After the poor crops that year, Perren Baker of Nemiskam commented wryly, "In 1912 we had wheat but no railway. Now we had a railway but no wheat. . . ."[26] No one had any wheat the next year either. Just when the future looked dimmest the bumper harvest of 1915 arrived and induced the railroad to move eastward.

By year-end the steel had almost reached Pakowki, a burgeoning burg on the northern tip of the massive, incredibly shallow, alkaline lake of the same name. On the wings of rumor, "imperialists" from Seven Persons and Manyberries swept down and erected a large store and a pool hall. Potter and Company, grain buyers from the Hat, slipped into town and began doing business in a tent, shared by a preacher on Sundays.[27] For a time they did well, because over the next year the town would ship 566,000 bushels of grain.[28] The place briefly flowered, then fell into eclipse as the head of rail moved on.²⁹

The next community to spring into life was Orion, a few miles eastward, amid more thickly settled country and somewhat richer soil. Teenager Wilfrid Eggleston witnessed the birth of Orion. Speedily four grain elevators, four general stores, two pool rooms, two Chinese cafes and hotel accommodations, and a drug store were thrown up in an imposing new block. The most impressive structure of the lot was Charlie Robb's new general store, and it was here that young Eggleston worked. With the crop failure of 1917 it was evident that Orion had vastly overbuilt, and the store hand was let go. Just before Robb closed the venture, Eggleston became a clerk for the Standard Bank in town on November 1, 1917. Business was not brisk. Shortly after the new year, Eggleston, bored and underworked, was transferred to a post in Kronau, Saskatchewan.³⁰

These hints of instability warned that the wind was changing, that it was at the moment of reversal when the chop on the shallow, brackish sloughs simply rose, roiled up, pushed from front and rear, without the uniform splash of the whitecaps revealing their direction. Not noticing, most westerners still dwelt on the earlier boom and the mammoth harvests of mid-war. Charles S. Hotchkiss, Alberta publicity commissioner, was typical. "When the war is over," he said frankly, "we may expect immigration to assume its old proportions."³¹

As the lean and seasoned veterans returned to the land, this expectation seemed to be unfolding. "Isn't it true that in most Canadian homes life goes on to-day pretty much as it did five blank years ago?" *The Hanna Herald* asked. "[T]he stalwart sons come to the breakfast table with the same noisy greetings though there is perhaps a shade deeper ring to their voices[.] Returned from war, the head of the family sits in his old accustomed place at story time, perhaps bringing a new kind of prince and knight for the youngsters."³²

When enough ex-soldiers had trickled back to the Clivale hamlet, south of Hanna, the ladies of the district staged a home-welcoming

and a dance at the school house.[33] At nearby Burfield, early on
Easter morning 1919, Sergeant A. L. R. Davidson, scant days before of the Eighth Field Ambulance Corps, beheld a motley caval-
cade approaching his farmstead. Some riders brought four horses,
others five and still others six. Some brought an implement, others,
two. As they arrived, they greeted Davidson with a hand, a grin,
and a deep appreciation. They had come to seed his crop. "Slowly
and steadily," wrote the community correspondent, "up and down
the field, the great procession moved until at noontide, when, either through natural impulse, or by the delightfully scented breezes
wafted on the wings of Boreas, the toilers were informed that the
mid-day meal was being prepared." To the house the yeomen filed,
where they sat down to a splendid feast prepared by the women of
the district. Sated, they returned to the fields to resume plowing
and seeding, and some hours later they assembled the teams for a
memorial photograph. Till sundown they worked before seating
themselves again. "After a second repast no less tasty to the weary
workers," wrote the correspondent, "the outfits could be seen
wearily wending their way homeward until the shades of the night
lowered and obscured their view." In all, the twenty-seven
samaritans sowed sixty-five acres.[34]

Elsewhere there were similar benefactions. At Fraserton thirty-
two farmers and their teams, representing the local UFA, plowed
and disked eighty-five acres for J. G. Cudmore. The peace time
army was then treated to a sumptuous dinner by the local Women's
Christian Temperance Union. Since Cudmore had already seeded a
hundred acres to wheat, the Fraserton scribe concluded, "It did not
take Mr. Cudmore long to switch from raising [hell] in France to
raising wheat in Alberta."[35]

With the same alacrity and strangely unmindful of the stagnation
along the Lethbridge-Manyberries line, the railroads turned to the
task of building new lines and extending their transportation
empires. Like worms, projected routes wriggled all across the dry
areas—from Hanna north to Warden Junction, from Scapa east to
Sedalia and Loverna, from Leader (once Prussia), Saskatchewan,
south through Hilda and back to Bigstick Lake, from Mantario,

Saskatchewan, west to Acadia Valley, from Lethbridge north to Bassano, then to Coronation and south to Empress.[36]

It was one of the supreme ironies of the rush to lay steel across the dry belt that the hand of none other than William Pearce was at work. Gone from his writing was the cursing of the farmer, gone the warnings that this was cattle country. Now as surveyor for the CPR he looked at the settlement, he looked at the Canadian Northern, and he plotted lines to serve the former and foil the latter—a sentiment the Canadian Northern shared in reverse. Though he could never bring himself to forget the dryness, the entrancing heresies of the moisture clique had touched his mind, and he let slip a newfound belief that—"Of course the heavy [crop] growth will with good farming, in time stand sparsity of rainfall much better than at present."[37]

In early 1919 news leaked out that the CPR would shortly commence work on a major branch from Acme to Drumheller, then east along the Red Deer River through the Berry Creek country all the way to Empress. Behind the scenes was the "new" Pearce, the arch-draftsman dissecting the aridity, the master of detail, charting the way down the Red Deer, not to Empress, but veering northeast at Bullpound Creek toward Coronation.[38] Whatever the exact destination (neither the settlers nor the railway seemed to know), the proposed line, in the last stages of negotiation according to Minister of Railways H. H. Halladay, would be a godsend to the south country.[39]

Even more important for the dry areas was the new Hanna-Medicine Hat route of the Canadian Northern, soon to be the Canadian National. After the bumper crops of 1915 and 1916, settlers in this region had complained bitterly about marketing difficulties, for the increased production campaigns, they said, could scarcely achieve their object without extended rail lines. By 1918 over six hundred homesteaders had abandoned their land, exasperated with forty to fifty mile hauls and the emptiness of earlier promises of rail service. Still the population of the region was at least two thousand farm families, and the value of buildings north of the Red Deer alone was estimated at $3,500,000. The area comprised 400,000

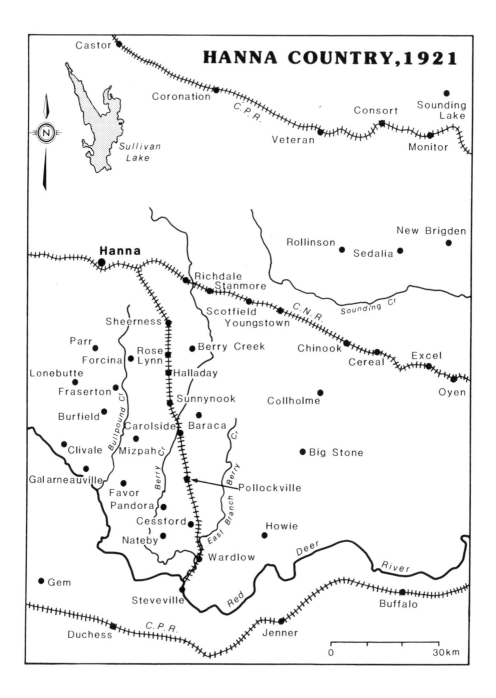

HANNA COUNTRY, 1921

acres of "prime" importance and contained 18,000 cattle, 10,000 hogs and 150,000 horses. Consequently, the UFA, municipalities along the proposed road, and the local press pushed the project with all their might. As the Hanna paper said, the region was "one of the greatest wheat growing districts in Alberta."[40]

Grading started that summer, and the roadbed was finished to the Red Deer River. Track would have been laid in early winter, but influenza invaded the work camp, and the crews temporarily disbanded.[41] When interest reignited in spring 1919, the town of Hanna disgorged a bevy of bigwigs southward to Sunnynook, Pollockville and Cessford in search of investment opportunities. Promises were made of speedy locations, and the spirit of the boom was reborn.[42]

A month later, the newspaper correspondent for Sunnynook related a dream he'd had of the future: "I was motoring on the boulevard of Sunnynook, which was beautified by rows of trees, while on each side, as far as the eye could see, were fields of golden grain which were fast being harvested." Working easily and smiling as they cut down the gilded pods, the farmers reflected the radiant goodness of the world. As the dreamer drew near the town, he "passed one of its magnificent parks, a haven of rest for the weary. . . ." Just then he was hit by a passing vehicle, and he awoke in the resplendent Sunnynook Hospital where he dimly heard a doctor say, "He will live." Waking with the vision of lushness still fresh, he repeatedly sang the refrains of the old, happy song, "When Dreams Come True."[43]

By mid-July the excitement generated by the approaching railroad reached a crescendo. "We are thrilled thru and thru with the train siren shrieking out its welcome from the new siding at Fendall's," wrote the reporter, "and it is all we can do to restrain ourselves from dropping our shackles of labor such as cultivators, harrows and kitchen aprons, to rush to the spot where the gangs are laying the steel." Two months later, the crews were down to Pollockville, and the townsites of Fendell and Sunnynook had been surveyed.[44]

For a brief embarrassing span, Sunnynook was renamed by the

CNR, Konowall—humorously dubbed "Knowital" by neighboring hamlets. Under the unusual new rubric, the town news collector for the Hanna paper reviewed the past as the new decade dawned. He had arrived in July 1912. That fall, the founders of *The Hanna Herald* passed through en route from Bassano, sixty-seven miles away, lugging their printing presses and paraphernalia through an early deep freeze. Staying with their future scribe, the publishers were treated to a dish of hard tack which sorely tested their will to continue. Since then, the scribe believed, there had been many advances in rural life, and the area, despite the last three difficult years, had progressed beyond homesteaders' original expectations.[45]

By the end of 1920, development of the south country was remarkable. The influx into Hanna itself was so striking that all housing accommodation was engaged and an energetic building campaign was undertaken.[46] The population was estimated at at least 1,800, up from 711 in 1916.[47] Rails were laid right to Steveville on the Red Deer River, and a bridge crew was despatched to that point.[48]

Early next year, the boosting of the Cessford, Pollockville, Sunnynook country reached a climax. Full page and two page advertisements bedecked *The Hanna Herald*. Cessford was lauded as "the metropolis of the land of promise [athrob] with strength of age and enthusiasm of youth." Almost five hundred industrious farmers, it was claimed, had settled in the environs since the coming of the railway. Centring the municipality of Berry Creek, Cessford was led by the likes of the aptly named W. J. Winning. "Here we produce some of the finest wheat on the continent, and cattle which command the highest price in the market places of the cities," he exclaimed.[49] A heavy investor in farm implements and hardware, and the Ford car agent, Winning bore the distinguishing mark of the boosters who preceded him elsewhere—he sold farm lands and insurance.

At Pollockville, J. R. Yigler moved the first building, a general store, onto the townsite in 1919. In the fall of 1920, the Bank of Toronto led the boomers, followed by two restaurants, two feed barns, two harness makers, a large butcher shop, pool room and barber shop, and the massive general store of Robert Pollock, one of the earliest settlers in the whole district. On December 30, 1920, a new community hall was built. The man honored to drive the first spike was Andrew Hedman, president of the lively Board of Trade and, of course, real estate agent for town and farm properties.[50]

Sunnynook too had come a long way since J. O. Robertson and son had arrived in 1909. The first grain shipment had been freighted sixty-five miles to Bassano, and when the Goose Lake line reached Youngstown to the north in 1912, the distance was shortened to thirty-five miles. Boasting two lumber companies and restaurants, livery and feed stables, a doctor, a drug store, a lawyer, and a bank, the town was as typically Anglo-Celtic as Alderson to the south and Carolside claimed to be to the north. The latter crowed that the district had "no obnoxious foreigners or detrimental aliens," but obviously allowances were made.[51] Despite its Waspish sentiments, Sunnynook tolerated Dick Wong's laundry. "We heep sabbee good washee," Dick advertised, "We hab lotsa soap, lotsa wata, lotsa ebathing for good washee." Lest Wong should feel too comfortable in the new hub, above his ad was another for "The White Restaurant, where white help entirely is employed."[52]

The Sunnynook advertising section in January 1921 began and ended with the disturbing news that the Bank of Toronto, resident in town since spring 1919, had just withdrawn, leaving only the Union Bank. It was a powerful indication of the reality behind the rhetoric, of the flagrant lies in the promotion, and of the incredibly short time in the sun these towns had.

6   In the Thrill Zone of the
       On Rushing Calamity

See You at the Fire　　　　THE TRUTH WAS that the advertising
campaign in early 1921 for the in-
fant towns along the Hanna-Medicine
Hat line was grossly, even maliciously
misleading. True, the growth of communities during 1920 had
been remarkable, but it was patently false that "everyone seemed
happy, good natured and prosperous." And it was even worse deception to say that "a total crop failure [had] never been known
since the first white settlers in 1909." Failures had come almost immediately, starting in 1910, and continuing in 1914, 1917, 1918,
and 1919. By 1921, Sunnynook was hardly "everything its radiant
name would indicate."[1]

Further south at Cessford, promoter W. J. Winning had no
sooner peppered prospective settlers with optimistic bombast

about the glories of the region than he testified sullenly before the Southern Alberta Survey into the dryland crisis that he had indeed suffered heavily in his farming operations in the past four years.[2]

The bubbly local correspondence in *The Hanna Herald* had been thinning out for over a year, and by summer 1921 it was only a trace of what it had been. Tax sales in the country south of Hanna began to appear by September, just months after the ecstatic forecasts of inevitable boom. On September 1,450 quarter sections in Lonebutte municipality were listed in a pending sale for arrears and costs, for amounts totalling anything from $525 to $2.86.[3] Another 415 quarters in Berry Creek municipality were listed on October 13, most with $20–$40 against them.[4]

The year before, the paper announced its own relief fund for the settlers in the drought area south of Hanna.[5] It reported conditions "reaching alarming proportions." The municipality of Flowerdale was completely out of seed grain, and the banks were refusing to finance either feed or seed.[6] By spring 1920, circumstances were so desperate in southern Alberta and southwestern Saskatchewan that large scale relief operations had to be mounted by the provincial and federal governments. In Alberta, offices were established in Medicine Hat, Lethbridge and Youngstown. In Saskatchewan, Hatton was the distributing point for relief for the hard hit municipalities of Big Stick, Enterprise and Bitter Lake.[7]

Everywhere the difficult years took their toll. In Carlstadt the editor of the *News* wrote at year-end 1914—"Trying to run a business without advertising is like winking at a girl in the dark. You may know what you are doing, but no one else does." The brief ad appeared unaccompanied on a full page, a pointed message to local businesses to "show their wares."[8] Three years later, after the *News* had changed hands several times, the new editor, R. H. Thornton, complained of a whopping jump in paper costs and an equal drop in advertisers, with the result that the paper was reduced from eight pages to four.[9] Grain marketed from Alderson in 1917–18 was a mere 72,000 bushels, down from 679,000 bushels in 1915–16. A year after, only 14,000 bushels left the four elevators, and in 1919–20, just 9,000 bushels.[10]

Ironically during the good times the town's only doctor, S. F. McEwen, decided to accept a position with the CPR physician in Calgary. Alarmed, the municipalities of King and Sunny South agreed to guarantee McEwen $1,300 if he would stay. In return, he would charge residents of those jurisdictions half price.[11] The arrangement promised deliverance from the growing backlog of unpaid debts, so McEwen relented. Some, however, branded the deal a piece of blackmail; others deemed it a bluff for quick lucre; and still more refused to have the land taxed at 25¢ an acre just to keep a medicine man in town. Consequently the plan worked badly, and in mid-1918 McEwen left Alderson, poorer but wiser.[12]

The editor of the *News*, like others of his ilk a natural booster, was distraught. Three weeks later he wrote the paper's obituary. With two-thirds of his subscriptions overdue and no chance of collection in the fall, and with twenty-three businesses in town and only seven paid advertisers, Thornton wrote glumly, "We have our course, we have finished our fight and we have lost."[13]

If Thornton had stayed that year, he would certainly have left the next, after the great fire. The drama in that chapter of the town's decline may well have begun earlier in the summer of 1919 when another crop failure became evident. But for one witness it began Friday, August 24, 1919, near dusk.

Nineteen-year-old Inga Carlson had just stepped to the upstairs window of the Johnson Hotel on Broadway where she stayed as a maid. Peering down, she saw a strange encounter between the operator of the hotel, Mrs. Johnson, and her son Herbert. Mrs. Johnson's arms were full of fine linens which her son was loading into a wagon. The woman seemed anxious, and once when she glanced up and saw Inga, she looked worried.[14]

The event puzzled Inga, but no more than the strange trips Mrs. Johnson was making to the graveyard. The lady's favorite son Harry, aged thirty-three years, had died of the flu ten months earlier, leaving her utterly weepy and unsettled.[15] Often in Inga's presence she would excuse herself saying she was going to talk to Harry. A quarter of a mile to the east she would walk to the cemetery on land Thom Swanby had donated to the village. The

Alderson in the doldrums, the western edge of town, 1920. NA 1644-2, Glenbow-Alberta Archives.

surroundings were less forbidding than might have been, for the burial ground had been beautified that summer—there was a large impressive gate leading to a circular drive in the centre of the plots, and the silent community was laid out in paths of cinders, gift of the railway.[16] There Mrs. Johnson would commune with the dead.

On the morning of the 25th, Mrs. Johnson instructed Inga not to go upstairs, a most unusual request because cleaning the upstairs was part of her job. One other instruction Inga received earlier—and that was to have her suitcase packed and by her door, always. Perhaps the admonition was well enough intended, given the generation's obsession with the fire demon, but Inga saw more in it later.

What happened as noon approached, no one knows for certain. Mrs. Johnson was in the kitchen preparing dinner as usual, and she slipped out, down the street to buy a very few groceries. Upstairs, against Johnson's wishes, Inga was cleaning, when she suddenly smelled smoke. Dashing downstairs, she saw flames leaping from the kitchen, starting from the overheated stove, as the paper later revealed. Out onto Broadway she rushed shouting, "Fire, fire!"

She ran into Mrs. Johnson who asked, "Where?"

"In your hotel!" Inga shouted.[17]

A chain reaction now ensued, described by sharp-eyed Charlotte Cotter, whose special column in The Hat *News* likened the sequence to the blasts of war.

As the townspeople mobilized, the flames, fanned by hot summer winds, quickly spread to Drummond's hardware and then down the street. In an instant the whole block on the westside of Broadway was ablaze. Drummond's store and residence, Hutchinson's general store, Rosenberg's ice cream parlor, the restaurant of John Goehring's widow, Hansen's store, McDiarmid's hall, H. B. Brigham's office, and the shop *The Alderson News* had occupied only a year earlier—all went up like kindling.

Working feverishly, the bucket brigade soon surrendered the block and concentrated on saving adjacent buildings. Across the street, the American House, the drugstore and the pool hall were badly scorched. Fearing the fierce heat, the Union Bank staff draped wet blankets over their heavy plate windows and the windows upstairs. Once the west-end livery barn ignited, but the flames were doused. Behind the barn was the Atlas lumber yard, but it, the Massey Harris Building and Stubbs's hotel were saved.

At the centre of hell was Drummond's hardware. While the firefighters swarmed over the heaps of belongings jettisoned into the street, the flames reached the gasoline in the store. The explosion blew out the plate glass windows and projected deadly shards everywhere. Reverend George Steele, village secretary, and Bert Cole, were badly cut. Even as Doc McEwen, who happened to be on hand, patched them up, the ammunition in the store went off like fireworks on the Fourth of July. Buildings thundered down, and fiery projectiles ignited bags of clothing and other flammables cast into the thoroughfare.

When it was over, the loss amounted to $75,000, six families living over stores were burned out, and nine major structures and several smaller ones were razed. All but one of the major edifices were insured.[18] For Mrs. Goehring it was the second disaster in short succession. Two years earlier, her husband John, one of the first pioneers, had slipped into a hole in the Bow River while wading. Someone threw a rope, but lost hold of it. When they found Goehring's corpse the next day, the other end was wrapped tightly around the wrist.[19]

Meanwhile, in the confusion of the fire Inga Carlson had left her packed suitcase and had saved two potted plants. In the aftermath, her father listened intently to her suspicions and then, fearing for her life, told her to seal her lips. When he met Mrs. Johnson in the street, she moaned,

"I have lost my hotel."

"But you were insured," replied Carlson coolly. "Inga lost everything."

Later A. J. Drummond, a former mayor, begged Inga to reveal what he suspected she knew. Obedient to her father, she whispered nothing.[20] Others too were suspicious, and a year or so later Rev. George Steele told the Department of Municipal Affairs about fires of mysterious origin.[21]

In November Mrs. Johnson and her son Herbert moved eastward to Kingston, Ontario, where they took over the Albion Hotel.[22] No one ever proved the suspected arson, but several carried the thought to their graves. There were just so many fires those days.

In spring 1917, the central block on the main street of Seven Persons was destroyed.[23] In April 1921, the Beaver Lumber Company buildings, plant and stock were wiped out at Sunnynook.[24] Almost exactly the same time the most disastrous fire in the history of Hatton, Saskatchewan, site of one of the CPR's famed experimentalfarms in the 1880s, consumed nearly the whole of the west side of main street, eating away the business section and threatening the residences. One family that had lost a baby boy two weeks earlier lost their store, their home and everything else. Perhaps symboli-

Fire at Seven Persons, 1917.
NA 4017-5, Glenbow-Alberta
Archives.

cally the name of the town was printed in the Hat *News* upside down.[25]

About this time a sardonic saying circulated around neighboring Redcliff—"We'll see you at the fire tonight."[26] It was a measure of the desperate turn agriculture had taken in the drylands.

The Nightmare of Western Canada

YET THE FARMING problem after the war was in another sense very general. Across the Canadian West, settlers complained bitterly about the drop in wheat prices from over $2 in 1918 to well less than half that in 1922 and 1923.[27] Simultaneously the price of goods they purchased had greatly inflated during the war and was much less affected by the ensuing period of deflation. Farmers were especially prone to make comparisons with costs in contiguous American states. One claimed indignantly that prices in the T. Eaton catalogue from Winnipeg were 20 to 40 percent higher than those of the Sears-Roebuck catalogue from Chicago. Riding in a car which could be bought in both Canada and the United States, he noted a price advantage in North Dakota over Manitoba of $375, along with a gasoline price only half as great.[28] A bag of sugar, a Saskatchewan farmer complained to the

Minister of the Interior, cost $4.90 in New York, $5.50 in Montreal, and $10 or $11 in Eastend.[29]

The disbanding of the Wheat Board, high freight rates and haulage costs irked others. Farmers on the Etzikom-Orion-Manyberries line scored the CPR for its failure to extend the track into Saskatchewan with the result that their wheat had to be rerouted all the way to Lethbridge before swinging east again. These woes were shared by settlers in the Tripola-Tide Lake area, impatiently awaiting the half-built CNR line south of the Red Deer River to Medicine Hat.

Added to these troubles was a big jump in taxes. Local improvement taxes around Nobleford increased from $2 a quarter section to $27 and then to $36 in the years before 1922.[30] George Coutts reported from Pandora, south of Hanna, that in 1919 he was paying 18 or 19¢ an acre; by 1921, it was 40¢.[31]

At the same time, there was a precipitous drop in land values. In the Neutral Hills, for example, the average price per acre for the usual turf in 1915–19 was $12.89, down to $9.85 in 1920–21, and only $7.51 in 1925–29.[32]

Naturally for the dry areas these concerns were little compared to the drought. From Calgary to Swift Current the years 1917 to 1922 almost invariably featured below normal precipitation, indeed, often record or near record low moisture falls. Only twice since 1890 was it as parched in Swift Current as in 1917 and 1920; or in Medicine Hat as in 1919. In Lethbridge 1918 was the driest year ever, before or since, totalling only 7.63 inches of moisture.[33] At Suffield, near the epicentre of the Alberta dry belt, ten miles east of Alderson, the average rainfall in the crop growing season in the ten years before 1924 was just 6.36 inches. Between 1917 and 1922 it was only 4.11 inches, with May, June and August all registering less than one inch on average.[34]

Compounding the drought were scorching high temperatures. While the Hat mean daily maximums for July in the bumper year of 1915 had been 77.7 degrees F., the ten subsequent years *averaged* 86.6 degrees. In 1917 the average maximum temperature for July was 92 degrees, a figure exceeded only twice in the first forty years of the century.[35]

The inevitable consequence was crop failure. In 1915 Southern Alberta yielded over 35 bushels of wheat an acre, with many examples vastly greater. In 1917 the average fell to 10.7 bushels; in 1918 to 4.9 bushels; in 1919, 1.4 bushels. In the last year, yields in Lethbridge, Enchant, Macleod and Medicine Hat areas were nil, and when the yields of 1920 and 1921 were 6.3 bushels and 4.6 bushels, calamity was rife.[36] After 1916 these grim harvests averaged almost always considerably less than those of Canada or Alberta as a whole.[37]

The vile accompaniment of the return of the land to desert was an assortment of plagues which like those of Biblical Egypt poured down upon the people without mercy. In 1916, almost as an omen, Olaf Skjenna, Sr. of Buffalo, north of Medicine Hat, witnessed a mammoth cloudburst which "looked like a very big giant pouring water over the land with millions of big buckets." Gophers were drowned and birdlife was killed over a large area. Not long after, Skjenna saw a herd of horses, chased by "millions of big mosquitoes," so many of which landed on his mare that he could not tell her color. "I stood there for two hours," he wrote, "swatting mosquitoes in order to save her life."[38]

There were other winged predators too. By mid-summer, flies were everywhere, in the barns, on animals, in houses, on humans, pestering the life out of everything that moved. On August 19, 1919, Arthur Ion, north of Alderson, recorded that he, his wife, and son killed 1,500 flies, 500 each.[39] The year before, grasshoppers had invaded Saskatchewan and Manitoba. In Alberta the infestation started in the southwest corner in 1919, and by 1921 it engulfed almost the whole south. "You could hardly see the sun for the grasshoppers," one settler south of Manyberries remembered.[40] In 1921 H. E. R. Davies of Enchant seeded his land three times, and each time the hoppers devoured the sprouts.[41] Devastated, Wilhelm Kowalewski wrote from somewhere near Walsh on the Alberta-Saskatchewan border to he knew not whom. He just addressed his plea in German to "honorable Sir," Regina. With no

A rabbit drive near Lomond, 1920s. NA 1308-25, Glenbow-Alberta Archives.

feed, his grass burned, he, his mother, his wife, and six children were up against it. "[A]ll my crop is destroyed," he moaned, "worms and grasshoppers are eating everything. . . . Kindly help me as soon as possible, I pray you from the bottom of my heart."[42]

Disillusioned by repeated failure and the apparent uselessness of further effort, farmers would not cooperate in control measures.[43] Abandonment of farms further intensified the pest problem. A. F. Meek wrote from southwestern Saskatchewan that he was "surrounded by three sections of land that never saw 'a spoonful of poison.'" As a result, his seed was lost, his crop destroyed, his labor and time wasted—a fact of life for hundreds of settlers over thousands of acres in the district. "If not exterminated," he said, "the gopher will drive us out."[44]

Meek was hardly exaggerating. One year the single municipality of Excelsior, near the Hat, counted 15,000 tails bagged in a children's contest from spring to mid-July. Together the top five nimrods, including a girl, recorded 6,984 kills.[45]

Perhaps the most unusual plague was rabbits. On Christmas Day

1924, the young twins of Adam Bond, travelling by rail from Manyberries to Lethbridge, looked out their coach and beheld the ground in every direction covered with the critters. All Forty Mile municipality was overrun with them.[46] Two years later, Arthur Ion counted four hundred rabbits between his house and the well. A few days after, an eagle soared in from the north, terrorizing another herd almost twice as large, chasing it across the west pasture, past the well and along the fence to the house. The stampede, Ion wrote, "sounded like a train going by." Behind the barn a lone victim fell to the predator.[47]

For several seasons war was waged against the bunnies. In winter they gathered by the hundreds in the coulees where similar numbers of hunters tracked them down, corralled them, and clubbed them senseless. Students playing hookey often participated in the hunts, collecting and selling the skins for hide leather, and selling the carcasses for fox feed. Under the auspices of a government agent, one chase near Winnifred netted 756, and perhaps half way through the winter drive, 3,600 rabbits had fallen. Casualties, of course, were unusual amongst the hunters. Charles Reardon, however, cut himself, was apparently infected by blisters on the rabbits, and died shortly thereafter.[48]

If the infestation of gophers and rabbits afforded some recreation and excitement, the darting of pursuer and pursued, the swinging of primitive weapons and the butchering of quivering pests drew attention from the way that nature was engaging her own quarry, the dry farmer. Those who took time to straighten their stooped shoulders, to lift their dusty heads from their laps, and to think, understood that the most pitiable victims in all the interplay in the dry areas were themselves. Even then, few truly comprehended the significance of their hour in history.

An exception was W. R. Babington. A man of grand schemes and large estates who had earlier practised the art of testimonials on behalf of John Hall, Babington was in his eighteenth year south of Medicine Hat when the meaning of the moment came cascading from his troubled mind. Like the scientist who tasted poison to record for posterity its terrible effects, he was fascinated by the impending catastrophe about to envelop an "empire." It was the nervous agitation and raw excitement in the face of doom that he found perversely thrilling. "We are even now," he wrote six days before Christmas 1920, "in the thrill zone of the on rushing calamity.... And now, right now, Western Canada is rushing heedlessly, unknowingly into the very jaws of the most crushing debacle recorded in the history of the West...."

Babington then turned to an old theme from the Territorial days. "We generate the cold waves and the warm waves for Eastern points," he said, ignoring a generation of local editors and promoters who had tried to discredit such notions. And there was still more to the strange power of his locality. As he wrote, "We are sensitive to the changing currents of diversity and prosperity that seem to centre at the magnetic pole of Medicine Hat." Mysterious it was, but there was a sense in which it rang true—whenever the Prairies suffered from drought, it was always more noticeable around the city with all hell for a basement.

Babington was particularly tormented by the weeds which he said were "holding carnival" and which would soon engulf whole townships. "The Canadian West's hide will soon be hanging out to dry on the branches of the weeds she has created . . .," he predicted. A big farmer at the Hat, with big steam engines and steam plows, he had even bigger fields of Russian thistle and tumbling mustard. "I was justly conceded to be the champion weed-King of this immense region," he admitted, though he almost had a rival for the dubious honor in James Amos, a neighbor seven miles westward. Amos, too, grew "some elegant crops of Russian Thistle," as luxuriant the past four years as the wheat was withered. Amos was finished, destitute, Babington had just been told. "I only had one dollar in hand or in sight and I spared a tear or two with it for poor old Jim. He has gone 'over the top' and is wounded nigh unto death—the first of our band to give in but it is for the children's sake." It was the drought and the weeds and some unspeakably vile incubus that did it.

The incubus was "the Nightmare of Western Canada." "It is here—" he stuttered. "It has demonstrated its destructive power—

its marvellous multiplying powers—just a little worm—a variety of cut-worm—the Pale Western Cut-worm." First noticed near Lethbridge in 1911, this menace was largely responsible for the crop failures from 1917 to 1920. In Montana frantic farmers built fires by night to attract the moths that laid the eggs that became the worms. Flapping by the cloud load, they entered the flames and perished, and when the fires had burnt out, their charred remains encircled the roasting pits three feet deep.[49]

The Worst of Life and Death

THE COMBINED ILLS of the era ensured that deprivation would be widespread. G. W. Hess of Flowerdale municipality, south of Hanna, considered his own case hopeless. He and his wife had invested $12,000 in the land, and by December 1921, they were flat broke. They had been forced to sell their barn a year before in order to continue farming, but the ploy was unsuccessful, and their land had just been sold for taxes.[50] Mrs. Edward Body of Birdsholm, south of Foremost, wrote the United Farm Women's Association in Calgary explicating another predicament. "With three little children and another one coming in December," she said, "I cannot pump water for sixteen head of stock and so my husband cannot go out to earn money, and there are liens on the stock so they can't be sold."[51]

John Kramer of Herbert, Saskatchewan, related his deep anguish to Premier William Martin. It went back to his first crop in 1913 which had just been stored in the granary when a prairie fire leveled the storehouse, the stable and his home. So complete was the loss that the family had to borrow clothes from the neighbors to get to town. Leaving his dependents with the grandparents in Regina, Kramer borrowed money to buy seed for 1914 crop which a few months later was dead in the field, victim of one of the hottest, driest summers ever. Like most other drybelters, he had a good crop in 1915, but owing to his penury he was obliged to sell it in the fall at exactly half the price his friends got in the spring. That fall another big prairie fire laid ruin to fifty miles of contiguous countryside.

Fighting the flames by hand, Kramer and his wife were unable to save their feed, and in the struggle the wife stepped into a gopher hole and was badly hurt. Four days later she had a child which at the time of Kramer's lamentation to the premier was four years old and helpless. "We have to feed her on cream and milk to keep her from starving and she can't use her legs at all [,] neither can she sit up on a chair or talk," said Kramer. "[W]e just have to carry her around and handle her like a new born baby."[52]

Reinhard Frerichs and his family had homesteaded near Social Plains, Alberta, north of Medicine Hat, about the time the Kramers arrived across the provincial line. For years they lived in poverty. In 1919 and 1920 they had no crop at all, and in 1921 they harvested 400 bushels of wheat. From these meagre pickings they were to pay the thresher $110 and the bank $300 for seed and feed. Every year they had fallen deeper in debt, and 1921 was especially bad. Not even the garden stuff prospered to help feed the children. They tried to secure a loan as first payment on a place beyond the desert, but their mortgage company had ceased operations in the district. Anyway, as Reinhard explained to his wife, even if the loan had been forthcoming, the debts would have to be settled first and there would not be enough left for a first payment. "When you send somebody out here to inspect the land, he will find this land is no farming land," Mrs. Frerichs wrote Premier Greenfield. "It eats all them years the dear seed and never gives it back." Begging the premier not to throw away her letter, she alluded darkly to a personal affliction, grave but unnamed—"I am waiting 2 years now for a crop to see the doctor and I have to wait another year. Maybe by that time it is to[o] late already, that a doctor cannot help any more."[53]

In September 1921, the Red Cross conducted a health survey in several crop failure districts of southern Alberta, from Lomond and Retlaw in the west to Bow Island and Winnifred in the east. Examining school children in the drylands by using height/weight charts, they discovered nearly two-thirds of 638 pupils to be suffering from malnutrition. On the richer irrigated stretches around Purple Springs and Taber, the figure was barely over one-third of eighty pupils. The tabulators also totalled more than a thousand defects of throat, teeth, nose and eyes—an average of one and a half defects a child.[54]

As poverty grew in maddening times, the children suffered piteously. Officers of the Hanna detachment of the Alberta Provincial Police often thought of the Hilsabeck case and shuddered. Their inspector who had seen his share of grief considered it "one of the most cruel and heartless cases that has ever been brought to the attention of the public."[55]

Just after New Year's, 1924, William Francis Hilsabeck of Clivale, south of Hanna, went berserk when his son Archer, aged seven, and daughter Irene, aged nine, lost the key to his violin case. In a satanic transport, he beat the two mercilessly, without let up, concentrating on his young son. He hit Archer everywhere, choked him, and burnt him, as battered Irene later testified. Then, spent, his boy unconscious on the floor, the offering done, his wife weeping, imploring him to stop, he carried Archer to the bed. A neighbor was summoned, arrived at about 10 P.M., and before the hour was out, the little boy was dead. Dr. George Harrison Wade of Hanna performed the post mortem and declared that a hemorrhage in Archer's head had killed him.[56]

After alienists of the Provincial Mental Hospital at Ponoka examined Hilsabeck, he stood trial and was found guilty of murder. He was taken to Fort Saskatchewan to be hanged on September 30, 1924.[57] Twelve days before the execution, Governor General Lord Byng, impressed by the blatant insanity of the act and perhaps mindful of the dementing conditions surrounding it, commuted the sentence to life imprisonment.[58]

Then there was the Maier case of Hatton, Saskatchewan. Herbert Maier, Jr., a delicate twelve-year-old epileptic perished on December 9, 1924, after appalling neglect and abuse.

In the last seven months of his life, Herbert knew the deepest misery the Fates permit a human to know. His father habitually beat him, even when seizures gripped him. Starved, he dragged himself to the granary or the fields to gorge on grain. Flung into the winter cold for stealing meat, he was comforted by cattle. Once his feet froze, and for weeks in the night he cried from the pain, receiving only threats of more violence if he did not keep silent and let the others sleep. Finally, the ill-treatment and malnourishment, compounded by acute pneumonia, ended the child's earthly existence. When the father told investigating Corporal Balsdon of the Saskatchewan Provincial Police that fits killed the boy, Balsdon knew better.

Amid a heat wave in late May 1925, the King's Bench sessions were held in the Grand Theatre of Maple Creek. Condemning Maier as an unnatural parent and a lowly craven, Judge Bigelow sentenced him to seven years for manslaughter.[59]

These cases recalled Mrs. Bolosky, a widow in the Polish community of Tide Lake, north of Alderson, who some years before had murdered her two children before committing suicide. Transfixed with poverty, the pending loss of her homestead, and the recent death of her husband and another offspring, she left a note of incoherent phrases crying that she did not want her children to freeze to death.[60]

All places and eras have their ghastly examples, but for the land of Cain after the influx these were its specific contributions. In each instance, some pointed to the black spirit of the region that had surely possessed the slayers. For those of such a mind, there was a dreadful and dawning awareness that these sacrifices, and others, would never have been exacted without the first and primal error— the settlement of so disheartening a plain.

7 The Sorcerer and the Clouds

Governments and Gifts

IN THE END, it was the heap of accumulated maladies, the ruination of W. R. Babington's "empire," and its dark reflection on all prairie agriculture that drew the most attention. That a core of the basic industry of the two provinces had come to such a pass so shortly after the bacchanalia of the boom and the wartime victory was scarcely conceivable. As the news crept into the offices of potentates, provincial and federal, they discounted it as both aberration and hyperbole. So many of those in power had knelt so long before the gods of expansion and improvement that they viewed the carpers almost as heretics, pedlars of perversion and claptrap, anticapitalistic scaremongers of the worst order. Of course, the collapse of the dry country made such liars of so many of them that reports of it were hardly appreciated.

116

Efforts were made to keep the spreading disaster hush-hush. In Saskatchewan, meetings between government nabobs and affected farmers and businessmen were kept out of the press, and suggestions of debt relinquishment were systematically quieted because of the effect abroad, should the investors of the world stumble onto the real story. In Alberta as in Saskatchewan, settlers, furious with the lack of attention to their woes, demanded investigations. After visiting southern Alberta in 1919, John Glambeck of Queenstown deemed the crisis "far worse than stated in the press."[1] When a Liberal government MLA toured the area and found only three cases of destitution, William F. Rabbitt of Etzikom waxed indignant. "On that date there were thirty cases of *destitution within a radius of ten miles of where I am writing this letter,*" he wrote the pro-farm *Western Independent*. Apparently provincial Minister of Agriculture Duncan Marshall was making an investigation, but Rabbitt wanted to know when. "When all the stock have starved to death?" he asked.[2] Three years later, the new Agriculture minister, George Hoadley, who certainly knew better, denied that there was an exodus taking place from southern Alberta.[3]

After five consecutive crop reverses, C. W. Peterson, longtime prairie resident and editor of *The Farm and Ranch Review,* wrote in 1921, "A fight is being waged in some of these dry areas in Alberta and Saskatchewan that the general public knows little about." With their backs to the wall, the settlers were staving off the leviathan. "If ever there were cases calling for sympathy and the generous out pouring of the milk of human kindness, these are surely in the very front ranks," he wrote. "From the bottom of my heart, I wish them Godspeed."[4]

What even Peterson did not know and what few others have known since, was that between a fifth and a quarter of all the townships in southeastern Alberta—a whopping 138 of them, covering 3.2 million acres—would lose *at least* 55 percent of their population from roughly the time he wrote until 1926.[5] These and the farm abandonment figures even the Great Depression never equalled. On both sides of the provincial boundary perhaps 120,000 settlers and their families were enveloped.

From within the bunkers that were their homes, farmers began the search for their salvation. At the annual convention in 1919, the United Farmers of Alberta decided to enter the political arena. Already swelling, excitement in the UFA locals intensified, as settlers from Irvine, Seven Persons, Whitla, Winnifred, Bow Island and elsewhere anxiously awaited the next election. Following the death of Arthur Sifton who had left the Alberta premiership to join the federal Union government, a federal by-election was called in the ancient storm centre of Medicine Hat.

Led by the likes of Lorne Proudfoot, son of a Scottish father and Irish mother, graduate of Van Kleek Hill Collegiate Institute in Ontario, and longtime secretary-treasurer of Collholme municipality, the farmers mobilized. North of the Red Deer in his district, Proudfoot exclaimed in early 1921, the settlers were "thoroughly organized and will fight to the death for a farmers' candidate." Already he had received pledges from 98 percent of the farm voters in his territory.[6]

The choice of the nominating convention was Robert Gardiner, a forty-two-year-old Scot who had come to Canada in 1902, homesteaded in the North Battleford district in 1903 and bought land in 1911 near Excel on the Alsask-Hanna line. A local municipal leader, Gardiner had been associated with the farmers' cooperative movement since his emigration.[7] Stressing the litany of agrarian grievances, he was driven by the spectre of drought.

On June 27 Gardiner wiped out his opposition, and joy, so long a captive of the desert, was loosed. Astounded, the provincial Liberal government, seeking to stop the wind from the Hat before it became irresistible, called a snap election. With just three weeks in hand, the UFA worked like fury. In Medicine Hat the farmers and organized labor each fielded a candidate and agreed to support the other. The farmer's man was Perren Baker who had been defeated by Gardiner at the federal nominating convention a few weeks earlier. A veteran of the great land rushes, a resident of Nemiskam since 1910, Baker was a graduate of McMaster University, chairman of his local school board and a councillor for his municipality.[8]

Stumping the riding in his Model-T, Baker was accompanied by "an earnest little labour man who denounced the financial interests, big business, the 'old line parties' in general and the Liberal Government of Alberta in particular."[9] Across the dry areas, several strong UFA candidates joined Baker in pursuit of office—Maurice Conner, an ex-American Methodist preacher, representing Warner in the south; George N. Johnston, an ex-Ontarian and former Saskatchewan teacher, representing Coronation in the north; Gordon Forster, an ex-O.A.C. student and five-year president of the Berry Creek agricultural society, representing Hand Hills in the west; and Lorne Proudfoot, the organizer for Bob Gardiner, representing Acadia along the Saskatchewan border.[10]

On election day Charles Stewart's government was soundly thrashed. The dry areas and fringes were championed by more than a dozen new, exuberant farmer MLAs bent on renovating the world. In the Hat, Perren Baker and his Labor running mate, Billy Johnson, an amiable ex-farm boy turned locomotive engineer, were carried on jubilant shoulders through a tumultuous crowd. Perhaps reflecting on the ghastly wards he now represented and sobered by the magnitude of the task besetting him, Baker was thankful but subdued: "I distinctly remember thinking as we rode high amid the shouts of adulation that the same crowd, with no more reason, would be quite capable of howling us down with cries of hatred and derision."[11]

Meanwhile the novice southern MLAs were buoyed by the words of their new leader, the premier from the north—Herbert Greenfield. "The government is prepared to stand by its attempts to solve the problem of the south," he promised, "and if, after we have tackled that problem in its fundamentals . . . the south country should fall, then we are prepared to fall with it."[12]

In Saskatchewan a similar course beckoned. Had Premier Martin dallied another moment before calling an election, or had the disaster in the southwest been as widespread as that in Alberta, his government would surely have fallen too. As it was, Progressives in the federal election of 1921 swept the region, with A. M. Carmichael representing Kindersley and N. H. McTaggart representing Maple Creek, tallying phenomenal majorities.[13]

But the Saskatchewan provincial Liberal party dealt more quickly

Charles Magrath, longtime
Lethbridge entrepreneur and
chairman of the Southern
Alberta Survey. NC 2-657,
Glenbow-Alberta Archives.

than its Alberta cousin with the dry area crisis. It promoted the euphemistically dubbed "Better Farming Conference" at Swift Current in July 1920, and the conference led to a similarly nicknamed royal commission undertaken by W. J. Rutherford, dean of the provincial College of Agriculture. Following suit, the new UFA government quickly commissioned a survey in November 1921 under Charles A. Magrath, long-term resident and former mayor of Lethbridge, assisted by George R. Marnoch, chairman of the Lethbridge Chamber of Commerce, Arthur A. Carpenter, a judge, and William H. Fairfield, director of the Lethbridge Experimental Farm.

The Southern Alberta Survey completed its report in January 1922 and was followed in succession by a commission on banking and credit as it affected agriculture, in November 1922; a massive Interior Department study of the heart of the dry belt radiating from Alderson, in December 1924; and a provincial inquiry into the same parts, completed in December 1926. To these were added at least a score of minor reports and investigations. Alberta may have begun its formal study of the problem later than Saskatchewan, but by mid-decade its documentation of the calamity was five or six times as deep and mountain high.

In a way, all this attention was no more than might be accorded any "heartland"—though it certainly perverted the meaning of that term. It was not that the metaphor of the dry belt as a strange heartland ceased to have meaning or grew less insightful—far from it. At first the heartland was strange because it was an unlikely locus for agrarian splendor; now it was odd because it was a shambles still in the spotlight. In the beginning, the heartland was expected to lead in productivity and growth; in the end, it led in debt and decay. Dominant once in the light, it now was even more dominant in the dark. The proof of its heightened hegemony, in fact its first official phase in the dark light, was the incredible attention the region drew from commissions of every rank.

Enough recommendations issued from these inquiries to fill the coulees. Either the commissioners or the victims demanded better credit facilities, freight rates and schools, more summerfallowing, mixed farming, rye growing, water storage reservoirs and meteorological stations, agricultural representatives, community pastures and experiments in suitable grasses, cooperative marketing, the empowering of municipalities to prevent cultivation of sandy soils, the reassessment of land values and taxes, and the provision of new homesteads.

The most insistent cry and the one to which governments responded most readily was for seed and feed. The federal government advanced Saskatchewan farmers over $520,000 in seed grain, fodder and relief between 1918 and 1920, and their less numerous Alberta cousins over $300,000; it also assisted the transportation of hay into the drought areas and of livestock out.[14] The provinces, however, bore most of the expense, and in just the thirty rural municipalities north of the South Saskatchewan River near the border on the Saskatchewan side approximately $340,000 worth of relief was poured out in the two years before October 1920.[15]

In return for the handouts, each government took liens on the crops until the amount was repaid. By mid-June 1922, about ten thousand liens had been filed with the Alberta Department of Agriculture alone, covering groceries, feed oats, hay and coal. Within eleven months of the UFA takeover, twenty-seven hundred cars of hay and a thousand cars of feed oats totalling almost 2.2 million bushels had been moved from northern Alberta to the south.[16] As Bow Island residents later admitted, area relief in the twenties dwarfed that during the Great Depression.[17] By early 1923, Alberta government aid had skyrocketed to nearly $8 million.[18]

Some of the southern UFA members had no sooner grown accustomed to the trees in Edmonton than J. R. Boyle, Leader of the Opposition, began harping against government paternalism toward the south country and warning that seed relief, feed relief and augmented grants for education and medical assistance could not go on forever. Unless nature came to the aid of the south in the growing season of 1922, the government would have to reconsider its policy.

The comment visibly annoyed the southerners, and Dr. J. S. Stewart, a Conservative from Lethbridge, snapped that the south would rejuvenate sooner than the rest of Alberta, and when it did debts of every stripe would flee before the returning tide of prosperity, and the province would not lose a "red cent."[19]

It was all silly pride and pointless bombast, for elements within the Cabinet were already doubting the resilience of the region. After five years of famine, they saw the province tumbling into an abyss of debt and insolvency. Only hours after Boyle's admonition, Attorney General J. E. Brownlee admitted that expectation of repayment in favorable years was a faint hope.[20] That year the provincial accounts showed a deficit of $2 million for the second year in a row.[21]

Recoiling from the heaviest debt load in the history of the province till then, the UFA huddled solemnly in caucus in mid-winter 1923.[22] When they emerged white-faced and drawn, they were one with Agriculture Minister George Hoadley who had shocked the south in January with the decree that there would be no more doles. As one member declared, "the door is closed absolutely this time."[23]

Some in the disaster zone saw, if not wisdom in the move, at least a certain inevitability. As in Saskatchewan, settlers had been hand-fed for several years and had come to expect it.[24] Other times relief had been forked out to the undeserving or to those who ignored so-called sane tillage methods. Some municipal councils failed to survey their districts to determine the truly needy; others left the whole operation to the municipal secretary. Consequently, the unprincipled secured their supplies with ease.[25] Still more serious in the end was the fact that unrepaid relief advances became a charge on the municipality and a millstone around the necks of fewer and fewer ratepayers.

Reaction to Hoadley's decision was mixed. Like Matt O'Reilly of Sunnynook, a good many settlers felt enervated by government relief.[26] J. R. Johnson, reeve of devastated King municipality told Greenfield, "The people are sick and tired of having to go to the Red Cross and Government for relief as we are only wasting the best part of our energy, vitality and lives to develop a country which is proving a positive failure."[27] Also secretary of the Blue Grass UFA local, centred on Alderson, poor Johnson was so battered and bewildered that he was in no mood to be consistent. Hours after Hoadley's announcement, he ejected another missive from the ever-deepening sinkhole. He told the UFA central office in Calgary of the antagonism toward Hoadley, of farmers' desire to evacuate but their inability to do so, and of Hoadley's compounding the problem by squeezing off aid.[28]

The relief program kept farmers in place for several years, but it hamstrung the province and bankrupted its municipalities. Ultimately its major assumption that all the settlers needed was a little boost to float them off the shoals was unfounded.

Water By All Means

EVEN BEFORE THE relief program played out, thoughts were focused on another remedy, one which the commissions, the governments and many settlers perceived as the quintessential solution—irrigation. During the dry early 1890s, intense interest in the subject had been first generated by William Pearce, Calgary mogul of the Interior Department and

The nightmare of drought riveted minds on a "certain" cure-all—irrigation. B 1174, Glenbow-Alberta Archives.

others like Charles Ora Card, leader of Alberta Mormons, Charles Magrath, then up-and-coming entrepreneur of Lethbridge, and Alexander and Elliott Galt. The ensuing wet cycle which enticed thousands of drylanders into the desert retarded the irrigation movement considerably. Nonetheless, advances up to the war were significant, if modest. The Galts' system in the Lethbridge-Cardston area, bought by the CPR in 1912, was operational. Lake Macgregor was filled, miles of canals were excavated, and the gem in the CPR's irrigation districts, the Bassano dam, was set in place.

When the dry years of 1917, 1918, and 1919 evinced famine on dry land and relative feasting on wet, dry farmers all over southern Alberta and southwestern Saskatchewan clamored for canals and sluice boxes. The Taber irrigation system was established in 1917, followed by the Lethbridge Northern in 1919, the Mountain View in 1923, the Magrath in 1924, and the Raymond in 1925.[29]

No matter how waterless a locality or how distant the tiniest streamlet, settlers met in droves to discuss the application of the magic elixir to the land. Teams of reclamation surveyors tramped through the dust, taking readings, making projections and birthing schemes. Eyeing big Sullivan Lake between Castor and Hanna, they plotted the drainage of what by *The Hanna Herald*'s own admission was "probably the most worthless body of water in Western Canada." Though closely rivaled by foul Lake Pakowki east of Foremost, and Bitter Lake north of Maple Creek, the judgement was just. Sullivan Lake was roughly eighteen miles long, seven miles wide and knee deep. So rank was it that beasts of burden shrank from it. Only the Canada Grey Geese loved it—and possibly those who hunted them on its shores.

Dominion reclamation experts determined that the lake could be poured neatly into Berry Creek, thus irrigating one of the driest parts of the desert. The twenty mile barrier between eastern and western sections of the slough would be eliminated, and roads could be punched across the dry bed, greatly easing the transportation problems in the area. The bottom lands of the gargantuan marsh could then be farmed.[30]

Nine months later, E. T. Drake, director of the reclamation service, reported that engineer J. S. Tempest had discovered that the soil beneath the lake was so impregnated with alkali that he doubted if it could ever be rendered arable. Moreover, residents further south, along Berry Creek objected strongly to the contamination of their stream by millions of gallons of scarcely diluted salts.[31] In the end nothing was done, and the lake remained the haunt of the Canada Grey.

Two dominion water experts also examined the possibility of diverting flow from the North Saskatchewan across the Red Deer River to irrigate the Tide Lake area as far east as Leader and Cabri in Saskatchewan. They concluded that the topographic features of the area made it "entirely unsuitable for the economic construction of any irrigation system . . . by canals of any source whatsoever. . . ."[32] When Rev. J. W. Morrow considered the feasibility of irrigation for the empire around the Hat, he concluded it would "not solve 5% of the problems here."[33]

Even most projects that had been established teetered and nearly toppled. In the CPR Irrigation Blocks, the eastern portion of which centred on Brooks and extended almost to the doorstep of Alderson, the company was faced by a revolt of its ratepayers who claimed that if their contracts were not renegotiated they would move to Bolivia![34] In 1924 the Eastern Block granted an adjustment amounting to three years' water rental and five years' interest, and it dropped the price of dry land in irrigation units from $25 to $10 an acre. When these measures failed to resuscitate farmers, the company was forced to reclassify all its lands in 1927, to reduce the price of watered parcels from $50 to $35 an acre and nonirrigable parcels to just $5 an acre.[35]

The Lethbridge Northern project, comprising 100,000 acres of irrigable land and 200,000 acres nonirrigable, had no sooner gotten underway than ratepayers stated they could not pay water charges of $5.25 an acre. The final capital charges of the project were reported as high as $100 an acre to be divided among three hundred settlers. As the farmers threatened to leave en masse, Attorney General J. E. Brownlee openly feared that the government would be saddled with a $12 million white elephant.[36]

By that time the massive Canada Land and Irrigation Project west of the Hat was utterly insolvent and virtually dead in the dust. At decade-end the irrigation projects, headed by the Lethbridge Northern whose debentures had been guaranteed by the Alberta government, were subject to a royal commission.[37]

All this time frantic efforts were being made to entice burnt-out drybelters to enter the projects, an act equivalent to leaping from the flames into the frying pan. Not all settlers had the sense or experience of E. E. Noble of Chinook who frankly told the Southern Alberta Survey that he had seen many irrigation districts in his time, but none where the first-comers had made a success.[38] As another settler grunted, irrigation was undoubtedly a good thing, but "sky water was cheaper."[39]

Mesmerized by this maxim, enterprising businessmen from Medicine Hat hatched another "remedy." Of all the solutions conjured up for the dry belt problem none combined mystery, sorcery and inanity in similar measure. Perhaps the crucial character in the saga was F. S. Ratliff, a Falstaffian figure with a boundless optimism to match his girth. He was a Nebraskan who had farmed as a young man, been a policeman in Omaha and a sheriff at Colfax, Washington, before succumbing to the deadliest of all sins—real estate promotion. After brief stints in Spokane, Portland and Moose Jaw, he landed in Medicine Hat in late 1913, and became manager of the Dominion Harvester Company which manufactured shells during the war. Following the war, he suffered a relapse and opened a real estate office in the city.[40]

Sometime in 1920, perhaps earlier, Ratliff, in his late forties, became interested in one of the marvels of the age—Charles M. Hatfield, a professional rainmaker. A native of Eagle Rock, California, Hatfield, according to the worshipful *Wide World Magazine,* first came to prominence in 1904 by wagering with Los Angeles businessmen that he could break the drought then gripping southern California. Speedily assembling the necessary chemicals, he hurried to the foothills of the Sierra Madres, and sixty hours later the skies obediently opened, pelting down 1.64 inches of rain. The next winter the businessmen offered $1,000 if he could deliver eighteen inches of rain between December and May, a period which averaged just ten inches. Again he complied with ease.

Sometimes, it seemed, he had only to come within view of the clouds, and they would squeeze themselves dry. Once he had a contract for delivery within a fifteen day period. Saturday, the first day of the contract, the railway crew refused to spot the car containing his apparatus, and the unloading was delayed till Monday. On the Lord's Day, as if some prior notice had been filed skyward, a drizzle began and continued until the allotment was reached. Though the contract merely specified the amount of rain needed and said nothing about Hatfield's having to unpack his gear, the drought-breaker graciously refused his fee.

Unfortunately, Hatfield's own clients were not always as wellmeaning. Like the San Diego city council in 1916, some were pure mercenaries. For $10,000 the city fathers wanted the source of their domestic water supply, the Morena Reservoir, filled to the brim, but since this tank in the mountains held a small ocean, the council kindly allowed Hatfield a year to top it off. In January alone, thirty-six inches of rain fell and four billion gallons of water tumbled into the tank—a five year supply. Still the rain fell, and soon nearly five feet of floodwater was passing over the spillway. A flood resulted, immobilizing the Santa Fe Railroad and washing out 110 city and county bridges. Then the Otay dam burst, destroying a fortune in property and drowning a dozen people.

When the time for payment came, the city reneged, claiming there was no written contract. Presuming that the city preferred him to bring suit rather than the scores of the dispossessed and the descendants of the deceased, Hatfield pocketed nary a cent in the hour of his consummate triumph.

Another time, at Crow's Landing, California, farmers offered Hatfield $250 for nine inches of rain, nearly twice the annual mean. For twelve inches, they upped the ante to $1,500. After eleven inches fell in a short span, there was so much water in the fields that farmers could not plant their crops. They quickly held a meeting, paid Hatfield $1,500, and ordered him to desist.

Hatfield's methodology was mysterious. Near a pond or lake and on the highest ground in the vicinity, he erected two to four towers on top of which he placed many shallow pans, not unlike gold pans. Into the pans he sprinkled a potion of secret chemicals which were connected to earth for what one savant called "radio-activity although it may be nothing more than galvanic electricity." The art of inducing the sky to weep, Hatfield claimed, was learned from library books, some studied during his boyhood in Minneapolis, and from practical tests of his own arcane theories.[41]

On January 12, 1921, Hatfield signed a contract with the United Agricultural Association of Medicine Hat to generate the greatest increase in precipitation possible. The territory of the blessing was to radiate from the city, now "the artificial storm centre," for one hundred miles, reaching well past Hanna and Gleichen, to the doorsteps of Fort Macleod, Kindersley and Swift Current. "The operations of said Hatfield," stated the contract, "tend to contribute a 100 per cent increase over and above the natural rainfall." Crediting

Charles Hatfield, master of the clouds, Chappice Lake, 1921. NA 2003-67, Glenbow-Alberta Archives.

the rainmaker for half the precipitation that fell between May 1 and August 1, it offered him $2,000 for every inch of moisture that fell. The maximum consideration was $8,000 for a four-inch rain. Magnanimously, the contract also declared—"All rainfall in excess of four inches no extra charges whatever."[42]

What troubled Saskatchewan Deputy Minister of Agriculture F. Hedley Auld was that the contract offered what might be expected six years out of seven.[43] Indeed, the average May-July rainfall for Medicine Hat over a forty-one year period was 6.05 inches; the average for Jenner over nine years was 6.17 inches; even the bone-dry Alderson-Suffield region over ten years got 4.89 inches.[44] When a Gull Lake, Saskatchewan, resident pointed to this fly in the ointment, the drought-breaker replied that the average rainfall was not considered at all since the past four seasons had been much drier than usual. Reassuring readers of the *Medicine Hat News,* he predicted a cascade of eight to ten inches of rain. Remarkable as his past achievements had been, he professed immodestly, "these operations that are to be conducted in Alberta this summer will be the most pronounced and convincing in the increased production of rainfall ever attempted by me."[45]

In late April, Hatfield arrived in Medicine Hat, accompanied by a light drizzle. He was welcomed royally at a sumptuous luncheon at the Corona Hotel where representatives of the churches, the government, the city, the Canada Land and Irrigation Company, the *Lethbridge Herald,* the *Medicine Hat News* and the farmers embraced him in an orgy of fulsome praise and local puffery. F. S. Ratliff acted admirably as master of ceremonies and toastmaster. Politician C. S. Pingle said the eyes of the government were upon him; Superintendent Cameron of the CPR wired that Hatfield must have arrived in the Hat because it was raining in Calgary. Local Lawyer L. N. Laidlaw suggested that others of his calling present were hoping to represent those about to become the loss leaders in the approaching flood. As for himself, he would defend Hatfield free of charge.[46]

A few days later, Hatfield and his brother erected their largest tower ever, north of the city at Chappice Lake. Unable to contain their curiosity, Ratliff, photographer Brown of the Royal Studio, and a minion of the ever faithful *News* motored directly to the lake where Hatfield had assumed command of the weather. The rainmaker was convinced that drought amid such natural fertility was totally unnecessary. "It's a grand country for these operations," he said. Asked about his location at the lake, he beamed—"It's one of the best I've ever had; I'm perfectly satisfied."

The two drought-breakers were comfortably ensconced in a neat, roomy cookhouse, rigged with eaves. Visitors were welcomed and enjoined to bring their picnic baskets and cameras. When questioned concerning the petition of several farmers that they be al-

lowed to finish seeding before the first downpour, Hatfield mercilessly replied, "Let it rain."[47]

And rain it did, short hours after Hatfield stepped from the
tower. Local communities exulted and sang the praises of the sorcerer. "Mr. Hatfield . . . is certainly on the credit side, and given full
praise for the splendid rains of May 5th and 6th, which this district
hasn't experienced in years," wrote the grateful Winnifred correspondent of the *News*.[48] Baseball fans in the area had just renamed
their circuit the Rainmaker League.[49] At month-end the correspondent's jubilation was unbounded—"The weather! Oh, well every-
body knows it rains about every other day. Hatfield is certainly
making good."[50]

It rained so much that month that Medicine Hatters petitioned
the sorcerer to schedule downpours for night time only.[51] Even in
the parched Alderson-Suffield area a full two inches fell in May,
double what had fallen in 1920 and over eight times the 1917–18
totals.[52]

Almost as soon as the crops peered above ground, F. S. Ratliff
began touring the region and reporting on their progress. By June-
end he was predicting bumper crops north of the city.[53] Nowhere
was there anything approaching calamity. His view, however, was
overly roseate, distorted by a terminal boosterism and an over-
whelming desire to see Hatfield succeed. The fact was that the rains
had stopped in June.

At nearby Suffield only 0.65 inch fell that month, the second
lowest since records began in 1913. In Medicine Hat, June was one
of the hottest ever. The average daily maximum temperature was 84
degrees F., exceeded only in 1919 all the way back to 1883. July
continued the trend as the Hat maximums averaged a sweltering
86.4 degrees F., and at Suffield precipitation fell to a seven-year
low.[54]

In late July, F. Hedley Auld was in Shaunavon, Saskatchewan, at
the same time as Hatfield who had extended his operations to that
point. Hatfield was complaining that his towers had been placed by
local dolts in poor locations.[55]

Near Redcliff, only the South
Saskatchewan River was wet in
1921 and 1922. PA 19127,
Public Archives of Canada.

Settlers on both sides of the provincial line now saw their folly.
W. C. Gibbard of Richmound, Saskatchewan, considered Hatfield's methods "an insult to farmers' intelligence," and Ratliff's
means of collecting money to support the venture a veritable skin-
game perpetrated by city slickers.[56] "The farmers in this district are
exhausted with finding faults with Hatfield 'the rainmaker,'" added
the once grateful, now apostate Winnifred correspondent. "His
first play is enough! Winnifred farmers won't bite again."[57]

At Alderson the mood usually flamboyant of columnist Charlotte
Cotter was more subdued, more reflective. "The harvest work is so
slim that it is hardly worth speaking of; to mention it only makes all
feel badly. Best plan, try and forget it as soon as possible."[58]

There was one movement left in the farce, and that was the payment of Hatfield. Though not in Alderson-Suffield, in the measuring stations that counted, the region had received a scant four inches of rain, and the sorcerer was entitled to the full $8,000 of his
contract. It was a measure of the usual city and speculator misunderstanding of the man on the land, and of the latter's own misconception of his own requirements that a contract could be con-
ceived asking for much less than a miserly nature normally accorded. In the final analysis, the United Agricultural Association
had requested a drought and paid for it.

Mindful of the din of discontent, Hatfield returned $2,500. Still under his spell, Ratliff's association now admitted that they had chosen Chappice Lake as the centre of operations and that "the location was not a good one." They then renewed Hatfield's contract for the coming year, imagining that they had at last inspired Hatfield to actually produce rain. For every inch after three they offered $4,000 to a maximum of $12,000 for a six-inch fall.[59] Even the maximum, however, was less than the longstanding Medicine Hat average.

Mercifully public sentiment forbade the sorcerer's return, though black humorists might have wished he had come and planted his measuring rod near Alderson the next year where he would have collected not a cent. It was all reminiscent of Mark Twain's adage that everyone talked about the weather but no one ever did anything about it.

8   It Does Not Matter How
You Farm It

IN A SMALL WAY, those farmers who donated to Hatfield's coffers were decrying another "solution" to the all-encompassing calamity that was slowly devouring their world. For some, the reliance on the sorcerer was an admission that there were no farm methods appropriate to the desert, that changing what one did on the ground was useless without changing what fell from the sky. To the agricultural experts who had devised dryland farming techniques before and during the settlement period, such an admission was pure heresy. In truth, however, it was they who were the heretics.

The brew of lies, shams and frauds distilled by the land speculators might almost have been pardoned, since no one expected more from their class. But the piffling pedantry preached by the so-called dry farming experts, inflated like blimps with their

134

own importance and accorded rank by an almost obsequiously deferential society, was another matter. True, the science of soil culture was rudimentary, and the experts, like others commenting on the settlement of the dry belt, simply did not know enough. Yet what they thought they knew they took great pains to publicize. And it is one thing to be wrong and quite another to write books about it.

Somewhere deep in the universe the blaring of these blowhards of the settlement era still reverberated. They had been the heralds of the occupation. Their words had been emblazoned on the sheets of the departments of agriculture, the agrarian press, the regional and local papers, the minutebooks of agricultural societies, and the notebooks of careful settlers. Drawing to themselves all the import that their books, articles and speeches seemed to represent, they reckoned they had bared the secrets of taming the "desert."

Several of these false prophets had taken their seminary at the Ontario Agricultural College (OAC), the great propaganda mill of the joys of country living. The core of its doctrine was the belief that there was "a force inherent in the human mind which could make the elements subservient to man's purposes"—the dictum of agriculture Professor Thomas Shaw.[1] Buoyed by the recent spate of inventions including enhanced binders, electrical gadgets, and thousands of mechanical patents, many of its progeny attended the settlement of the West, almost as missionaries, padres of the land, with a vibrant rural theology. There, in the new departments, schools and colleges of agriculture, on the new experimental stations or the staffs of farm papers, these rural zealots fashioned their own Nicene Creed—*I believe that the new tools of science and discovery can surmount any obstacles; I believe that the land being occupied can in fact be occupied; I believe that God is in nature and that nature nourishes man physically, emotionally and morally.* With much to commend itself, the creed had a fatal flaw: an overweening faith in the power of man.

Naturally, too, not all the tenets of the creed were cherished with equal vim. Stalwarts of a more practical bent set about confirming what to many was the first proposition—namely, that man could render livable the arid west of the Territories, the barren tip of the fabled Great American Desert.

W. R. Motherwell was one who accepted this challenge. An OAC graduate, a statesman of first rank, a longtime minister of Agriculture of Saskatchewan and later of the Dominion, Motherwell kept meticulous account of his attempt to demonstrate the fertility of the North-West Territories. From 1891 to 1909 at Abernethy, near Indian Head, this dry-farming wheat baron averaged almost thirty bushels of wheat an acre, never once suffering a failure. Even in the drought of 1892 and 1894, he reaped twenty-six bushels an acre. His record he and others held in esteem as proof positive of the invariable reward of proper technique.

Motherwell's technique was similar to that of friend Angus MacKay. The latter had come to the Territories in 1882, establishing a large farming company near Indian Head. After drought decimated his crops in 1883 and 1884, the Riel Rebellion prevented his seeding the next year. On land left idle, he reaped twenty-six bushels of wheat an acre in 1886. Realizing the benefit of the summerfallow as a means of moisture conservation, he devised a near failsafe scheme of farm management, especially after becoming superintendent of the Indian Head Experimental Farm in 1888. Including some diversification, the system hallowed deep plowing, summerfallowing and weed eradication.[2]

Naturally, McKay and Motherwell fancied they had disproved the central claim of Captain Palliser about the existence of a forbidding desert on the southern plains. Fervently, they believed that their dryland methods of moisture conservation stood for all the southern Territories—Eastern Assiniboia, Western Assiniboia or Southern Alberta. And on the eve of the occupation of the *real* dry belt, leagues westward, most of their claims were warmly supported by Professor H. W. Campbell, a Dakotan, who preached water conservation by carefully conducted summer tillage. Barnstorming the new communities in Southern Alberta at provincial invitation, Campbell instructed summerfallowers to pack the subsurface to generate capillary action from water below and to leave a dust mulch on top to retard evaporation.[3]

All three of these mortals—Motherwell, MacKay and Campbell—attracted a worship of sorts. When Campbell journeyed to the Hat in 1909 to bless the land and summon it into production, his approach was likened to the second coming. He and the others even talked in Biblical terms. It was as if they had slipped into the craggy coulees, communed with God, and returned with a carving of commandments. A dryland expert in the settlement period without a set of tablets, indeed, was a runt of a human being, out of step and out of fashion.

Most of the commandments resembled those of Professor W. C. Palmer of North Dakota Agricultural College which appeared in 1912 in the *Carlstadt Progress:*

TEN COMMANDMENTS OF THE DRY FARMER
1. Thou shalt Plow Deep.
2. Thou shalt Keep the Surface Soil Loose and Level and Lower Soil Compact.
3. Thou shalt Add Organic Matter to the Soil.
4. Thou shalt Summer Fallow When Rainfall is Less Than Fifteen Inches.
5. Thou shalt Grow Corn or a Cultivated Crop Every Two to Five Years.
6. Thou shalt Grow Clover, Alfalfa or Some Leguminous Crop Every Few Years.
7. Thou shalt Grow Early Maturing Crops.
8. Thou shalt Keep Down the Weeds.
9. Thou shalt Keep Stock.
10. Thou shalt Plant Trees.

Palmer ended with the assurance that "Who obeys these commandments shall reap abundant crops."[4]

To this bidding, there was an addendum, divined by other prophets of Baal—sufficient moisture at seeding assured a crop, and obviated the need for even a drop of summer rain.[5]

For years, many pedants bombarded dryland farmers with these and slightly modified preachments. Thus when tillers experienced crop failures in 1917 and 1918, the experts turned to their old sermons and concluded that no one had listened. In a snit, Motherwell, Saskatchewan minister of Agriculture, told the Saskatoon *Star* in September 1918 that drought or no drought, "success or non-success is chiefly, if not entirely due to straight good or bad farming."[6] Even Seager Wheeler, the yeoman marvel from Rosthern, categorically stated that he had "frequently made the statement that it is possible to grow a very satisfactory crop in any season. . . ."[7] And F. Hedley Auld, deputy minister of Agriculture, was just as certain. As he told one farmer in 1918, drought was simply a poor reason for crop failure.[8]

Self-righteously, authorities reminded stricken settlers that the principal control for drought was the summerfallow. "We must not forget that in many parts of Alberta and Saskatchewan there was no reasonable certainty of reaping a crop until summer fallows were introduced, and we do not think it safe with your limited rainfall to get along without them," said James Murray, superintendent of the Noble Farms in Southern Alberta.[9] Summerfallows assured crops even in bad years. After many seasons at the Indian Head Experimental Farm, Angus MacKay unequivocally stated that proper fallowing at the farm "never failed to give good results no matter how dry the year was."[10] Even more adamant were respected farmers like J. P. Robinson of Cadillac, Saskatchewan. "Anyone doubting that from half to a full crop may always be assured as against drought by proper summer fallowing," Robinson said, "is the victim of marked self deception."[11]

When the Survey Board for Southern Alberta completed its report in 1922 it declared the summerfallow to be a basic necessity. Then, echoing an earlier injunction of Motherwell to farmers in the drier regions, the Survey implored settlers to "spring fallow," that is, to cultivate the land early to take advantage of early spring moisture.[12]

It was all old advice, indeed, but good advice. How neglectful the farmers had become, how forgetful. When James Murray travelled to the Better Farming Conference at Swift Current, he decried the wretched fallows: "From the railway one cannot see above a thousand acres of land plowed lying bare, but one can see thousands of fields growing mustard high enough to hide the gang plows that are turning it under," he exclaimed. "These are the summer fallows[!]"[13]

Groping in the Dark MANY SETTLERS DEEPLY resented the experts' response to their dilemma. In the first years of the drought they detested the unwillingness of the departments of Agriculture in Saskatchewan and Alberta to admit that crops had failed repeatedly over large tracts. They chafed at the implication that they had never heeded the lessons of dry farming, that like mental cripples, they had to be told over and over the simple steps they had missed. They detected an insensitivity, a smugness, and ultimately a disturbing ignorance in certain experts, particularly in Motherwell. They took offense at his suggestion that they had failed because of their own inanity. Those who truly understood the drylands, burned under the collar at his cocksuredness and his old, old tale of the "remarkable discrepancy" in adjoining crops, the one overflowing with milk and honey and the other burnt-out and dry as flour—the perfect reflection, Motherwell said, not of a lucky shower on the first as farmers were wont to tell, but of proper tillage practices on the first and abysmal methods on the second.

R. Fenerty of Bickleigh, Saskatchewan, was among the annoyed. "If the Hon. Minister were to visit this vicinity, he could be shown numerous identical cases where exactly the same methods were used on both farms, but where rain fell in sufficient quantity on one farm and not on the adjoining one," he wrote. Dramatic local variability of rainfall was a fact of life in the dry areas. In blaming crop failure on shoddy methods, Motherwell was "shooting very wide of the mark." Then, wedding his ire to his experience, Fenerty uttered the unutterable, the supreme blasphemy—"It is simply proven in this locality and we doubt not in others, that the best known methods of agriculture will fail to bring results some years."

Fenerty next turned on the long-lauded summerfallow. Still tracking Motherwell, he presumed that "good farming" meant summerfallowing, early plowing and thorough tilling. Squaring these precepts with existing conditions, he wrote, "we find that the men in this locality, who are according to the above standard, the best farmers, men whose fallow was plowed earliest and most thoroughly cultivated, are by far the heaviest losers this year, and have harvested less grain than those whose land was less thoroughly tilled." The paragons of so-called "good" tillage practices reaped less than many of the oft-maligned, indifferent farmers.[14]

Others too began to eye askance the traditional clear summerfallow. At Medicine Hat, one tiller told the Southern Alberta Survey of his son who had an excellent summerfallow the previous spring and had offered a dollar for every bit of fallow that went to sod. "He had his summerfallowing done and everything looked prosperous," said the father, "and along comes a big wind and blew him out." The father himself had a field of light land between his house and the school. Said he, "The wind would come and pretty near bury us under."[15]

Abetted by the fallows, soil drifting became a serious problem after the war. Dust storms rose in fury, dwarfing the worst that had ever come before and equaling the worst that would come later.[16] At the Western Canadian Irrigation Convention in July 1920, John Bracken, former Saskatchewan University professor, new president of Manitoba Agricultural College and future premier of Manitoba, reported that he knew a district where 50,000 acres had blown out.[17] Just before the convention, a ferocious wind stripped a million acres in southern Alberta.[18]

At the height of the blowing, the bitter legacy of Professor H. W. Campbell was revealed. His insistence on sub-surface packing and surface mulching to interrupt moisture loss by capillary action had been heard by thousands as they first homesteaded. Assisted by the Alberta Department of Agriculture, by the farm and local press, by eager agricultural societies, and by the early dry farming congresses, Campbell had succeeded beyond his wildest reckoning in converting the masses to a system which left the earth covered with a light mantle of dust. By the time of the Southern Alberta Survey in 1921, settlers still on the land saw their folly. Matt O'Reilly of Sunnynook, for instance, told the Hanna hearing that "he had followed the Campbell system on his farm but it had nearly broken him."[19]

Of course, by then Campbell had long since fallen from favor with the new community of agricultural pundits. Many suspected his involvement with American railroads. Others questioned his theory. "The capillary theory," E. C. Chilcott of the U.S. Department of Agriculture wrote in John Bracken's *Dry Farming in Western Canada*, "is undoubtedly responsible for more false reasoning about dry land agriculture than any other one thing."[20] Water vapor loss through capillary action, Chilcott pronounced, was inconsequential in the desert. Years later, agricultural scientists would dispute Chilcott's own wisdom, and for tillers who followed the history of expert promulgations it must have seemed that the scientists, like mythical Cronus, were forever devouring their own progeny.

At any rate, in this time of trouble it was Campbell's turn to be feasted upon. As the scapegoating began, he ironically had accomplices still in high places. Virtually en masse, dry farming experts before 1917, from Motherwell and MacKay to Professors W. C. Palmer of North Dakota Agricultural College and John Widtsoe of Utah Agricultural College, had recommended deep plowing, either partly or principally to facilitate penetration of rain into the soil and to prevent excessive run-off. And pundit after pundit had promoted undue surface cultivation.[21] By the early twenties, the baneful results of the repetitive tearing and rending and stirring of the soil were increasingly apparent. P. M. Abel, an expert himself, explained: "When Hon. W. R. Motherwell was earning himself the sobriquet of 'the moisture minister' by preaching moisture conservation to all and sundry, we used to talk about dust mulches. Since that time dust mulches have contracted the habit of climbing astride every passing breeze."[22]

For the soil experts the dilemma was plain: summerfallowing meant survival, but it stripped the land and robbed the soil of nitrogen. For many settlers, on the other hand, the practice had no redeeming feature. "It is becoming increasingly and ever more painfully evident," wrote the joint committee of the Grain Growers' Associations of South Cypress, "that we are working along wrong lines in our endeavours ... that the best summer fallow falls pitifully short of solving the problem even in years of fair rainfall...."[23] "You use two years' moisture for one crop, but i[f] the moisture does not come," John Stewart of Nemiskam told the Southern Alberta Survey, "summer fallowing is not better than any other method of farming." Hot winds swooping across their preordained glide path through Alderson and Suffield sucked the fallows so dry that not once from 1919 to at least 1921 could they be cultivated after July 1st.[24] Whatever farmers did, summerfallowed or springfallowed, results were terrible. As G. Harrad of the Pincher Creek area told Premier Greenfield, if he summerfallowed the land blew away, if he spring plowed it dried up.[25]

In time, many farmers came to the conclusion of Thomas Lannan of Ingebrigt in the Great Sand Hills area, north of Maple Creek: "It does not matter how you farm it, the result is the same. This year the summerfallow seeding was the first to go, and you can see fields of sumerfallow that will not yield anything."[26]

A second major farm management solution the experts offered was fall rye. At the Western Canada Irrigation Congress in Nelson, B.C., in July 1918, Motherwell trumpeted this savior as one solution to the wind menace.[27] Sown in autumn, the hardy rye crop anchored the soil by spring when danger from drifting was acute. Equally impressed, John Bracken published a photograph in *The Farmer's Advocate* showing a badly drifted oats crop next to fall rye which was practically unscathed.[28] C. McConkey, agronomist at the Claresholm Alberta School of Agriculture, also noted that fall rye used the autumn to spring moisture largely lost to spring grains. Growing vigorously in May and June, it combatted weeds and was less susceptible to summer drought, and ripening earlier, it was less subject to fall frost and distributed the harvest over a longer period, thus reducing labor costs. It was also resistant to cutworms, rust and smut.[29] Thus, by 1921 agricultural authorities in Alberta and

Saskatchewan were imploring banks, mortgage companies and rural municipalities to give every assistance in planting the crop.[30]

Unhappily, practitioners often shunned this "solution" too. Several Alderson farmers tried fall rye, but were dismayed by the very light yields.[31] P. H. Tolley of Macleod reported that one year grasshoppers took it, and another the winter killed it.[32] Before long, even the experts were keenly aware of the latter problem, especially north of the Red Deer River.[33] W. H. Walker of Ceylon, Saskatchewan, worried that fall rye had to be sown during harvest when there was little time and when the land was so dry that germination was likely in only one year out of three or four.[34] Rye was also worth much less than wheat as a cash crop. "All talk of mixed farming and rye growing is futile," summarized Thomas Lannan of Ingebrigt in 1921. "A whole township would not feed the stock of four farmers and if you can raise a rye crop, you are also sure of a wheat or oats crop. There is no rye in this part any good this year."[35]

Lannan's condemnation simultaneously belittled another common expert solution—diversification. "Thou shalt Keep Stock," the comandment thundered. "My personal opinion," said F. Hedley Auld, "is that too many farmers are depending entirely upon grain growing."[36] The fixation on grain was an outcome of wartime demand and high prices, but with the post-war downturn, farmers needed to diversify just to feed themselves. Unquestionably, mixed farming was the wisest form of agriculture in western Canada, asserted the CPR's General Superintendent of Lands.[37] "A few cows, a few pigs, some hens with a variety of crops necessary for these various classes of livestock," concluded Auld, "will provide the greatest measure of safety." A monthly cream cheque, an occasional egg cheque and a litter of pigs for sale in autumn, all ensured a reasonable living.[38]

Many Alderson farmers heard similar cheer, heeded the counsel and turned to mixed farming to save themselves. They found, however, that in addition to their families, they had to save their stock.[39] A Gouldtown, Saskatchewan farmer spoke for the whole dryland empire when he said, "We are up against it for feed three years out of four, and stock keeping is not profitable if one has to be always buying feed to keep them alive. . . ."[40] Had the land been in wheat in the years when there were crops, many settlers felt they'd have been miles ahead.[41] Water shortages and poor prices, others moaned, precluded stock keeping. Mixed farming too was more costly than wheat farming in the buildings it required, the windmills, the chopping mills, the fences, the corrals, breeding stock and labor.[42] It meant harder work and longer hours. It was riddled with hazards—with predators, infections, epidemics, and freeze-ups. The winter of 1918–1919, the most terrifying since 1906–1907, indeed, froze to death half the stock in the dry belt.[43]

Consequently, by 1920 the Grain Growers' Associations of South Cypress declared the mixed farming solution "hopelessly out of the reach of most of us who in the past ten years have exhausted our never too plentiful resources experimenting as it were in the dark for proper methods. . . ."[44] The conclusion was apt for many areas of the drylands.

Unravelling the Mysteries

THE RESULT OF the calamity was a remarkable shift in farming wisdom and a whittling of "experts," both professional and practical, down to size. As the early twenties wore on, many experts appeared somewhat nonplussed, humbled, and less sure of themselves. Perhaps a soil scientist of the calibre of University of Saskatchewan Professor Roy Hansen ought to have fathomed the "burn outs," circular areas of varying dimensions, completely devoid of top soil and vegetation, about which farmers had complained for years. Yet, beginning his soil survey in southwestern Saskatchewan, he betrayed a profound and disturbing ignorance. "An interesting thing to me," he wrote, "are the 'burn-outs.' I have often heard them mentioned but this is the first time I have had a chance to see such extensive areas of them. We hope by gathering samples to learn more about them." In passing, Hansen noted settler claims that fall rye "came through best where sown in the stubble or among the thistles and poorest where sown on clear summer fallow." Revealing the shaky stance of agricultural experts in the process of changing their minds, Hansen admitted, "There must be a certain amount of truth in this judging by the experience of a number of farmers."[45]

To unravel the mysteries of dryland farming, illustration stations had been established by the federal Department of Agriculture in southern Alberta after the short crop of 1914. Unfortunately, they availed little. In 1924 virtually all the stations experienced crop failures. At Jenner, operator Jerry Fisher reported four bushels of wheat on summer fallow and nothing on land cropped the previous year. At Orion, operator George Wagar reported that the 320 acres cropped were operated at a loss of $1,400. Shuddering, the director of Illustration Stations remarked, "this loss would be sustained in spite of the most approved methods and efficient performance available. The old and offhand statement that crop failures are the result of careless indolence supplemented by ignorance of advanced methods should be dropped."

If good farming meant clear summerfallowing, plowing early and tilling vigorously, as the moisture clique said, then one or more conclusions, rejected outright by the experts, beckoned—it was possible to fail using "correct" methods; the so-called methods were a snare and a delusion; or no methods would ever work some years. The last, the director of Illustration Stations believed in his heart when he concluded that the basic cause of crop failure over southeastern Alberta in 1924 was lack of moisture, pure and simple.[46]

After the 1926 crop disaster, the director, alluding to the earlier teachings of Motherwell, Surface and others, commented, "the statement is sometimes made that with a good moisture content of soil carried over from autumn to spring a fair crop is assured. In more than one instance the 1926 results have failed to bear out this theory. From the past season's work it appears that a certain amount of summer rain is essential if a good crop is to be harvested." The few farmers who read this profound "discovery" and recalled the pipedreams of the settlement era must have shaken their heads in utter dismay. Yet they should not have been too critical, for there was a valuable demonstration by the show farms that year—Robert Montgomery of Sunnynook abandoned his altogether.[47]

F. Hedley Auld, who had specialized in relaying the pontification of the Motherwells, MacKays, and others to disgruntled farmers in 1918, captured as well as anyone the consternation of experts. He told the Prelate, Saskatchewan village secretary, "I used to think as you do that those who farm properly would get some crop every year." The key to one farmer's success over another, he now reckoned, after his ears had been repeatedly buzzed about variability of dry belt rainfall, was a lucky shower or two. As for "proper methods," he was no longer sure they would work. "We can only recommend a system which we believe is best suited to the district, and allow the individual to take a chance whether it will pay him in the long run to follow it."[48] How far Auld had come from the age of certainty when he had wielded the lessons of the dryland masters with such aplomb!

It was another of the ironies of the slide into oblivion that S. E. Greenway, former Saskatchewan Extension director, paragon of the country life movement, and high priest of the values of enhanced rural living, was assigned in 1926 as a lowly crop reporter for the *Free Press Prairie Farmer* to survey the wreck in the Youngstown, Alberta, area. No one ever saw more clearly the degradation that had befallen a dream. Still with the spark of the ameliorator in him, Greenway noted the supreme need for leadership in dirt farming. G. S. Coad, operator of the Illustration farm, he regretted, was instructed by superiors to use the methods that had proven successful at Indian Head. "It is no criticism of Mr. Coad to say that the general results of his plot work thereon the Indian Head plan *is a fair demonstration of what not to do. . . .*" Deeply aware of the widespread abandonment, Greenway looked despairingly at the "magnificent set of agricultural school buildings, now used for housing cockroaches."[49]

Greenway's sarcasm betrayed the expert state of mind by the mid-twenties. Openly critical of mismanagement, he blamed the authorities themselves for refusing to discard outworn methods. Like Auld in Saskatchewan and the director of Illustration Stations in Alberta, he had lost his assurance, his confidence in mind over matter. It did not particularly strike these men that God was in nature or that the soil elevated man. All seriously wondered if the land that had been occupied was habitable after all. And if they ever pondered Thomas Shaw's dictum that there was a "force inherent in the human mind which could make the elements subservient to man's purposes," they must have considered the old professor slightly daft.

The fact that the settlers had discovered the reality of the desert first was unsettling to the experts. The latter had always had a clear idea of the nature of the crucial relationship with commoners. A recurrent theme in Canadian history, their interaction, they assumed, was an encounter between those who knew certain principles, skills and techniques, and those who did not know them; it was the old process of enlightenment, of transforming hearts and actions with flashing intellect and palpable truth. In the history of the dry areas, these assumptions, unfortunately, were all too often invalid. The usual experts' view that the locals were simply uninformed and irrationally resistant to education was not always justified. Nor was the experts' perception that like professors they were merely assembling irrefutable, even unanswerable evidence, or that like priests they were only exorcizing myths from bumpkin minds. In fact, the development of the Canadian West was full of encounters which purportedly pitted the skilled against the unskilled, but which really sometimes confused those roles, rendering the expert's task most trying and over-extending his authority. It was the experts' cross to bear that recurrent farmer opposition to scientific, rationalized agriculture was not always based on sheer and shameful ignorance.

Swept by feelings of confusion, doubt and dejection, the agricultural experts, of course, were troubled by other factors, including the termination of the Agricultural Instruction Act and its life-giving funding, the lack of public appreciation of their work, the lack of focus in the agricultural training institutions, and the gen-

C. W. Peterson, editor of *The Farm and Ranch Review,* foresaw the consequences of the calamity. NA 4945-1, Glenbow-Alberta Archives.

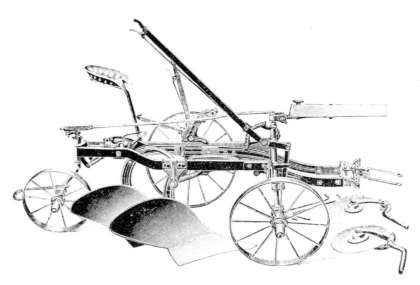

WESTERN CHIEF STEEL GANG PLOW

A legacy of the disaster—the gradual disappearance of the plow. PA 2590-3, Glenbow-Alberta Archives.

eral agricultural depression. When Dominion Cerealist Charles Saunders, gifted founder of Marquis wheat, renounced agricultural research and bade farewell to Canadian plowmen in a pool of despondency in April 1922, his speech recalled the dry belt catastrophe. He spoke of the "profound discouragements of recent years" which had exhausted his "buoyancy and enthusiasm." He remarked how his "best efforts to bring about improvements [had] been fruitless." And he lamented that scientists and others had been too preoccupied with "the brilliant results" of the past generation, thus discouraging further work.[50]

Consequently, the leadership Greenway called for emerged very slowly, warily, and after much trial and many a backward look. In June 1923, C. W. Peterson assessed the impact of the disaster in *The Farm and Ranch Review*. "Farm overhead is mounting up with leaps and bounds and every economy must be studied," he wrote, stressing heavy interest charges and high taxation. "Agriculture the world over has come to the parting of the ways. It will be a case of the survival of the fittest." With the desperate need to produce and transport at the lowest cost, inefficient usages had to go. Already it was becoming common knowledge that the usual practice in the dry areas of leaving half a farm in fallow every year was economically unsound. "I am staking much on the new system of 'ploughless farming,'" Peterson wrote. Excessive cultivation, especially of nonproducing fallows, was simply too costly. Groping for a solution to the perplexities of poor markets, poor production and foreign competition, Peterson suggested that "quantity production at a lower cost per bushel may win out in the end." Furthermore, the half section farm in the dry areas would likely prove inefficient in the long run. "We must study Henry Ford methods," he said prophetically, "and apply them to farming the best way we can."[51]

These methods were essentially fashioned in the crisis of the twenties. The Koole brothers near Monarch started strip farming, alternating strips of wheat with fallow to control wind erosion. Plowless farming was initiated to save tillage costs and to leave stubble on the surface to hold the soil. A variation with the same purpose was shallow tillage. When Asael Palmer of the Lethbridge Experimental Station heard reports of bad drifting on shallow tilled fields, he discovered that farmers had burned the stubble and weeds to ease cultivation. In the process of divining what his pedantic predecessors did not know, Palmer learned the virtue of the trash cover. Gradually, the farmers turned away from moldboard plows, deep tillage, packers, harrows and drags which pulverized the surface, and toward duckfoot cultivators, new rod weeders and blades which retained surface residue. Discarding heavy steam engines, they turned to light tractors. Experimenting with listers which created wind resistant ridges in the soil and with one-way discs which left some vegetation intact, they eagerly adopted the Noble Blade, a V-shaped scalpel which sliced off weed roots underground, when it emerged in the next decade. These measures encapsulated much of the new dry farming wisdom, and significantly, most of them came from inventive men on the land.[52]

In the end, the sacrifices of the strange heartland—of the Tilley East, Berry Creek and other parts of southern Alberta—brought with them tiny pearls of great price. These pearls of wisdom could help unlock the secrets of the south country and reveal her character to those who cared. It was a paradox that so many were worth so little in the heartland itself.

At best the smithing of the new tools and the sculpting of the new wisdom represented a containment of the desert, not its vanquishment, a truce on the flanks of the dubious region, not a change in its barren heart. An indistinct line zigzagged through the centre of southern Alberta, south of Hanna between Bassano and Brooks, through Lomond and Foremost. West of that line, the new tools and the new wisdom would settle for the foreseeable future the old tiff between William Pearce and the sodbusters. Pearce was only partly right in seeing this region as a mecca for ranchers solely, for as it turned out, it could also support farmers. But east of the line, Pearce's original assessment of the land (though not his revised views as a CPR man) proved essentially correct. There the turf was intrinsically ranchland. And there the new tools and wisdom of grain husbandry, ground from all the tears and the misery, could hardly succor either the expatriates of the region or the misguided souls who from time to time sought to reinhabit it.

9   The Blowing Sands of
Financial Ruin

A Cold-Blooded View

A S THE HOPELESSNESS of the farm methods solution was revealed, another aspect of the problem swelled like a pulsating tumor, drawing attention and demanding excision. The tumor was the product of another, much more stressful encounter than that between farmers and experts, for it brought into conflict the moneymen and the settlers over the issue of who in the end would inherit the dry belt.

At the conclusion of perhaps the worst season in the unremitting drought, in September 1924, E. G. Gordon of Iron Springs wrote a long, telling letter to *The Lethbridge Herald*. Summing up the history of the Prairies, he concentrated on the pioneer spirit, praising its alacrity for work and its willingness to sacrifice. After the settlers came the implement dealers and the bankers—all three with the same faith in the West as a safe investment and the proper site for

a grand, cooperative enterprise. However, when the dry areas succumbed, from Hanna east into Saskatchewan and south into the
United States, the bankers had revealed their true colors. Said Gordon, "Why don't they come out into the open like men and
proclaim to the world and to the farmer, 'We called this venture a
safe bet: we placed our money here believing that you would make
good. Your success means our prosperity and we took an even
chance with you in a losing game. Now we will go "fifty
fifty"—when no crops, no interest.'"

Gordon noted the recent raising of $3.5 million by California
bankers on behalf of the cooperative projects of the fruit farmers.
Such zeal in the depressed Lethbridge irrigation districts would
surely bring people, industry and prosperity, he thought. Alas, the
sentiments of Canadian bankers were contrary and unprogressive.
Gordon singled out the utterance of Colonel Hatch, vice-president
of the Canadian Manufacturers' Association and a prominent bank
director—"The western farmer, as a rule, has no interest in the
country. He eats out of a tin can, gets all he can from outside the
country and sows his wheat in the spring. This he harvests and
markets and goes to California, spending his money outside of the
country." To Gordon, Hatch was an ignoramus who lived by the
dictum, "Grab all you can and keep all you get." He and his hapless
eastern bank directors knew less about the western farmer than
about "a dinosaur egg."

Gordon turned to his experience with a beef-witted banker's en-
voy: "Last week a large car came charging up, containing a chauf-
feur and a large, monocle-eyed young man. It was evident from his
swagger that he was a scion of British aristocracy, and a stranger at
our gates. I was just over the fence hoeing potatoes, when he came
up, touched me on the shoulder and said: 'Pardon me, my dear
man, but may I trouble you for a match?' After lighting his cigar, he
continued: 'Bah Jove! This is a remarkable country. The bloody
farmers are riding in motors and hiring their work done, d'ye
know? I'm a deuced stranger here, but on the other side I'm Sir
William G. Patton, Knight of the Garter, Knight of the Golden
Fleece—'

"'Wait a moment, Bill, allow me to interrupt you,' said I. 'I don't know anything about the Garter stunt, but that Golden Fleece is all right. Dad Lathrop will place you in a separate class at our fall fair. May I ask your business?'

"'Certainly,' replied Sir William. 'I came to look over the country and report to the bank directors of the eastern cities the condition of the farmers and the crops. One of the directors is my father's brother. . . . I came directly from Quebec to Calgary, where I hired a motor and came to Nobleford. My route takes in Taber, Brooks, Duchess, Wainwright, then north and west to Edmonton.'

"'Thank you, Sir William,' said I. 'How long were you driving from Nobleford?' (A distance of 20 miles.) 'Just thirty minutes,' was the answer.

"'It must be a sort of mushroom, short order report you are making if you are giving the country the once over from an auto moving at forty miles an hour.' But Sir William was already vanishing down the east road in a voluminous cloud of dust."

Gordon then addressed all the eastern banking Shylocks: "Bank directors, we have met your representative but we think it would be more business-like if you would come and get the conditions of the western farmer at first hand. Eat and drink and stay down upon the earth with him till both are well acquainted. If you behave yourself you are as good as the farmer. We still live on the sunny side of the road, and we are not going to the bow-wows, and though we are loaded and held down by debt, we do occasionally come up for air.

"You know that wealth and the farming industry are not on speaking terms and the distance between the two is daily lengthening.

"Leave Main street, fill your lungs with Alberta ozone, and make the trip of inspection yourself. Before you start, go to the library and get John Stuart Mill on Philosophy and read the chapter on Deductive Logic. Then go to the bank and ask the manager for that book, 'Agriculture in Its Agony.' It will give you much-needed information.

"We know something about the miracles of irrigation—the desert blooming as the rose, and two blades of grass growing where formerly there was but one. We are not asking for any orgy of romance nor agricultural fireworks. We care nothing for pictures of men lost in alfalfa fields, pumpkins that require the strength of two men to lift, nor a berry patch that would put Paradise in the shade. The project farmer needs a sane, helpful talk that will encourage the down-hearted, steer the misguided, pacify the irate, capitalize the enthusiasm of the successful and find credit and fair markets for the financially embarrassed. This is a man size job. Can you do it? Any of my neighbors can give your bank managers better instructions than you do. Can you take this land, support and educate a family, pay back debts, besides taxes and interest? You refuse to loan money on this land, then you must consider land a liability not an asset. Yet you ask us to work on nothing, with nothing, and produce something."

Gordon then illustrated the bank motto, "grab all you can and keep all you get." Joe Miller had been raised in Manitoba, had gone to Minnesota with his father and later homesteaded in southern Alberta in 1907. By dint of great effort he kept his wife and four children comfortable during the six bad years from 1917 to 1922. In 1923 he had a good crop but could not quite cover his amassed deficit. Struggling sixteen hours daily to feed his stock and to ready his land for a greater crop, he was met one day by the sheriff with an order, courtesy of the bank and implement dealer, to seize his stock.

That night as the family knelt in worship, Joe searched for something to be thankful for. "Joe," said his wife Mary, "Old Speck came up to the barn with a new calf." So they thanked God. The next morning the sheriff reappeared and drove Old Speck away.

That day they began preparations to leave the farm, rather than stay so handicapped. Performing the last rites, Mary and a young daughter walked to the small cemetery which held the body of the youngest, little Fred, gone now only a year. When Joe closed the kitchen door for the last time it was like closing the lid of another casket.

As the wagon and old team they were left with rolled down the lane toward the road, Joe said to Mary: "Isn't it awful! Sixteen years of careful planning and hard work gone. All useless, useless."[1]

As the dry belt crawled with clamoring creditors seeking payment and with sheriffs seizing grain and chattels right and left, the hounding of hapless farmers grew so harsh that even a bank manager felt driven to appeal, if confidentially, to the attorney-general for compassion.[2]

Settlers sought to let go before they lost all, but found their debts had lashed them to the rigging of their floundering farms. Jacob Schellenberg of Herbert, Saskatchewan, was one of many who wished to move to a new location. Begging the permission of the Bank of Commerce which held an interest in his farm and was demanding payment, he was told by the manager that he could go if he mortgaged all his chattels to the bank. "I fear however that if I give the chattel mortgage to him he will cripple me so badly that I can never pay my debts," said Schellenberg. "Also the same will happen if I do not give the chattel mortgage and he obtains judgement."[3]

Over and over farmers were given the choice of keeping the pittance they had or keeping nothing at all. A grim option it was, blighting their courage and optimism, breeding a sad shiftlessness. One farmer south of Youngstown, by perseverance and able management, survived the succession of bad crops until 1921 when he was unable to pay the interest on a loan. His creditors threatened to foreclose. He replied, "Well, I owe little besides what I owe you, if it is the land and buildings you want you are welcome to them, my outfit is clear and I can get ready to move almost any day."[4]

In the long chain of creditors, local merchants were at the last link. At Milk River, the owner of the largest general store in the district said frankly, "There can be no difference in opinion among all classes when the grave conditions in the South are stated. They are simply appalling and almost beyond human understanding...." Wishing to be lenient to her hard-pressed debtors, she said, "I simply held back this fall on collections, only to see the banker, lumberman or implement man grab it all by threatening suits or court action."[5]

Merchants fumed that they had been obliged to accept promisory notes from the farmers but could not get credit on them from the banks.[6] Others growled that when a farmer had a carload of wheat the banker had often taken a lien on the crop for an advance for wages or twine. The lien gave the banker first crack at the proceeds, and more than once he had taken it all. Merchants snorted that food supplies they had advanced in the summer were just as legitimate a charge on the crop as advances for twine or wages. In fact, workers would not even stay if they were not fed.[7]

Like the seeping, poisonous damp gas, the financial disaster choked everything that moved. Ever in the centre of devastation sat Alderson in the Tilley East country. By the end of 1925, the local bank was ruined, the town fathers totalled $14,000 in unpaid taxes, and the tributary municipalities and improvement districts had been claimed by the noxious air. King, Sunny South and Britannia had amassed a fortune in uncollected revenues—$13,000 in hail taxes, $19,000 in wild lands taxes, $63,000 in supplementary revenue taxes, $104,000 in municipal taxes, and $146,000 in educational taxes. Together they owed $474,000 for seed grain and relief, and in turn, their citizens owed them similar amounts. Tax arrears in the four surrounding improvement districts amounted to $336,000, while Dominion and Provincial relief claims reached $646,000. The total debt on the public accounts alone was over $1.7 million. In addition, the liability by way of mortgages, caveats, mechanic's liens and writs of execution charged against just the homesteaded land was a whopping $2.75 million or $640 a quarter section! As E. J. Fream, chairman of the Tilley East Commission said summarily, "This represents a liability greatly in excess of the value of the lands and is more than the land can earn."[8]

If the rest of southern Alberta and southern Saskatchewan was better off, the indebtedness of the whole region was nonetheless absolutely gigantic. Mired, the two provinces wrenched and twisted and agonized for some deliverer. But, as if the process of being sucked down caused some embarrassment, provincial officials for a time turned to the outside world a face, if not smiling, at least unperturbed.

In late 1921, Saskatchewan Premier Martin summoned representatives of the legion of creditors—the government, the Retail Merchants' Association, the Saskatchewan Association of Rural

Municipalities, the Grain Growers' Association, implement dealers, lumbermen, stockmen, wholesalers, mortgage and loan companies. Fearful of bad press, he urged that the meeting be given little publicity. Then he told them where he stood. The weight of debt crushing farmers could not be liquidated. "This government has never believed in a moratorium and we do not believe in it now," he pronounced. "It would be an admission that the province is bankrupt." Outside firms would shy away; goods would enter the province only for cash in advance. The country had been largely developed by outside capital, and "anything done to scare it away" would not be in Saskatchewan's best interests. Said he frankly, "We need capital for many years to come."[9]

Some months earlier, Martin had admitted to individual farmers that the government larder was empty. The days of liberal feed, seed and relief were ended. The Farm Loans Board, moreover, was stretched to the snapping point.[10] At one juncture in 1921, more than fifteen hundred applications could not be filled. By early 1922, the Board had dished out $8.5 million, but the largess was over. "I am quite sure," Martin predicted to one applicant, "that for some time to come it will be able to lend very, very little."[11]

Already important elements in the civil service viewed the situation as quite cureless. In the mind of one who had learned as much as any about the disaster, F. Hedley Auld, there was even the seed of a savage, final solution. Ruminating over what might facilitate the adoption of a viable form of agriculture in the arid lands, Auld fell back on two phrases—"the mills of the gods," and "the survival of the fittest." Deeded land was so cumbered that it was impossible to transfer it to grazing land. Clinging like barnacles, the debts attached to the land guaranteed a profitless future and rendered the dry areas the most expensive grazing proposition under the sun. "The remedy then, would appear to lie in permitting the unproductive lands to go through the normal course of foreclosure, thereby becoming purged of some of their debts and being offered for sale at what they will bring," concluded Auld. "This I realize is a rather cold-blooded way of viewing the matter."[12]

Quaking Shylocks

THE TEMPER OF most Albertans that spring was less melancholy. The province had just turfed out the Liberals, and the Survey Board for Southern Alberta, following the Saskatchewan Better Farming Commission, had just handed down its report. In a much more hopeless case than that in Saskatchewan, there was ironically and fleetingly more hope. As the new United Farmer Government gazed, awed and trembling, at the hydra-headed monster afoot in the southlands, it slowly waded in and struck a few blows, and then taking in the vast power of its adversary, it stepped back and struck another commission.

This one dealt with the banks. Completed by Professor D. A. McGibbon of the University of Alberta, the study milked the popular venom excited by the mere mention of farmers' financial overlords. "Four years ago it was 'borrow money, get cattle and hogs and produce, produce, produce,'" exclaimed one irate drybelter in late 1921, "now it is 'you owe us money so sell what you have for whatever price you can get and pay, pay [,] pay.'"[13]

Banks were too liberal when crop prices were high and too miserly when prices tobogganed. They forced farmers operating on small margins into stock, and when the bottom fell out of that market, the farmers were ruined. Banks offered only short-term loans of three or four months, whereas farm operations extended twice that long. Banks charged interest rates above that allowable; they deducted the interest before the loan was granted, an infuriating process known as discounting. They were controlled by malevolent corporations in the East. They withdrew unannounced from districts, or they changed managers so often that a consistent policy was impossible.[14] So said the crowd of critics.

Staging six of his sixteen inquisitions in the dry belt, McGibbon found force in farmer complaints about excessive changes in branch overseers. It seemed as soon as a manager was broken in, he was removed. If he was overly obliging, he was replaced by a miser bent on "cleaning up" the branch in a month. If he had made promises, his successor never heard of them. If he had learned whom he could trust, his replacement knew nothing. Canvassing the 360 branches in Alberta in 1922, McGibbon discovered that over 80 percent of managers were post-war appointments. Nearly a quarter were at their first managerial posts. Moreover, between 1916 and 1921, almost two hundred new outlets were established, most in 1919. Anticipating the same bonanza that fed farmers' hopes, head offices opened nine hundred new branches in the western provinces. That meant, admitted one banker, "nine hundred green managers to be tested—in some cases weeded out—and carefully trained. . . . And it takes nearly as many years to make a good bank manager as it does to make a good farmer."

McGibbon was unimpressed. He cudgeled the banks for their pell-mell expansion which fed credit inflation during the regime of high prices. In some districts, he noted, peering southward, handsome returns had accompanied bumper crops. "Farmers increased their investment in land, and, largely financed by the banks, made heavy outlays in the expectation of a repetition of the same favorable conditions." When lean years ensued, these over-extended settlers found themselves in trouble.

When McGibbon queried a minion of the Bank of Commerce at Youngstown about the dubious practice of discounting, the man raised his eyebrows and snapped that patrons who disliked discounting were not forced to deal with the bank. Whatever the murky legality of discounting, the take it or leave it attitude was combined with a flagrant disregard for the Bank Act. Despite the Act which fixed maximum interest rates at 7 percent, many banks, especially in the south, were charging 10 percent.

There were other abuses. Citing the testimony of Charles Harod of Macleod, McGibbon revealed how trying the banks could be. Harod had been dried out five years running. Despite long association with the Pincher Creek Union Bank, he disgorged a tale of the institution's apparent abuses which astounded McGibbon. Having paid off an earlier loan, Harod had received several offers of more credit from the bank. He hedged until spring, however, when the bank manager expressed sudden reservations—even though Harod had three quarters of land clear and the bank had retained title to the property. At last Harod secured a loan of some two thousand dollars. After being dried up again, he was "hard on the rocks," needing more credit. The bank manager replied that he must have a chattel mortgage first, but when he got it he refused the credit, preferring to increase his security against Harod's $2,000 loan.

Without money from a friend, Harod would have been forced to leave his land idle in 1921. Because of the banker, he added, he had just lost $50. Having a little nest egg in the bank for expenses, he was "afraid of the bank putting their hands on it for interest," and so against his better judgment, he withdrew it. "As luck would have it," he said dejectedly, "I lost it." Had he left the cash in the account, within a few days, he assured the commission, it would have disappeared.

The dark side of bank involvement, McGibbon understood, had another face. Some of the abuse farmers heaped on financiers was unwarranted. Farmers were gulled if they thought the confiscation of current accounts for old debts was commonplace. And they were dead wrong if they reckoned banks had not offered a hand in carrying them through the drought and depression. In 1916 current loans running over a year totalled $17 million; by 1922 they reached $52.5 million.[15] Shortly thereafter, Sir Frederick Williams-Taylor, president of the Canadian Bankers' Association, reported that 419 of the 1,219 banks in western Canada were operating at a loss.[16] From 1919 to 1922, even the stodgy old Bank of Nova Scotia had excesses of loans over deposits in the West unequalled in the entire recorded period, 1900–1939.[17] By 1922 there was not a single bank that did not believe it had opened an artery for the drylands.

Regardless of how much the bankers appeared in the popular mind as cormorants for lucre, the fact was that they too had been buffeted nearly senseless by the cataclysm. No bank was more deeply embroiled in the dry belt than the Union Bank of Canada. H. A. Robson, a director and chief counsel for the harried institution, candidly told McGibbon that "doing business at any rate of interest, no matter whether ten or twenty percent [was] bad business" in the south. "I imagine that if the banks had entirely stepped out of Southern Alberta they would have been hundreds of thousands of dollars ahead, but farmers and cattlemen would have either starved or had to trek out," said Robson. Farmers might be bitter, but they would have produced nothing that year without the banks. Bewailing the fate closing in on him, Robson declared, "It certainly was an exceedingly risky and unremunerative partnership for the banks to go into dealings with southern Alberta farmers merely on the possibility of some day receiving interest at ten percent per annum on their money." Given the mountainous risks, poor markets and poor crops, Robson dubbed the bank attitude "highly generous, even to the degree of simpleness."

As McGibbon retorted, there may have been "a spirit of quasi-benevolent feudalism" imbedded in Robson's remarks and his cavalier disregard for legal interest rates, but from the viewpoint of the financiers, Robson spoke the only truth they knew.[18] And he understood a great deal more than McGibbon about the precarious position of his own bank.

Operations in the dry belt were anything but models of classic, textbook banking. The annual accounts of sixteen Union branches, six Royal and one Trader's branch, or about 40 percent of Alberta dry area outlets, revealed seven consecutive years of excesses of advances over deposits from 1919 to 1925. A common rule of thumb held that if a bank had $400,000 in deposits and $300,000 in loans, it would be profitable. Not once in the seven years after 1918 did these branches come near the ratio. In fact, deposits averaged $3.3 million and advances, $4.4 million, a ratio precisely the opposite of the desirable. As the large scale permanent abandonment of the desert became apparent, huge write-offs suddenly appeared on the books. Bad debts reported by the twenty-three firms totalled $160,000 in 1920, $655,000 in 1924, and nearly $1 million in 1926.

After the Union Bank merged into the Royal in 1925, the latter quickly laid to rest its atrophied appendages. Ten of the twenty-three outlets were sealed like empty tombs in the mid-twenties; two more were evacuated by 1930; and four more in the thirties. At least four others, in Winnifred, Jenner, Grassy Lake and Alderson, either did not survive to the merger or succumbed shortly after.

Loss leaders in the dry belt were the Union Banks. NA 3596-167, Glenbow-Alberta Archives.

The tragic details of the fall of Alderson's Union Bank have defied resurrection, but they must have resembled those of Sunnynook's branch in the Berry Creek country northward. Open from 1919 to early 1926, the Sunnynook Union Bank registered one of the most dismal branch performances in the history of the West. Not once did average deposits come close to advances. For its entire earthly existence, deposits averaged $50,500 a year and loans, $125,000. In the first five years, before the head office reined in the runaway loser, the spread was even greater, with deposits annually totalling about 30 percent of advances. In the year before the bank was interred, bad debts reached $18,300, a sum equal to nearly half the average annual deposits in the first five years.[19]

Naturally the populist UFA wept less for the moneybaggers than for the people. Bankers always seemed so inanimate. They made their own rules and loaned money on their terms. Dealing primarily in lower risk, short-term loans, they could adjust to exigency before too long. The rate at which they participated like pirates in seizures might be controlled somewhat, but little could be done if they withheld credit. Anyway, the fiscal institutions which caused most distress were likely not the banks at all, since at this time they could not loan money on the security of land and thus were uninvolved in the most traumatic of dispossessions—land foreclosure. The real enemy was the unholy mortgage company.

Mortgagemen and Ted Fream

IN LATE WINTER 1922, a delegation waited on George Hoadley, Alberta minister of Agriculture. Mortgage foreclosures since war-end, they reported, had reached the mammoth value of $15 million in Edmonton and $18 million in Calgary. Edmonton citizens had lost through tax sales 80,000 of 110,000 lots. In the rural areas, the foreclosures equalled the Calgary and Edmonton losses combined, and through tax sales Albertans had forfeited 10,767 farms comprising 1,653,150 acres.[20] Before long, a report on the Alderson region, east of Tilley between the Red Deer and South Saskatchewan Rivers, would disclose that fully 450,000 acres of a total of 784,000 taken up was in process of forfeiture.[21]

By late 1920, William R. Babington, veteran farmer, resident of the Hat district since 1903, owner of vast acreages of dust and monstrous tractors, was in financial difficulty. His wife Barbara, also a property owner, had just been given an unsolicited extension of time for payment of interest and principal by the Standard Trusts Company of Winnipeg. Pondering the collapse about him, he admitted, "I am rendered penniless by these afflictions." Yet he made a startling offer to the managing director of the trust. Adding two more titles to the honors of Medicine Hat, he called the city "The Garden of Romance, and the Dreamland of the West." "I can dream more money into being in a minute than 99 pessimists could squander in ten years," Babington said. For several seasons he had seeded over a thousand acres to wheat and flax, only to discover that of his eighteen years near the Hat eight were total failures and only three were ideal for wheat.

Quoting an utterance of the late H. Y. Sudduth, the eminent alfalfa authority, that alfalfa seed was optimally produced under "extreme heat and drought sunshine conditions," Babington declared—"You will concede that we are 'It' for alfalfa seed production—no room for argument." Virtually any year he believed he could have netted four hundred to seven hundred pounds of alfalfa seed an acre at an average wholesale value of 40¢ a pound, or not less than $100 an acre.

More significant than even these revelations, Babington claimed to have invented a machine which would annihilate the weed and cutworm menace, combat grasshoppers and remedy soil drifting. He needed money to secure a patent. Emphasizing secrecy, he requested a loan of $1,000 on a quarter section east of the Hat.

William Harvey and his fellow directors of the trust were so intrigued by Babington's epistle that they sped a copy to F. Hedley Auld in Regina. They were as entranced by Babington's chilling account of the nightmare of western Canada as Babington was by the approach of doom itself, but as for Babington's proposal, that was something else. The trust, alas, does not seem to have acceded to the request.[22] Two years later, Babington was one of nearly three thousand names on Attorney General J. E. Brownlee's list of the bankrupt.[23]

At almost the same moment another of the former champions of the Hat, as big a promoter as Babington had been a farmer, real estate man F. M. Ginther, was through. Packing his bags, he slipped into the States, regretting that he had not left earlier. In Texas his sharp eye for money-making schemes reasserted itself, landed him in the growing oil business, and brought the comforts he had lacked in his last days in the weather factory.[24]

Meanwhile, the financial complications spun by the disaster had all the simplicity of a Gordian knot. Seldom before in the country had the intricacies of the law of contracts and of bailments been so minutely pored over and so utterly laid open; seldom before had longstanding assumptions about justice been so cantankerously disputed. In what priority should creditors be ranked? What protection should the law afford to mortgagees and their clients, what obligations did the provinces have to outside investment capital?

These questions and others reverberated throughout the strange heartland and then the province. Each answer was specific to the heartland but became general to Alberta—that is, responses required in the former became applicable to the latter. The heartland dictated to the whole, and the disadvantages of remedies in the region rebounded on all.

Even to the previous Liberal government, it was clear that an enormous tension existed between the legal rights of contract and the survival rights of the settlers, between the sovereigns of capitalism and the trodden vassals of the electorate. In this opposition, punctuated by howling indignation from both quarters, contractual rights and sovereigns tended to give way. Taking the part of its people, the UFA did what it could to ensure the primacy of the individual and of the province over outside capital.

Before 1919 the borrower in a mortgage contract personally covenanted to repay the loan. If he defaulted, he lost the property *and still had to pay.* In 1919 and 1920, the Alberta Liberal government forbade mortgage companies to enforce the personal covenant until they had recouped what they could by selling the property.[25]

Secondly, both the UFA and the previous government systematically interfered with the priority of the first mortgage. Statute after statute they enacted, giving cost after cost precedence over first mortgages—including hail insurance premiums, hospital aid relief, the wild land tax and charges under the Drainage Act and for destroying weeds and agricultural pests. The mortgagee's rights were further curtailed by prior liens on crops grown on mortgaged premises including liens for Dominion and provincial seed grain advances, for municipal seed, fodder and relief, and liens in favor of cooperative credit societies and to storekeepers for goods supplied during the crop season.[26] If in relinquishing his land the farmer had not tended to any of these charges, the first mortgagee inherited them.

Thirdly, before 1922 when property became exposed to sale for tax arrears, a notice by registered mail was sent to all parties with an interest in the land, giving them a chance to redeem the land by paying the arrears. Alarmed by the looming collapse of municipal government and by the spectre of provincial debt which had doubled since 1914, the UFA passed the Tax Recovery Act of 1922. The Act squeezed tax delinquents by streamlining the process of forfeiture—not to the mortgage company, but *to the municipality*.

Caught between the post-war depression and the dry belt calamity, Alberta mortgage interests were hamstrung. If the deliberations of the Canadian Bankers' Association often seemed to Albertans like distant ruminations from Mount Olympus, the reverberating choruses of the Mortgage Loans Association of Alberta were very insistent and very immediate. It was much more they and less the bankers, who led the counter attack against the government fiats, the grilling and bad publicity assailing the fiscal bodies from all sides.

Naturally the Mortgage Loans Association abhorred the impairment of the personal covenant as an unprecedented change in the law of contracts.[27] While the offending amendments were not quite the same as exploding the covenant altogether, it was too fine a distinction for the mortgagemen to fathom. They were loath to sell a property which had fallen back into their laps and which was now worth half the loan they had advanced on it. As a result, they were immobilized, waiting out a depression, hoping for a return to 1919 values, paying all the while the expenses attached to the depreciating land.

The Tax Recovery Act, mortgagemen damned as blatantly confiscatory. And the debilitating interference by a veritable catena of liens and prior charges, they deemed pernicious. As Secretary-Treasurer E.C. Pardee of the Mortgage Association snorted, "At one time the words 'First Mortgage' meant what they said."[28]

Workhorse of the UFA government, director of the Debt Adjustment Act, and chairman of the Tilley East Commission—Ted Fream. NA 4790-2, Glenbow-Alberta Archives.

The farmer government, however, was not through. Recognizing the sweep of the catastrophe, it enacted what to outside investors a few years earlier would have been unthinkable—a species of moratoria. The Drought Area Relief Act of 1922 was nothing short of revolutionary. It empowered a government commissioner to stay the hand of creditors, and it introduced for the first time in the province's history the principle of debt adjustment. The mediator appointed was the longtime servant of countless farm organizations—E. J. (Ted) Fream.

At age thirteen, Ted Fream had run away from home in Gloucester, England, and was deposited at Calgary by the CPR early one morning in April 1893. The fact that his uncle William

Fream was one of the leading British agricultural scientists of the day was probably etched in his makeup, but save for his public school education at Sir Thomas Rich's School, Fream was self-taught.

In the early days, he herded cattle, riding with books in his saddlebags. He grew to be a giant of a man, six foot three. Though he never objected if others imbibed in moderation, he never took a drink in his life. How strongly he felt on the point his cowpuncher cronies learned during one festive foray into Calgary. Fream was in the barber's chair having his hair cut when the others decided they would force-feed him several shots of booze. They strapped him in the chair and began pouring grog down his throat. Rearing up like a stallion haltered for the first time, Fream tried to kick off his main assailant. His spurs caught the joker square in the face, raked him horribly down the cheek and neck and scarred him for life.[29]

The event stayed with Fream all his days too, for he was by nature kind, fair-minded, and polished. Toward middle-age his hairline receded from his ample forehead, and save possibly for his old friend J. E. Brownlee, he became the closest facsimile the farm movement ever produced of a banker. A consummate amanuensis, Fream was the master of detail work, an administrative whizz who could write with equal facility with either hand and who could read a letter upside down as fast as if it were rightside up.[30]

He had been the first secretary of the UFA, secretary of the United Grain Growers' Limited, the Alberta Farmers' Cooperative Elevator Company, and the Alberta Fairs Association. A former editor of the Innisfail *Province* and of the Alberta section of the *Grain Growers' Guide,* he served the farmer government as a Public Utilities Board member, as the chief investigator of the Tilley East Commission, and as the first director of the Tilley East Special Area.[31]

He was a model of stewardship, the servant the farmer government went to again and again in its great distress. When he died fifteen years after the new Premier Aberhart dumped him from the Public Utilities Board as punishment for his loyalty to the fallen government, the great secretary was a poor man, gnarled and bent by the ravages of arthritis, so swollen and bed-ridden in the last years that even his ambidexterity was nullified. By then only the aging Brownlee and a few others knew what Fream had meant to Alberta.

In all the history of the province there probably had never been a role more exacting or more significant than that of the commissioner of the Drought Area Relief Act and the subsequent Debt Adjustment Act. The job involved corralling debtors and creditors and determining what the former could pay and the latter would accept. A major purpose was to bypass costly court actions which dragged on, choked up the judiciary, and siphoned off what little might have gone to bonafide creditors.

In August 1922, Saskatchewan Minister of Agriculture C. M. Hamilton visited Fream, and according to the latter learned the nature of the Alberta program and installed it in Saskatchewan.[32] In 1922 alone, some six thousand cases were handled in each province. Concluding the work of the Drought Area Relief Act in the first five months of 1923, Fream's office employed twelve to sixteen clerks who dispensed nearly fifteen thousand pieces of mail.[33]

That year the Act was replaced by the Debt Adjustment Act which extended the semi-moratorium throughout the province. Again Fream went in search of voluntary adjustments. In extreme cases, when his multiple skills failed him and crowding creditors lifted their fists to crush the farmers, he was empowered to issue a paralyzing certificate to prevent them from initiating foreclosure. After due advice, he would then distribute the proceeds of the debtor's crop among claimants. In 1923 and 1924, 190 certificates were filed each year, and by December 1924, nearly $500,000 had been doled out by Fream's office.[34]

No creditors were enthralled by the process, but those closest to the devastation understood its need. The more distant, however, were often flabbergasted at the imposition of so stern and anticapitalistic a measure. With links to outside plutocracy, the mortgage companies were most susceptible to this view.

Foreclosing the
Foreclosers

THE CLASH BETWEEN the mortgagees and the government was best revealed by none other than the Associated Mortgage Investors of Rochester, New York, and formerly Calgary, the brainchild of Kingman Nott Robins, the one-time apostle of the new Canaan and pamphleteer of the glories of Alberta, *circa* 1910. One of the largest investors in Alberta mortgages, the company had seen better days and better laws. In March 1925, G. J. Keys on its behalf wrote Ted Fream, setting the record straight. Keys informed Fream of the company's agreement with its investors in Canadian mortgages to advance interest when due and to protect the title of the land mortgaged. Recently the company had been embarrassed by having to advance considerable funds to cover interest payments which could not be collected from farmers. Moreover, many farmers had let their taxes slip, thereby endangering the title to the land and exposing the property to loss by tax sale. In December 1924, the company was obliged to fork out more than $50,000 in taxes. Strapped for funds, it discontinued all loans, concentrated on collections, and pondered reneging on automatic interest payments to investors. More money was poured into the coffers, but relief was fleeting. Spiralling to earth, the company cancelled its agreement with investors and offered to remit interest as collected.

Signing investors under the new arrangement, however, was painstaking. "Some of the investors who have been unwilling to enter into the new agreement," said Keys, "have demanded foreclosure, which the company is both legally and morally obliged to carry through." While the company recoiled from the draconian measure, Keys reminded Fream that the loans advanced in Canada for investors were made "in good faith." The sad estate of the debtors was due to their shirking of interest and tax payments. The company had played its part; now it was time for farmers to drum up their resolve and do likewise. Bitter, Keys wrote, "So many of the borrowers write us such antagonistic letters, ignoring entirely their own delinquencies and endeavoring to place the burden upon us rather than upon themselves; and some of them seem to feel no obligation whatever to the company who loaned them money to purchase their farms but rather a resentment of the fact that such a loan was made."[35]

Fream's response struck like lightning. Reminding Keys that he had not been around long enough to assess the situation, he said conditions in New York were not those in Alberta. "Your investors probably see before them settled farming communities where conditions have become stabilized and values are established . . .," he wrote. "We have not reached that position in Alberta. . . ."

Benefitting by past experience as an agent of the company, Fream then laid bare the role of the Associated Mortgage Investors in the past fifteen years in Alberta. In the early days, he noted, the company sought to increase the amount of the principal loaned so that interest at the rate of 6 percent would really amount to 9 percent of the funds invested. "It was difficult to make a farmer understand that while he was only a borrower to the extent of $1,000 and had agreed to pay interest thereon at nine percent, he was called upon to sign a mortgage showing that he had actually borrowed considerably more than that and that the interest rate was six percent only." As an agent, Fream himself had lost several loans when farmers balked at signing such a deal aimed apparently at showing a windfall of interest to investors, making room for the outpouring, and keeping interest rates on paper within legal limits.

When prosperity, high prices, and the cry for greater production came during the war, "the farmer who had been making good on a half section came to the conclusion, probably, in many cases influenced by the local real estate agent, banker or loan agent, that if he could do well on a quarter or half section, he could make twice as much if he held more land. . . ." Without the wherewithal, he turned to mortgage companies who reaped a bounty for some time. An "orgy of spending" developed, and credit was poured out on flimsy security in the expectation of a continuing boom.

Amid this outflow, Associated Mortgage Investors made such extensive advances that they were considered "easy marks," said Fream. One effect was that loans granted by the company were greater per quarter section than those granted by others. When prices nose-dived and depression began, most loan companies pulled in the reins and trimmed their accounts. The most notable exception to this policy was that employed by Associated Investors. The company, said Fream, "repeatedly told the borrower that so long as he was farming the land and was doing all that could be reasonably expected, he could never anticipate any trouble from the company. . . . The company always had plenty of money on hand so that a renewal could be arranged for and the loan carried on." Clearly the firm had ignored the stormy petrels of the downturn.

The situation remained so till December 1924. Until then, Associated Investors vexed Fream as director of the Debt Adjustment Act least of all mortgage companies in the province. Invariably the company was fair and conciliatory. "Then, like a bolt from the blue, the change came," said Fream, "and this happy position was reversed until, in the short time which has elapsed, I have found it necessary to open up more files in regard to Associated Mortgage Investors['] business and have more correspondence and trouble with the company than with all other Companies doing business in the Province. . . ." Then, reflecting a moment, Fream threw in all the banks and machine companies too.

With the change in policy, Fream was met with an attitude, "hostile and suspicious," resenting any moderating suggestions and ruthlessly bent on clearing up overdue accounts. Seeking some let-up from the unnerving pressure applied by the company, Fream warned of the grave danger of a move urged by many which would ruin all creditors—a legislated full moratorium. He spoke of the glum attendants of foreclosure—decreased revenues and augmented liabilities—the latter due to the tendency to charge everything to the absentee owner, the loan company.

Fream then related several specific complaints. Frequently the mortgage company had failed to look after its interests. There were examples of crop leases where farmers allowed banks to take the company's portion of the crop. Why did the company sit idly by? Fream wondered. "Why as is happening where mortgages are falling due although the interest is paid up to date and the borrower has been given to understand in the past that he need not fear any trouble in regard to the principal, is it necessary to repeatedly threaten such a borrower that foreclosure proceedings will be taken . . .?

"Why, where the debtor has actually delivered all he had contracted to out of his crop, and was left with a small b[a]lance outstanding, should it be necessary to tell him that unless this balance is paid within one week a Writ will be issued without further notice?

"Why, where the debtor has actually delivered one-third the crop and has paid during the year a considerable sum . . . from resources other than his crop, and is prepared to do the same thing in 1925, should it be necessary to repeatedly threaten him with foreclosure, with all the trouble and costs incident thereto?

"Why, where the debtor has done what he contracted to do under his crop lease, should he be told . . . though he has agreed to give the same additional security for the ensuing year, that foreclosure must be proceeded with unless further payments are made at once, even though the debtor has shown clearly that there is nothing further in sight and that if he disposes of any of his equipment his farming operations must necessarily be badly crippled . . .?

"Why, in cases where the debtor has made a considerably payment on account and a small balance only is remaining, is it considered necessary to tell that debtor that if he cannot clean up the account in any other way he should dispose of his seed grain . . .? If he should fail in his attempt to secure seed he will be handicapped considerably and the loan will be that much worse off later in the year. . . ."

Finishing, Fream pointed to another irksome practice. Wherever the legal department had written letters to a debtor and payment followed, a charge of 50¢ per letter was added to the debt.[36]

The government stood by its enactments. First, it had no intention of renouncing (yet, at least) $7 million of seed grain and fodder advances.[37] The Dominion government too had unloaded a fortune in relief but only with the understanding that the expense would become a first charge prior to a first mortgage.[38] Secondly, before the personal covenant changes, it was the grisly practice to strip the indebted farmer of his animals and equipment long before the foreclosure was finalized. Few in the populist and land-based

UFA could stomach the resultant endless train of heartbreaking seizures.

Most of the major works of the UFA—the Tax Recovery Act, the Drought Area Relief Act and the Debt Adjustment Act—were cast with two broad purposes in mind: the maintenance of local, municipal and even provincial government, and the salvation of the demoralized southern farmer. Most of the legislation menacing the security of the first mortgage, moreover, had been passed by the former Liberal government in response to the same crisis. Generally, the UFA had promoted the legislation during its close relationship with the Stewart government, and consistently it blamed economics and not laws for what ailed the mortgage people.

Quite frankly, the government distrusted the mortgage interests. What it heard over and over was that no mortgage company wanted land on its books. What it saw again and again was just that. In time, Fream and the government began to realize that as far as the campaign to save the south was concerned, remediation to restore the sanctity of the first mortgage would only serve to disrupt resettlement elsewhere in the province and to hamstring the emerging final solution in the dry areas. Fleeing settlers would be pursued by the fiscal furies bent on exacting their pound of flesh. And as for the final solution, the amassing of even more hundreds of thousands of acres in the hands of mortgage lenders would stultify the gradual collection of the dry tracts in the name of the province and their administration as a set of special areas.

While these realizations were dawning, Ted Fream resigned as director of the Debt Adjustment Act. He turned to the worst of the dry belt, and was soon up to his neck in the Tilley East Commission. Shortly thereafter, the Debt Adjustment office in Calgary experienced a crisis. A government auditor spied an irregularity in the books kept by H. J. Cardell, Fream's former chief subordinate and office manager, and an inquiry was held. Without guidelines, Fream, Cardell and the Bank of Montreal had arranged that farmers' money held in trust by the bank should bear interest. Cardell then used the interest as a nest egg for the operation of the bureau—for incidentals, salary advances, and year-end bonuses to staff. Little effort was made to repay the advances, Cardell believing that the employees would get in bonuses what was left in the account anyway. Over four years, unrepaid advances totalled $1,500, and bonuses for at least fifteen recipients, $800. The latter amount, the provincial auditor claimed, should have been paid out of legislative appropriations or by special warrant; the bureau's entire use of the funds, indeed, constituted improper diversion.[39]

The real villain was Cardell in whom Fream had laid too much trust, a highly intelligent man with "no conception of his responsibility as a civil servant," as the special investigator put it. More than half the unrepaid advances Cardell himself owed, and some, if not all the repaid monies, he pocketed. Fream held the vouchers to prove that the advances were to be refunded, but had left the details to Cardell. Gaining not a cent from the affair, Fream was left in the lurch and accepted full responsibility. Somewhat unrepentant, Cardell scheduled a payback, though his days with the bureau were numbered.[40]

By then, however, the larger forces at work in Alberta had taken their toll. The mortgage interests had tumbled over each other and the settlers in forsaking the dry belt and allowing the land to revert to the state for taxes. If the banks and the settlers generally confined their retreat to the southeast, the mortgagemen were through with the whole infernal province. In 1915 twenty-five loan companies had been dealing in Alberta. By early 1924, there were four.[41] The land credit structure in the province and the West generally fell to pieces. Labelling the crisis "absolutely appalling," C. W. Peterson of *The Farm and Ranch Review* declared in 1925, "it is today impossible to negotiate a desirable farm loan in the west."[42]

The grim goblin of debt adjustment and the wraiths of liens and prior charges and state confiscation had completed their night of terror, and the mortgage money was gone. In the end, the power of the calamity ensured that there would be no abiding contracts, just ever-changing conditions of chaos and misery. The struggle over who would inherit the dry belt—the mortgagemen or the salt of the earth—was finished.

Neither would.

10   Glory, Glory to Alberta

The Mentor Messiahs

Nɪɢɢᴇʀ! ʀɪɢɢᴇʀ! ʀᴀᴍ-ᴀ-ᴛᴀᴛᴇʀ!
Half past alligator!
Rim! ram! bulligator!
Chic! wah! dah!
Antelope Cut school!
Rah! Rah! Rah!

So chanted the children of Antelope Cut school of the Woolchester district near the Hat. Led by Cheerleader Victor Bohnet, they were celebrating at January-end 1925 the anniversary of the opening of the school. Then turning to one of their favorite songs, they sang "Glorious Alberta" to the tune of "John Brown's Body":

Glorious Alberta
Come and see the land that raises
All the world's best wheat.

176

Come and see the land that has
Strong boys and maidens neat.
Come and see the land where
Happy hearts and faces greet
In glorious Alberta.

    Glory, glory to Alberta,
    Glory, glory to Alberta,
    Glory, glory to Alberta,
    Long may she thrive and grow.

Here's where the climate is
The healthiest and best.
Here's where the land is richer
Far than all the rest.
Here's where true Canadians
[Live] in our great and lovely West.
In glorious Alberta.

    Glory, glory to Alberta,
    Glory, glory to Alberta,
    Glory, glory to Alberta,
    Long may she thrive and grow.

So let us sing a song of hope
Of love and joy and peace.
Let us sing of happiness
And may our wealth increase.
Let us love our sunny land.
May wonders never cease
Of glorious Alberta.[1]

It is one of the mixed blessings of childhood that youth understand so little of what spins the earth and have so little conception of their place in history. They can play in the garbage and offal and be in a world of palaces and jewels; they can wade through a sea of sand and be frolicking at some beach. Like Jimmy Sharp and Howard Brigham Jr. of Alderson they could be poking through the burnt-out excavations on Broadway years after the great fire of 1919, peering through charred rubble for bones and whispering weird stories of an ancient plot to torch the town.[2] Living in fantasies, the children could create any existence, however true to life or preposterous. And, "may wonders never cease," they could even recreate the rhetoric of the boom. Line after line, they could sing praises to the land of Cain without for a moment knowing that they had uttered the most egregious lies since the planners of Nineveh had first concocted their tales.

The mothers and fathers of these atavistic boosters had long ago discarded the bombast and the idle prattle about the legacy of the soil. After the older folk had been beaten into the ground for years, they left the puzzle of who would inherit the land to the gods. When they thought of themselves, as they often did, they began to wonder who amongst them would inherit anything. They looked at their bedraggled, deprived offspring as few generations of Canadians had, and they prayed that their young might not always live as they had lived, so lost, so deluded and so consumed with mere existence.

In the swirls of sand they beheld the faint outlines of a ladder leading up from their perdition. Through shifting openings in the clouds of dust they could see that it was rungless in places, rickety, tottering. The ladder was that increasingly maligned and ramshackle institution which the people clung to in the storm and which the storm itself threatened to topple—the one-room rural school.

It is too much to say that many honestly thought that teachers might be the deliverers that long-suffering settlers strained to see. Yet if mere school marms had become one-tenth of what their overseers in the educational establishment expected of them, they would have been acknowledged messiahs within a week of their first postings. In pleasant reveries instructors in the normal schools and summer schools and inspectors in the real schools dreamt of master teachers, ushered in nearly by suggestion alone, marvels who were rural-minded and improvement-minded pillars of progress. They dreamt of teachers so stealthy and so invisible that in one moment they could slip into the community without a ripple and in the next they could emerge cast in the deepest local dye and poised to lift the community to a higher plane.

Regrettably, eight months of normal school training in the early twenties prepared trainees to teach on the moon better than in the typical one-room prairie school. At the Calgary Normal School there was only one bonafide country school out of fourteen apprenticeship schools in the whole operation. At Camrose Normal there was nothing.[3]

In 1922 an unprecedented horde of recruits jammed the normal schools to the rafters. The depression and lack of clerical jobs, departmental pressure to induce permit teachers to take regular training, and rumors that the government loan to students was to be withdrawn and the normal school course stretched to two years were the motivators. Swamped at the height of drought in the dry belt, principals E. W. Coffin and W. A. Stickle of Calgary and Camrose deeply lamented their niggardly offering to prospective rural teachers.[4] At Camrose Stickle frankly despaired at his offering to *any* trainees for *any* posts. With swarming enrolment and only twelve public school rooms available, each room had twenty-one student teachers in the 1922–23 school year![5]

Stickle must have winced when he recalled the old complaint of local Inspector J. W. Russell about teachers accepting the status quo, falling dumbly in line with community conventions, accommodating crass customs and hobbling habits without a whimper. "There is not sufficient effort being made by our teachers in leadership work," Russell fumed.[6]

Of course educational reformers had tried to address this problem, but by the time of the collapse of the dry areas most of their works were in shambles. They had started with the simple assumption that city and town-bred teachers would do well to know the difference between a horse and a cow before their coronation as rural leaders. The communication of such nuances was to be the job of a new course of studies—agriculture—and its promoters had begun their pitch out west in the early teens. All were half-siblings to the architects of Nineveh, those moon-struck mongers of exaggeration. Under the spell of the settlement boom, they contracted logorrhea, a disgusting effusion wherein their tongues could not stop wagging about the benefits of agriculture.

It would take more than a book to enumerate the blessings they attached to the new study (and several volumes were written to prove it), but the most important gift was the power it lent to tacklers of rural problems. It made teachers relevant for once, dealienated them, invested them with a sympathy for the elemental industry, with a love of the soil and the "wisdom" of the dryland experts. School gardens welded the character necessary to withstand the slings and arrows of adversity. After all, every virtue God handed down from the mountain and more, sprang from the work of the soil—health, strength, riches, respect, resourcefulness, industry, forebearance, sobriety, temperance, justice, equilibrium, and "a thousand sober delights and honest pleasures," as Socrates himself once said. School gardens were canned goodness, bottled benisons, imparting super-human qualities to cultivators. Forging an alliance between home and school, and hallowing the stooped figure in the distant furrow as the first essential of the race, school gardens and school agriculture would show farm children the fruits of progress and inspire them to stay on the land.

The naiveté of it all must have drawn a hideous guffaw from the dark forces grinding away in the drylands. Nowhere in the country were school gardens worse than there. One drop in the ocean of pathos that swept the region was Miss Speiran's saga. Arriving from Ontario in 1916, fresh from normal school and eager to plant a garden in the coming spring, Speiran went to a district near Oyen, just then beginning the long dryness. At her school in spring 1917, she carefully built elevated rows where students planted their seeds after the fashion in Ontario where there was danger of flooding! Sentinels in the high winds of Alberta, the seeds never had a chance, and many were soon wafted into Saskatchewan. Despite massive intervention by students lugging water to the garden, plants that did root were victims of pests, gophers and drought. By mid-June Speiran gave up; once was often enough.[7] As Inspector M. E. Lazerte of Bassano wrote, "There are too many cases where the little mound of earth serves but to mark the grave of the seed or of the early departed plant."[8]

Closely tied to school gardening was the school grounds beautification movement. "The natural features of the site and its surroundings," a departmental bulletin said in 1916, "should be attractive and lend themselves to a landscape treatment that would cultivate a taste for the beautiful and make the school centre a place of which the district may be proud."[9] The school was to be a model of sparkling maintenance and tasteful landscaping for the locals to emulate at home.

In the impoverished areas beautification was a farce. No trustees ever illustrated the negation of the beautification movement better than the Lyman school board, south of Hanna. None ever so poignantly depicted what the school meant to the sinking dry belt community. The scene was a meeting on September 25, 1926, the setting another crop disaster, the mood notwithstanding deliriously comical, the occasion a sort of Last Supper, strangely jovial and insanely sardonic. The trustees began to blather about painting the school.

A heated discussion ensued regarding the hue, each man insisting on his national colors. "Owing to the great diversity of opinion and the apparent hopelessness of arriving at an agreement," the secretary wrote, "it was decided on the suggestion of the chairman to paint the school yellow, with the view of its blending with any deposit made on the door step or nuisance committed in the vicinity." The matter was settled, the beautification movement, answered—the school would become one with the surrounding dung. Excited, the trustees added a final flurry—they would paint a white elephant on the front. "This suggestion met with great enthusiasm," recorded the secretary, "and was immediately carried unanimously."[10]

Alas, the dry belt school and its grounds were neither a shrine nor a model, nor were they beautiful or enviable. For these tired trustees they were mostly a burden. Less than four months later, there were only ten ratepayers left, and on March 17, 1930, Lyman fell into the hands of an official trustee.[11]

The Fates also conspired against a third, related and somewhat more successful ploy to link school and community in defence of the land—the school fair. Instituted in 1916 under the Olds School of Agriculture, school fairs in Alberta numbered 129 by 1922.[12] Most dry belt school fairs had no sooner become the responsibility of the spanking new agricultural schools at Raymond, Gleichen and Youngstown than the government sealed the Gleichen and Youngstown schools in 1922.[13] Crop failure squeezed enrolment to death, and the institutions created to combat farming difficulties in the region fell victim to the problems they were to solve. In May 1923, Education Minister Perren Baker chopped the staff of provincial school inspectors from forty to twenty-five. The scalpel job forced the survivors to set aside their stitching of school and community and their dabbling in agriculture and to tend more to the basics.[14]

It didn't really matter that inspectors thought school fairs interfered with their itinerary—though that was an indication of how committed they were to making the curriculum relevant. The point was that school fairs that emerged in the dry belt were crippled. The agricultural component was so stunted and emaciated that it could deliver nothing its salesmen promised. It could not inspire children with signs of progress, could not exact pride in the work of the soil, could not genuinely interest children in farm life, and could hardly spur their return to the land. Counter-productive, it was for teachers a lifeline from school to farm that they could never grasp, that became in the end a chimera.

By the time of Hatfield's charade with the clouds, all the falderal in the name of relevance about honoring agriculture on the curriculum and having the school share in the glories of the land was a distant echo.

The Siege

THE FAILURE SAID something about the kind of school that emerged in the dry areas. It was not quite the institution that has been canonized in the local histories and local homilies. Like the aroma of lilacs in spring, the scent in these sources evokes perfumed, smiling memories that bespeak a house of learning that was all-encompassing and ever-integrating, drawing the people of the district together in one accord, linking them as though they were one rejoicing family in one building that was a school, church, dance hall and a community centre combined. There is some truth to this story, but in the drylands it was not quite this way.

In the long days of agony for schools in much of the region, they were sources of conflict, discord and gut-wrenching anxiety. Schools were not the darlings of the sons of the soil; they were the creatures of an alien, city culture. They were not havens of coopera-tion, they were dens of feuding and spite. They were not the makers of profound togetherness, but rather the precipitators of wide-spread dislocation. They did not integrate society, they helped dis-integrate it.

By 1922 the annual reports of inspectors at Hanna, Oyen, Irvine, Brooks and Foremost more resembled economic resumes than ped-agogical essays. Inspector J. F. Boyce of Bassano had never seen the like of it, though he had been around since the territorial days. Settlers were dispirited, disinterested, and they trudged, as if lob-otomized, with blankness stamped on their faces and purpose torn from the breasts. No one thought of taxes. In the burnt-out hulks of Bulyea and Berry Creek municipalities twelve of the forty dis-tricts were so far gone that they failed even to *request* school funds for 1923.[15]

It was not that people gave up without a fight. They often paid school taxes before other debts. Ratepayers around Chinook, east of Hanna, remitted almost all their school taxes, only to find their donations poured into a common chest and used as security for municipal loans pried from local banks.[16] Recognizing the soft spot of the settlers, municipalities even jacked up school levies beyond actual requirements in order to stake their own survival.

As the locals girded up for the siege of their schools, they crafted several strategies. All involved trade-offs, all were problematic, all generated anxiety.

The first ploy was to go cap in hand to the lenders. Trustees of the Creole Belle school district extending into both Bulyea and Berry Creek municipalities soon learned what that meant. In April 1919, the secretary rushed a letter to the Department complaining about the neglect of the Bulyea council to advance funds for the Creole Belle district. Greeted by silence, the secretary launched a second missive a month later, threatening to close the school unless funds were "forthcoming at once." In August the secretary cornered the inspector and apparently failed to extract a loan of $400 from the Department. In November the chairman and the secretary appeared on bended knee at the portals of the Bank of Toronto, Cessford, and were refused a paltry $100 loan for sixty days. At a special meeting two weeks later, the board again pressed the inspector for help. A week after, frantic and still unaided, it decided to make another pilgrimage to the Cessford bank with the chairman and secretary willing to sign in their own names and the other trustees to sign as collateral. Receiving a pittance, they turned again to the inspector and repeatedly begged him to move the Department to provide a $500 loan. At wits' end, the board decided near June 1920, after a few dollars trickled in, to pay the chairman and secretary instead of poor Miss Ellsworth, the teacher.[17] Ellsworth could wait now.

Nothing improved. In March 1921, the Berry Creek municipality failed to supply its portion of the school money, and on May 1 the disconsolate board turned the school management over to an official trustee.[18]

Larger, more visible districts had better leverage in exacting government assistance. Some played the nervy game of calling the government's bluff. With poor crops and escalating costs, the Bow Island board held a special meeting on September 29, 1919, to pore over finances. Because the town would not meet the requisition and the Department of Education would not loan the money, the board decided to close the schools. The teachers and government were to be notified, and the excuses that tumbled from the miserly lips in Edmonton were to be published. A week after, Inspector Williams grew a smile and promised to recommend a government loan of $2,000. Jolted, Chief Inspector Gorman sped to Bow Island. Armed with an understanding of drybelters garnered during his five or six year stint as Medicine Hat inspector in better days, Gorman banked on his reputation as a cordial and efficient administrator to be able to induce the town fathers to assume their responsibility. Instead he had to bank on his ability to induce the Department to bail out the town rather than admit the collapse of education in one of the largest communities in the southeast corner. The procedure was repeated in August 1920, involving this time the inspector, chief inspector and deputy minister of Education. Again, only after assurance that the Department would finance the schools till taxes came in, did the locals "consent" to operate the schools.[19]

After 1920, bluffing closure lost its panache. As conditions worsened, the trickle of terminated schools broke into a rivulet, then a river. In the Alderson-Tilley East area alone, Ted Fream counted forty-four closed schools—almost 80 percent of all districts—in his survey of the ruins of the dryland core in 1926.[20]

Struck by the appalling need, the government first increased the supply of loans and then, dizzy from spiraling debt and nearly out of control, it instituted retrenchments and loan cutbacks.[21] The call to the locals to dig deeper sometimes worked, for it was remarkable how doles sapped local efforts at tax collection.[22] But the policy also finished many schools for good. Over and over districts went through the terrifying process of discovering the limits of their ingenuity to provide funds. Few ever wanted to close the schools, but it began to dawn on the most resilient and forebearing that the harder they worked the less likely the government would help.

Some school districts turned into predators, aggressively coveting and invading adjoining territory in order to widen their tax base. Inspectors urged this "solution," and it sometimes brought a brief rush of euphoria, but when the adjacent land already belonged to another district there was no end of trouble. In the fourth year of drought, Forcina residents in the Berry Creek country hacked out a school district and erected a $2,200 school house. Adjoining districts were bled of population and taxable land, and the new district immediately sank into irretrievable debt. Month after month the new board struggled—seeking loans everywhere, trying to extend the period of debenture call, begging for the renewal of bank notes and the postponement of the teacher's salary.[23] It was all a bad dream from which there was no waking. Ten years later, as the secretary reviewed 1929 and pondered the future, he wrote dejectedly, "I think to commence this term we really have nothing."[24]

All the scrimping and squirming forced another fiscal remedy into the sunlight—the short-term school. Until the early twenties, dry belt school boards adjusted opening and closing days with the weather and the state of finances—criteria which guaranteed the profoundest irregularity imaginable.[25]

The irregularity did not impress the bureaucracy in Edmonton. Short-term schools may have been a viable option for the locals and a means of maintaining local control, but departmental nabobs and their emissaries, the inspectors, viewed them as the bane of the rural school, one of the chief reasons for the galling disparity between rural and urban schooling. As schoolmen sought to grind down that disparity they hiked normal school requirements and declared war on the infamous "summer schools."

Chief Attendance Officer D. C. McEacherne perused teachers' contracts and insisted that none grant more than ten weeks' vacation for the year.[26] When local trustees defied sections 182 and 191 of the school act, they were sued. "Fall in line . . .," Inspector Boyce of Bassano urged the Britannia school board on December 26, 1927. "If it is the desire of the Board of Trustees of Britannia to close down for the winter months please give me the details of their reason, such as the size of the children, the number and names of the grades, the distance of the children from school and their means of reaching the school, the number of grades above grade V and the state of finances of the district."[27] The older the scholars and the more the grades, the tougher the teaching and the longer the term—that was the thinking. Boyce's point was that destitution was no longer sufficient unto itself to warrant a summer school.

However handicapping, this imposition was slight compared to another government attempt to "help." Though it was aimed more at the mortgage companies, the Tax Recovery Act in 1922 forced another hard choice on the locals—cough up delinquent arrears or forfeit the land. It is unclear which option was the more popular. Some schools in the Lethbridge and Medicine Hat inspectorates were actually resuscitated by the pint of blood extracted from the people; elsewhere the settlers had already been bled dry. Blanched, ragged, and hardly human, they straggled across the red-stained sands to new communities, leaving the ones they had left even more broken. A single notice in the *Alberta Gazette* in 1923 listed 36 percent of the total land area of King municipality under threat of forfeiture.[28]

As the fabric of society blew apart, those abiding reached for the tatters and held on for all they were worth. This fleeting ritual schoolmen called "cooperation," the union of two or more partners hoping against all odds that a handshake might bring stability and rejuvenation.

The truth was that districts that "cooperated" never wanted to cooperate at all. They did not want to sell their school houses and did not want to change the district name.[29] If they wished to send their children to a neighboring school, they had to await a report regarding possible overcrowding and the always thorny issue of cost.[30] If they felt compelled to fold, they still had to decide to renounce all further local control or to operate a school jointly and thus keep a finger on their own destinies.

In February 1927, the Arlington board in the Berry Creek country met to discuss the advisability of cooperating with Square Deal or Jennings districts "with the idea of reducing taxes." Trustee F. Rudge objected to school in either jurisdiction since the distance was too great for his children to walk. Nonetheless, the secretary presented figures which must have deeply worried Rudge. The cost of running the Arlington school for a year, including teacher's salary, fuel, stationery, and audit was $740. The direct tax was

$468. By cooperating with another district, costs, including half the teacher's salary, half the fuel, and rental of the school house, were $425. The direct tax was only $153.[31]

Wavering, the board decided against cooperation. In January 1928, it deemed "that as long as the number of children as at present remain . . . it would be advisable to run our own school." Exactly one month later, it reversed itself and decided to cooperate with Jennings and to move the school house. In January 1929, while the cooperation was extended another year, the board reported that Rudge was gone.[32]

Once anything was settled it had to be resettled each new year. Thus the Connorsville trustees, also south of Hanna, agreed to pay the Corinth board 25¢ per day per pupil for the education of Connorsville children in 1923. But a few years later the Connorsville people considered the cost too steep.[33] As well, agreements fell flat when boards failed to pay the tuition of their children in outside districts. When the Moccasin Flat board reneged on the tuition of Una Hornby for the term ending June 30, 1919, at the Creole Belle school, the Creole Belle trustees decided five days later not to "consider entering into an agreement for the tuition of the children of Moccasin Flat . . . until the said bill be paid."[34]

It was the sad truth that the urgent need for money fragmented the community in every conceivable way. On October 7, 1922, the secretary of the Crocus Plains school board told a Berry Creek resident: "Some time ago we wrote you about your account with this district, but have received no answer. This school cannot be kept running without funds, so we have decided to give you until the end of October to pay this account. If it is not paid by then your children will be expelled."[35]

When there were no locals left to govern, or they did not want to govern, or they could not govern because of strangling debt or bitter quarrels, they were replaced by official trustees named by the Department of Education. Sometimes these officials were appointed where there was a particularly determined board which had stayed through thick and thin only to discover that its self-preservation formula of summer school or low salaries for teachers was unacceptable to government. Always they were the means by which control over schooling was transferred, sometimes wrested, from despondent, fearful, pathetic, bickering, carping, and sometimes courageous locals.

The reign of these departmental puppets was never intended to be permanent. It was to be brief, the result of an official policy, buttressed by local sentiment, to stabilize local school districts, to regenerate collapsing boards, and to restore the status quo before the drought.[36] It took years before enough schoolmen realized that that status quo could never be restored.

Together the floundering locals and paternal government were swept along through the white water and the rapids, acting out their pathetic sideplay, trying to make out what the other had said in the din, garbling a response, with one eye on the rocks ahead, another on the powdery, ashy landscape shimmering behind them mile after mile. In all the drama the locals almost certainly did not know what to make of the outstretched arm of government. The government sought to oil the passage of taxes into the public coffers, but the Tax Recovery Act threatened to slide the locals and everyone else right out of the south. The government swore that it was dedicated to the restoration of local control, but that rarely happened, and standardized attendance regulations helped ensure that it never would happen. The government pledged itself to universal, compulsory education, but then it cut back the loans that could make that education a reality. The government sought to answer chaos with order, but after many years of chirping from Edmonton, what the locals thought they heard was more chaos and more meaninglessness.

The Department, for its part, heard the cry and wondered who among the howlers were truly destitute. It heard the wailing of the children, the teachers and the parents, and it wondered how it could ever help them all and who it should help first. In the end, it adopted an infinitely complex scheme of treating districts on their own individual merits. Of course the scheme was somehow unsatisfying, for it meant ad hoc decisions, dependent upon different inspectors and official trustees working in different contexts with different demands. It meant policies that were never certain, never definite. And these qualities they and the people had had enough of.

The Plan

FROM HIS LOFTY perch in Edmonton, Education Minister Perren Baker had been eyeing these developments for some time. By the late twenties as the dry belt continued to radiate demands from an ever-deepening and darkening void, it had already dawned on him that the old order was on its death bed. Everywhere the little school districts were going down, closing one by one, disappearing into the quicksands with a bubble and a plop. What was needed was some master roper standing on firm ground to throw a giant lasso to the struggling souls, pulling as many together in a single toss, dragging them to where the sands were not so deep and allowing them to work out their salvation in the comfort of the numbers they had once known. Districts had to be consolidated. And not just two, three or four at a time—but dozens, even scores.

Baker knew intimately the size of his desolate precincts in the Medicine Hat and Cypress constituencies. He had lived near Nemiskam since one of the last great land rushes at Lethbridge in which he himself had participated. He had known all the original homesteaders and had come to love them as one loves a family or the comrades of some stirring adventure. With deep personal anguish, he had seen his people scatter to the four winds, beaten and spiritless. With whole townships denuded, he saw the incompatibility of the old tiny school districts with the new settlement patterns.

Baker thereupon brought to the legislature a school bill calling for the creation of large administration units. Twice the hue and cry from his own back benches forced him to withdraw the bill in tatters. People were loath to give up their control over the schools, and where calamity was not as rife they saw no reason for the change. Always with an ear tight to the ground, farm MLAs heard

Perren Baker, UFA minister of Education—sorely tested in the long crisis that enveloped the schools. NA 4790-2, Glenbow-Alberta Archives.

the quaking and chose to embarrass Baker rather than alienate their ridings. Ruffled, Baker bided his time. Sooner or later the large units would come, and with the general downturn of the Great Depression he knew that the time was not distant. The people would decide themselves when the moment was ripe.[37]

One might have thought that the districts tributary to Alderson would have been the first to amalgamate, but the stampede out had been so speedy, complete and irreversible that it eliminated the need for any schools over goodly stretches. It was just across the Red Deer in the Berry Creek country that the seed of the first monster divisions took tenuous root. By 1930, the municipal government there was so battered that it was defenceless in the face of more bad times. Two years later it fell, and the province's second special area was called into being under governor William Hewlett. The next spring Hewlett reported the educational system of the district near total collapse. Six weeks later, embarking on another parching summer, the Stanmore secretary-treasurer, writing to the Britannia school board, said it all—"No rain: No crop: No taxes: No school: Why do parents put such a penalty on children as to keep them in this desert? What a world: what a people."[38]

With such a mood, it was understandable when Inspector Lindsay Thurber travelled through the dust of Berry Creek municipality and east bringing his quiet message of a new deal, that there was near unanimous agreement amongst the destitute that they should relinquish their school boards, allowing him free rein in the establishment of a large experimental district. For years the new division had been incubating in the smaller scale amalgamations of the locals.

Thurber's was a monumental step. What happened in Berry Creek was critically important in the slowly developing government strategy to provide large school districts. It was the starting point, the opening of the door, the place where the plan would have to work or it would work nowhere, the ground where local resistance would be weakest. Elsewhere there would be bitterness, and truth to the charge that large divisions had been imposed—but not here.

The mortal who became official trustee of the sixty-seven defunct districts was a Nova Scotian. A graduate of Truro Normal School in 1914 and Acadia University, Lindsay Thurber was twice wounded in the First War before becoming principal at Hanna in the mid-twenties and inspector in the late twenties.[39] For an expert, his plan was very simple—centralize control, equalize the taxation burden, afford the siblings of the dustlands an education, and make as few mistakes as possible. In his pitch there was the old line which the genetic make-up of all experts forced them to utter—"Trust me, trust me." The words came like soothing syrup, and the people for a time said—"Yes."

From the moment Thurber accepted the mantle of power it was as if he had stepped into the Red Deer in floodtide, intending to walk across—so deluged with problems was he.

In a region where any houses of learning were an endangered species, parents, in keeping with the times, suddenly began demanding high schools. In 1921 the percentage of provincial enrolment above grade 8 was only 6 percent; by 1934 it was 17.6 percent.[40] Naturally the ungraded school became the high school, a problem compounded in the dry areas by poverty and poor crops which militated against sending children to bonafide high schools. Across Alberta in 1934, about 50 percent of one-room schools offered instruction above grade 8; in the drought areas, the figure approached 75 percent. In the latter, children faced Hobson's choice—take what they could get in the home school, or take nothing.[41]

The prospects of high school often stoked the fires of community rancor, for parents of very young children soon saw how school marms with high school students or exam fixations ignored the first and second graders.[42] Sometimes not just parents saw the discrimination. Rolly Jardine of Alderson never forgave his teacher for what she did to him in grade one. Preoccupied by the older scholars, she completely ignored him the whole year. He would get up, saunter aimlessly around the class, play in the sand box, sit down, go to sleep, get up and wander off home. Never did his teacher interrupt this shiftless, loitering existence. She taught him nothing, and what he learned on his own matched that. At year-end he had no rudiments, no reading, no writing, no arithmetic, nothing. The day of reckoning finally arrived and he received his report card. He had passed into grade two! Over the next years Rolly paid heavily for the horrific start.[43]

Thurber heard similar tales in his own bailiwick, but what rankled him as much was a similar blighting effect on the high school students. "In many cases . . ." he said, "the teacher lacks the professional equipment necessary, and in practically all instances she has no previous experience in this type of work."[44] The bleak prospects never daunted the parents when they pressured the green grads from the normal schools into offering high school subjects. What daunted the parents were the results.

When Thurber took over, his job was almost comically complex. He was to match the conflicting local expectations with the largely unknown capabilities of the teachers, then tailor a unique offering of high school subjects based on an array of factors from enrolment to number of grades taught, and apply the result to a society in complete flux.

Lindsay Thurber and
the Labors of Hercules

NEEDLESS TO SAY, satisfaction was not guaranteed. In September 1934, Mrs. Fred Galarneau wrote Thurber: "I thought it had been arranged for the grade 11 pupils at the Connorsville school to take what subjects they needed to make up their 21 units. It seems too bad to think they will have to take Latin 1 instead of French 2 and Miss Anderson doesn't want to teach Geometry 2 either *[sic]*. Don't you think we could have a teacher to teach these subjects or else arrange for a central high school?"[45] J. F. Steinbach of Pollockville was furious that "french was not been thought, there where many other children which would have attended school but when they find out french was not thought they returned home *[sic]* . . . ." Had he known, he would have shipped his daughter to Brown school where both French and Latin were taught—"so now she is just out of it . . .," he fumed.[46]

Related to high schools, the problem of providing student dormitories became acute. When scholars were miles from operating schools, Thurber had to try to provide dormitory accommodation near the schools. Abandoned buildings helped, especially for older children who could fend for themselves, or for families willing to move into town for the winter. In some places, shacks were carted to villages or buildings already there were converted; at Cessford, the Women's Institute building was used for a boys' dorm in the winter of 1933–34.[47] At Pollockville, a dormitory was established at Mrs. Siefeldt's. The children were to supply their own bed clothing and to assist the landlady whenever possible. The accommodation they received in place of a conveyance fee Thurber paid to outlying parents to transport their children to school.[48]

Unhappily at least one parent found Siefeldt's hostelry wanting. Mrs. J. F. Steinbach informed Thurber in April 1934 that her children were no longer at Siefeldt's. "I have brought Mrs. Siefeldt milk, butter, meat and vegetables and so ford [*sic*]," she said, "but she would allow so little that I quit bringing any more." Though Steinbach had paid an extra 10¢ a day, her children got only two meals Mondays and Fridays. "We furnish everything and the children do dishes besides," she complained. The meals were "poor" and it was getting too "expensive." As a result, Mrs. Steinbach said, "We have moved a shack in town and the children board themselves."[49]

Mrs. Clarissa Dunford did not want her daughter in a dorm in the first place. Explaining that she used her widow's pension "solely" for her daughter's schooling, she wrote Thurber, asking for a house. Checking his inventory, Thurber issued a teacherage.[50] While teacherages for this purpose were in heavy demand, the result was not always pleasing. Once when Thurber had a building hauled in he was smartly upbraided by the denizens of Square Deal district who believed that the building was "not warm enough" and "too shacky in appearance."[51] Another time, L. Larson of the Youngstown area wrote Thurber: "They are telling me that the Armstrong children are moving into the building where our girl and Miss Houcsh are staying at Crocus Plains." Larson wanted to subdivide the petite building into two apartments since there would be "too much of a mix up by having so many from different families cooking and eating in one room." By the following May, with the subdivision undone and unauthorized, Larson wrote again, indicating the failure of the dorm and the error of Thurber's ways. "Those Armstrong children," he raged, "have been fighting these other two girls ever since they moved in there. . . ."[52]

If this litany of discontent seemed picayune, Thurber was reminded again and again of the very human impulses which motivated it and which rendered his job so painful. As Edward Kloepper wrote, "we as parents are sacrificing a great deal too in having our children living away from home during the week creating always spells of anxiety."[53]

A more significant cargo than dorms in Thurber's incredible spree of building moving to provide for the decreasing population of Berry Creek was the schoolhouse itself. Alas, not always did Thurber tell everyone his plans; nor was it always certain whom he ought to tell, nor how he might manage the telling. N. W. Dornan had no sooner moved "on account of school and water," than he discovered that Thurber had moved the school! "I cannot exactly see the reason of the school being moved," a dumbfounded Dornan wrote from the square in the ground where the school had been, "as at this location there are empty houses where the children can stay during the school term."[54]

When Thurber decided to move the Mizpah school, ratepayer Tom J. Tompkins balked. "I have built up a farm for over twenty years," he said. The school "was bought and paid for with our money for our convenience. . . . I demand this school be left here, and I am taking up this matter with the Premier of Alberta to try and get a square deal." Thurber replied that the policy was not to deprive Tompkins's children of education; it was simply "poor business" to operate a school where there were fewer than five children or to erect a new school when there were vacant ones around.[55] A month or so later, Tompkins again opposed the removal which was "against the wishes of the ratepayers." The building was "the property of the landowners and ratepayers here. . . ." And he added, "I intend to stir up the private land owners and take legal action against you for damages if you take the school out of the Mizpah District." His threat was backed by a petition of six signatories, which Thurber ignored.[56]

The maintenance of school buildings was hardly less onerous. For years inspectors all over the West had berated local apathy; now at least one inspector discovered in a very personal way that apathy was often poverty in disguise. When Phyllis Dove began teaching in Wardlow in September 1934 she requested a coal pail, fireshovel, water pail, wash basin, pencil sharpener, dust pan, broom, blackboard stencils, school globe and "an axe or an axe handle." She also asked that the barn and chimney be cleaned, the school house be banked, three panes of glass be fitted into the windows, latches or knobs be attached to the two outer doors, the school fence be mended, and that the barn and other buildings be repaired. Many of these projects, she noted, were "too difficult for the pupils and me to attempt without assistance from some capable man with proper equipment."[57]

Faulty stoves were endless problems. One George Spinks investigated a smoking heater, an "Enterprise Scorcher," and discovered that it needed more draught and thus had to be nearer to the chimney. Placing it there, however, would leave it "right in front of the blackboard," and, added Spinks, "there seems to be no other suitable place for the blackboard."[58] At another school, another repairman removed a stove with great effort only to find the new one broken, the centre grates in bad condition, the shaker gone. "We have tried the new stove for two days," the man wrote, "and Miss Lynn says she couldn't stand it any longer. The smoke was terrible and the place was cold all the time." The repairman thereupon informed Thurber's office that the old stove was reinstalled. Someone in that office, probably secretary Heaton, later pencilled on the letter "NO ACTION TAKEN."[59]

Not everyone was as forebearing as Miss Lynn. Mrs. E. C. H. Owen of Rose Lynn complained to Thurber: "My children . . . on terrible cold days . . . had to bum a place to stay around town because they could not get the school warm enough . . ."[60] Snorted A. G. Kingcott, a former trustee, "I am not sending the boy again until you have made some different heating arrangements, and I am not waiting until next spring for you to make them. If I do not hear something definate [sic] from you by Monday the 21st I shall take the matter up with the Department."[61]

The condition of outhouses and barns was another bugbear. At Sunnynook the boys' outhouse had "no roof and no seat"—apparently prompting a wiseacre to remark that they didn't call it "Sunnynook" for nothing.[62] The toilets in another district, an informant wrote Thurber, "are in such a condition that the children are unable to use them and are using the barn instead, which I certainly do not think is either proper or sanitary."[63] Cecil Stringer told Thurber that the barn of the Square Deal school yard had housed

"15 or so horses . . . 5 days a week." For eight months these Augean stables had not been cleaned. "It is so bad," Stringer wrote in May 1935, "the children are beginning to leave their horses outside on the school grounds rather than wade into the manure."[64]

Without the buffering school boards, Thurber was directly in the line of fire when teachers were deemed inadequate. Everything from outhouses to foreigners to Christian fundamentalism was involved. One woman complained about Miss Snards who made her two children and another "clean the toilet for . . . a terrible bad boy who did some dirty work on the toilet." Once more the offense occurred, and Snards allegedly sent the boy, a German, home, before marching the innocent out once again with their scrub brushes. "Miss Snards is a great friends to them Germans [sic]," remarked Mrs. Joseph, who seems to have been of Syrian descent. When the Josephs and allies attended to some repairs on the outhouse, Snards is said to have broken it again. Even then her alleged crimes had not been fully enumerated—for there had been a problem with a well. Apparently the Josephs and Holts had started to dig a well for Snards on the government property. Snards, however, called in a Mr. Pearson for an opinion on the location of the well, and according to Mrs. Joseph, Pearson's choice was on "his own property" where he could "water his stock!" "Mr. Thurber," the aggrieved parents said, "we would like to know if [our] children have no right to go to school." Bewildered, Thurber wrote, "I will be down as soon as the roads permit."[65]

What happened is not known, but apparently the feeling against the poor teacher was pervasive. A few months later, another parent informed Thurber that if Snards were back in the fall her four children would not be. Though they had been taught by "seven or eight" instructors, this was "the first time they ever rebelled against a teacher."[66]

Another time, the Square Deal Citizen's Committee protested against "Mr. Thurber's action in placing a teacher in charge of our school who is entirely incapable of managing a school as proven by her last years' work here."[67] "I think we need a change here," another woman wrote Thurber. "We lived next to school last winter. I seen lots of things that wasn't right for one thing they never kept the time they started school any time and let the children go whenever they got company *[sic]*. Ours didn't learn anything all term."[68] This story was confirmed by A. G. Kingcott who added: "I always thought that the teacher had to teach the Infants *[sic]* their sounds but it seems not as my boy never had a sound the whole of last year—he can do his work which is set on the black board but the sounds he never has been taught." Further, Kingcott was angry that his young lad, in second year in grade one, "had to sit on a nail keg since last January," a period of seven months.[69]

So often the truth was unclear. Thurber was aware of an attempt to dump the Rose Lynn teacher in 1934. One woman, however, wrote, "we have no complaint . . . The real cause of the dissatisfaction among others is that she would seldom go to the 'Gospel Hall' on Sundays and went to dances. The children all liked her." Clearly "if the teacher would not subscribe to their religious beliefs she could do nothing right. . . ." "I have lived among them for thirty years," the informant said, "and believe me, anyone who could stand it even as long as Miss James, deserves a decoration."[70]

Sometimes Thurber got unusual, even incredible requests. Once a new minister cruised into the area and wished to buy a school. Five weeks later he wanted a "good-toned bell."[71] In October 1935, the teacher of the Square Deal school requested that since she could not keep the door closed in windy weather, Thurber's maintenance staff ought to spin the school around so that the door faced south. Thurber objected that spinning the school would ruin the lighting effect. When his maintenance man refreshed his memory concerning the position of the school and reported that if the building were turned the lighting would be perfect, Thurber requested that a porch be built.[72]

One dedicated hunter informed Thurber's office that he had "about a thousand gopher tails," and since Thurber seemed to be in charge of all southern Alberta he asked where he might sell them. Thurber's secretary replied: "I regret to have to advise that, although I have made inquiries around town as to the possibilities of your receiving some remuneration for the gopher tails in your possession I am afraid that no bounty is being paid on gopher tails. It is a shame, I know, as you have undoubtedly gone to a lot of trouble under a misunderstanding, however, should I hear that some association or other is paying a bounty I will let you know."[73]

Alas, the lessons that were emerging from the dry belt were far from funny. The truth was that the expertise of the professional schoolman was not enough to solve the problems of Berry Creek; that the realities of drought, depression and depopulation posed human dilemmas which all the expertise in the world could never eliminate; and that to the extent that more information was a partial answer, what was needed was an expertise far more comprehensive than professional schoolmen possessed. Thurber often did not know the consequences of his own actions. When the Forcina school district became almost competely depopulated, Thurber quickly sold the school for $300 without consulting the debenture holders. The latter were upset and suggested with some justification that had he conducted negotiations longer, more might have been realized from the sale. Consequently, Thurber had to provide more funds to avoid a possible damage suit.[74]

In September 1933, Deputy Minister of Education J. T. Ross warned Thurber that the payment of conveyance fees would create a dangerous, costly precedent.[75] Thurber nonetheless felt that since the scholars were losing their local schools, even the buildings, the new district should pay transportation costs. He thereupon provided conveyance of 50¢ per day plus fuel at the student's abode near the school. In 1935, with the Berry Creek Division running short of funds, Thurber reduced the conveyance fees to 25¢ and stopped supplying fuel altogether.

For the locals the decision was devastating. "The children came home stating that Mr. Thurber will not furnish them any more kindling wood," wrote one shocked parent.[76] There was a general feeling that he had broken his word, a sentiment he probably shared; nonetheless, he defended the move with some twisted thinking. "I am certain," his secretary covered up, "that the Old Idylwilde or Crocus Plain school when operated under the old system did not provide dormitories, fuel or assurance of all grades in H.S. educa-

Lindsay Thurber, some years after his struggle in the Berry Creek School Division. Z21, Red Deer Archives.

tion or did they operate under such a low school tax as we are operating under."[77] The truth was that the new system had promised better service for lower costs. Having set certain guidelines and made certain commitments, Thurber was now unable to keep them.

The job of official trustee in Berry Creek Division resembled the twelve labors of Hercules in the hands of a mere mortal. As an attempt to bring order out of chaos, and as the first of its kind, the large division was bound to be full of false starts, untenable solutions, unmet hopes. Swamped by complexities of every dimension, Thurber's office deliberately downplayed the theme of salvation through expertise. As secretary Heaton wrote one disgruntled ratepayer, it was "impossible" for Thurber to know everything.[78]

By the time Thurber was ready to leave the dry belt there was a cloud over his head. So many of the old problems had not evaporated, and new ones had materialized. As well, in his abundant dealings with the locals—concerning exemptions for exam fees, amount of boarding fees, even his attempts to make sure schoolhouses were not used for private gain—he offended some, he confused others, and some confused themselves and blamed him.

As he sat drafting his post mortem, he brooded. He may have had some sense of how his work in the strange heartland as official trustee—as attendance officer, purchasing agent, building supervisor, and financial adviser—would reshape the role of inspector into superintendent. He may have suspected that the next several large divisions would be carved out of the fallen empire of the drylands and that he himself would help in the process. He may have even divined that some day he would establish in his new post in Red Deer the first composite high school for rural students in western Canada, offering a semester system and a dormitory, a model for the rest of the country and a synthesis of accommodation to varying student needs. But he certainly did not think that he was in the process of turning into gold, nor lord forbid, that one day the University of Alberta would award him an honorary doctorate for his contributions to Albertan education.

It would not be at all undeserved, for he had burned in the fire as the locals had, learned through trial and error as they had, and in the end put the whole grim story together as comprehensively as any other schoolman who ever set foot in the region.

For now, quietly, and with much regret, Thurber put pen to paper and finished his report. He seriously wondered if an inspector of schools was the right man to administer such districts. He spoke of the drastic action that had to be taken so often, how it alienated the people, how hard it was to deal with those who had been hurt, how their bitterness remained like salts in the hollows. And then he pondered his own low estate, and slowly wrote—"Unless the Inspector is a financial wizard and has the guile of a serpent, he is in a difficult position."[79] Understanding something of his shortfall, he made his confession, and he left the desert.

11 Desolate Places to Be Buried In

ONE MONDAY AT May-end 1909, long before the calamity, the Royal Templars of Temperance held a ladies' debate in Medicine Hat on the resolution that the country girl made a better wife than the city girl. Speaking for the former, Sister Curry praised the rural lass as a paragon of good nature and sweet disposition, of vigorous health and pure and noble thoughts, free of affectations, scandal and divorce, and always contented. The city girl, on the other hand, was a wretched cook, a likely sot, an inveterate flirt and a social gadfly. She had lost her sense of domesticity, her ability and desire to work, her humility.

Before the debate ended, cruelties were uttered of the country miss too—how she dressed slovenly, how she lacked accomplishments, refinement and education, how her life was filled with boredom, drudgery, grinding labor and discontent, how she and others of her sex were pouring out of the countryside into the cities. These slights the judges were not disposed to hear clearly, for the sentiments were unfashionable and out-of-touch with the mood and propaganda attending the land rush already underway in the West for a decade, and now at the portals of the Hat. Accordingly, the backers of the delights of country girls and country living were awarded the victory.[1]

Seldom in history has a propaganda so powerful been so profoundly discredited in so short a time. For the bedraggled army of veterans now beating a retreat from the dryland empire lying in ruins, nothing was further from their tired thoughts than the joys of life on the land.

Annie (Odegard) Edwards had grown up in the Lomond district. Recalling the blazing summers and scorching winds from 1916 to 1923, she wrote, "these long, hard years absorbed all the pioneer spirit from most of us." Desperately poor, she remembered the neighbor boys who gave her mother two red flannel shirts to make two dresses for her sister and her. Once when she was late to dinner, her brother ate her beans, and she went hungry because there were no more. Often her mother would say she had already eaten so the children could have her share. "I can still see my mother out beside the house leaning against the siding, which was rough for want of paint," she wrote forty years later, "and looking out across the sand-covered stubble, weeping in silent desperation."[2]

One by one the settlers were visited by such grief. After eleven years of the meaningless toil of Sisyphus, James Roebuck of Whitla was finished. "My money and children have gone, and now my wife says this is her last year on this desert," he told Premier Greenfield in 1922. "Six years in succession without a crop, and only two crops since the country was settled up in 1909. I think that has been a fair trial."[3]

"Any man of ordinary intelligence who has been on the job here since 1917," Thomas Lannan of Ingebrigt told Saskatchewan authorities, "knows what this country is and knows that it will never do for farming." Casting a jaundiced eye at the governments that

had brought him to so bad a turn, he declared, "We have been opti-
mists too long. . . ."[4] A few hours later, Peter Harder, east at
Gouldtown, confessed in misery, "I think this is all we can stand.
We got to get out."[5]

In the Berry Creek district, Roy Peterson had fallen ill with the
flu. One noon hour after he had begun work again, still weak, he
slumped unconscious. Delirious, he had a vision wherein three
men instructed him to leave and to begin life again elsewhere.
When he awoke, he summoned the nearest available auctioneer. After the sale, the crier took his share in cash, leaving Peterson and his
wife Flora with thousands of dollars in uncollectable notes, signed
and co-signed by impecunious farmers. In a ritual attesting to their
love, Flora and Roy divided the notes, knowing full well that the
securities were only play money. When they stopped payment on
an estate euphemistically called "Roseland," purchased after the
1915–1916 crops, the acreage was forfeited. Leasing their half section homestead to ranchers, they hoped the taxes would at least be
paid. In time, though, the land reverted to the government.[6]

Some like "H. G. C." many miles east of Lethbridge, thought of
the time he first homesteaded. "How many of us ever looked up
precipitation figures for the district we bought land in or homesteaded in? Not one in a thousand. We sized up the country as we
found it. . . . I decided this district . . . was a first class farming section, so I 'copped' off half a section of it, stuck in my plows and
bust it up and have sat here five years learning by experience what I
could have learned in five minutes before I came in." Declaring that
1921 would be his last year in the sunny south, he was leaving for
the north. "My solution . . . is . . . to try it once more and then take
the count. . . . We'll all be buried down here in this dry belt if we
wait for the government to get us out. And parts of it are pretty
desolate places to be buried in."[7]

The fact that the government had misrepresented the region
bothered H. G. C., as it did any number of settlers. But in all the
yowling about Dominion and railroad advertising farmers seldom
mentioned the regional and even local promotion that had contrib-
uted to their folly. They rarely acknowledged that settlers them-

selves had demanded that the drylands be thrown open. And they almost never admitted that they too had participated in the lie—in the way they had boosted the boom, squelched the nit-picking "knockers," played the petty speculators, traded town lots, and awaited the unearned increment, even in the way they had mustered pride in having fashioned new homes and villages from nothing. Yet some of this participation had been natural enough, for the people could hardly be blamed for making the best of their situation. And without the federal and railway boomers and the blathering of dry farm "experts," fewer of them would have been brought to the block.

Now that the worst of times were upon them, those staying after 1922 continually searched the skies for relief. The next crop season opened with promise, and in early June the land was thoroughly soaked by a "million dollar rain," the heaviest in years, which deluged the entire Medicine Hat district.[8] In parts, much further west, the resultant vigorous growth held up, and in places like Retlaw, a life-saving crop was harvested.[9] But eastward, at Alderson, the grain was too short for the binders, and special harvesters called headers were again employed.[10] At Bow Island the yield on many farms was three to five bushels an acre.[11]

The following winter was one of the mildest ever, as the warm winds blew even in February.[12] By mid-May, perhaps the most devastating season in the lives of the drybelters was underway. So dry was it in Winnifred in May 1924 that some were not seeding.[13] Two months later there were no gardens, no pastures and no crops. High and scorching, the gusts were filled with smoke and dust.[14]

In the swirling sand storms, forty families left in July and August from the Winnifred district alone.[15] As the salt of the earth poured out of the southeast like an hour glass, witnesses were dumbstruck. "The population of the town and Winnifred country is so reduced in number it is hardly believable," said the Winnifred correspondent for the Hat *News*.[16] Reports from around Bow Island were so shocking that the *News* sent a reporter to tour the disaster, and for a hundred miles southeast from Bow Island, the scribe drove, viewing forsaken homesteads, cattle and horses: "Miles and miles of

The desert invades—Lomond in the last year of the war. NA 1308-6, Glenbow-Alberta Archives.

Bow Island on the eve of the exodus, 1920 c. NA 1644-17, Glenbow-Alberta Archives.

Empress in decline, 1922 c. NA 1644-59, Glenbow-Alberta Archives.

what looks like an arid plain confront the casual eye, partially tilled lands, where the owner took fright and fled less worse overtook him. Bits of green land are sometimes seen, resembling the historical oasis of the desert. Canada's uninhabited thousands of acres—oh the tragedy and pathos of it all. . . ."[17] As if in sympathy, Bow Island nearly burnt down twice that summer.[18]

That fall, Harold Long of *The Lethbridge Herald* drove nearly six hundred miles through the southeast. North of the Hat, at Vale, he chanced on a family which once had the post office, serving fifty farmers. Now there were three left. From Hilda to Empress the land seemed given over to ranching, but the ranchers were faced with little feed, low prices for cattle, high taxes, and uncertain renewal of their leases. One settler reported that he had purchased two calves a year ago for $10.50. All winter he fed them, and a little before he met Long he shipped them. One calf died in transit, and the other netted $2.50.

South near Seven Persons, Long met A. McNeil, one of many farmers uncertain whether to go or to stay. If he went, he, unlike others, could take his stock and equipment, but he forfeited his 480 acre farm worth $10,000 in 1917, his buildings, shelter belt and fourteen years of labor. Many of his neighbors had gone, and he himself had been as far north as Red Deer reconnoitering the country. "But it's tough to think of giving this up when I know I would raise 4000 bushels of wheat or more every year if we just had a little more rain," he said. "Right up to 1917 I though[t] I was sitting on the world."[19]

On the eastern fringes of Lethbridge territory, from Etzikom to Burdett, Long encountered more abandoned farms than on any other day's drive.[20] North across the Red Deer River, where he did not go, up the finished part of the Hanna-Hat right-of-way, a voice from Nateby advised citizens not to be surprised if they saw farmers along the line carting their grain to elevators in wheelbarrows.[21]

After the fall exodus, the spring of 1925 began most auspiciously. At April-end the ground moisture around Winnifred was considered the best in fifteen years.[22] Shortly after, a rejuvenated local correspondent chirped in song: "April thunders bring summer

Dried out settlers from southeastern Alberta reach Cardston in the burning summer of 1924. NA 114-17, Glenbow-Alberta Archives.

wonders."[23] Conditions remained ideal as a forty-six hour rain deluged the whole region a week into June, and when the wetness continued, a bumper crop seemed assured.[24]

Then, as so often had occurred in the past, the rain halted, and the temperature soared to 100 degrees F. Day after day in July the beautiful crops scorched, writhing under the intense gaze of Old Sol. On the 17th, the Winnifred district experienced the worst dust storm in years.[25]

The next year continued dry and windy, with depressing sand storms and soil drifting, particularly around Bow Island.[26] The summer was again roasting hot, but this time without the benefit of spring moisture. One Winnifred farmer claimed in mid-July—"If it rained a lifetime some fields would not thresh a bushel."[27]

That year hail damaged more than thirty thousand acres of grain in southwestern Saskatchewan. At Scotsguard, fifty-four farmers lost 100 percent of their crop in the worst hammering in history.[28] Hail fell in the Lucky Strike area south of Foremost, Alberta, too, and was accompanied by rain so torrential that it ran off the land as if it were a table top. Crops remained so thin, short, and burnt that the general merchant told Cora Hind of the *Free Press Prairie Farmer* that conditions were the worst in sixteen years. For twenty-five miles north and east, all the way to Foremost, there was not a single good crop.[29] It was no different right to the Goose Lake line between Hanna and Oyen. Not surprisingly, when S. E. Greenway inspected that area, known as the "golden wheat line," he estimated that 80 percent of the homes had been abandoned.[30]

All across the south there were tearful farewells. The final evenings were often passed in music, piano and song solos. The friends played games, whist and bridge, they laughed at local wits, they danced to local orchestras, and they sang songs like, "God Be With You Till We Meet Again." They gave gifts that none could afford, and walked home in a sorrow that none ever forgot, weeping, sobbing, shaking their heads.

It was remarkable how often the men of God were present at the parting. Because the occasion was invariably moving and deeply spiritual, it seemed appropriate that a man of the cloth should at least appear and at best preside. It was a recognition of one of the pre-eminent joys in life, the sanctity of fellowship and the inherent richness in loving others, revealed so poignantly at the moment of separation. When the priests themselves were departing, the celebration was exalted, lambent with good will and reverence for the stewardship that was passing to other shoulders, or if no one else was coming, to the community yet abiding.[31]

When Reverend and Mrs. W. J. Rayner left Winnifred in the ghastly fall of 1924, the community celebrated their memorable service with the young folks, the CGIT, the Tuxis, and the Trail Rangers. Playing games and eating apple pies with their grateful hosts, the Rayners were presented with a beautiful cut-glass salad bowl. Reverend Rayner replied in the gentle manner the congregation had come to know, and Mrs. Rayner followed, close to tears.

"The gathering was the brightest affair ever held in Winnifred," wrote the correspondent, deeply touched.[32]

At Retlaw, a farewell party was held in the Bardin Hall, over-flowing into the adjoining vacant store, for Dr. and Mrs. M. Bardin. At midnight they were given a valuable cabinet of community silver. After more dancing and games, all parted with "Auld Lang Syne."[33]

Over and over it was the same. The numbers in this great sorrow were hard to take in. The Saskatchewan side was not subjected to the continued scrutiny and vivisection accorded southeastern Alberta, but losses there were still severe. In census divisions 4 and 8, 190 townships comprising 4.37 million acres, or 40 percent of the total land area of the divisions, lost at least 10 percent of their population between 1921 and 1926; 102 townships lost at least 25 percent; 62 lost at least 35 percent; and 14 lost between 65 percent and 100 percent.[34] The burnt-out areas were concentrated along the Alberta border and in the triangle with Swift Current at the apex and one line to the entry point of the South Saskatchewan River into the province and the other to the Montana-Alberta border.

Despite this drought pyramid, the total population in the two census divisions remained very nearly the same, one up, the other down, reflecting actual increases in more favored sub-divisions and in villages such as Admiral, Cadillac, Consul, Abbey, Pennant and Success.[35]

In Alberta, the losses were many times worse. Census divisions 1, 3 and 5 lost 16,798 souls between 1921 and 1926. Even this 21 percent depletion obscured much heavier exodus in the worst hit townships. Almost all the emptying occurred in about half the townships. Two hundred and sixty-eight townships, or 42 percent of the total, comprising well over six million acres, lost at least 35 percent of their people; 138 lost at least 55 percent; 48 lost between 75 percent and 100 percent.[36]

Still these figures underestimated the total evacuation from the height of population, likely in 1918 or 1919, to the depths of 1926. Two studies of the huge Tilley East region between the Red Deer

Nels Anderson "harvesting" near Alderson not long before he left, 1920. NA 4791-1, Glenbow-Alberta Archives.

and South Saskatchewan Rivers, from Tilley to the Saskatchewan border, provided such a measure. Township by township B. Russell and W. H. Snelson, minions of the Interior Department, surveyed in late 1924, disclosing that of 2,386 resident farmers not counting their families, only 645 remained.[37] The Alberta Tilley East commission, headed by the workhorse E. J. Fream, estimated in early 1926 that considerably fewer than 500 were left—indicating a population loss of over 80 percent across an area of over 1.5 million acres.[38]

What was striking about the exodus was that in so many cases it seemed directionless. A. K. Buckham, grazing supervisor, was one who saw it, and he could never drive from his mind the thought that *these people do not know where to go*. One meets [them] on the roads anywhere South of the Lacombe-Kerrobert line to the Milk River at the line. They are on the move." One caravan was rolling from Gull Lake, Saskatchewan, to Kamloops, B.C., where conditions were every bit as bad; another was moving from Iddesleigh to the alkaline blimp, Lake Sullivan. They had no conception of the breadth of the disaster; they did not realize that one could drive for days in any direction from the heart of it, and never reach the periphery.[39] They had no guides, no locators. Even when they had detrained for the first time in the land of Cain, they at least had locators. Some of the more deliberate had searched out a harbor, but the effort often did not pay. Matt O'Reilly of Sunnynook reported that many from his area had travelled the north from Edmonton to Prince Albert, searching.[40] But most were paupers and had nothing for a down payment, even when they found something to their liking.

Whether departing settlers knew where they were going, or got what they wanted, they still left, and patterns slowly emerged showing the direction of their flight. A group of drylanders from near Vauxhall moved to forty acre stump farms in Washington state.[41] Several from the Alderson area, including Nels Anderson, moved to irrigated farms at Tilley or Brooks.[42] A coterie of Dutchmen from the New Holland district north of Alderson went to Crossfield and Monarch, and R. S. Tribe from the nearby Tide Lake area moved first to Ogden then Olds.[43] Settlers from Lucky Strike were attracted to the Carrot River Valley in Saskatchewan.[44] During the evacuation of late summer and fall 1924, the Cardston district received two hundred settlers.[45] Further north, the Stavely, Claresholm, Champion and Cayley areas greeted many of the same people who had trekked out from those areas in 1909–11. Northwest of Edmonton, Westlock was a favored target. Several from the Jenner-Tide Lake-Berry Creek area moved to Viking.[46] Most, however, slunk back into the States from whence they had come. In the five years after 1921, the American-born population in the Alberta dry belt declined from just under 20,000 to 11,500.[47]

Judas and the Sheepmen   FOR THOSE WHOSE taste for the desert was not sated, there was a process of adaptation to the aridity and the expanding emptiness. The sea of desiccation provided extensive grazing, as always. With vacant lands at every point of the compass, the slowly revolving empire would soon come full circle, and the stockmen would take the land they thought was theirs in the first place.

The federal Department of the Interior gave up on farming in the region just after most settlers and somewhat before the province of Alberta. The victory of the federal Liberals in late 1921 reversed a move initiated by former Minister of the Interior James Lougheed, a reincarnation of Frank Oliver, bent on liquidating the remaining cattle leases in the region.[48]

The ranchmen sang the praises of W. W. Cory, the deputy minister of the Interior and thanked him profusely for his hand during the crisis.[49] Cory had two reasons for siding with them—he'd had his fill of tearful tillers from the area, and he wished for the sake of his job to show his new chieftain, Minister of the Interior Charles Stewart, how quickly he could support a new policy diametrically opposed to the last one. Before long, several lackeys under Cory condemned the dry farmer as a waster of "time and energy . . . not an asset to the country [but] a liability." "As long as he continues somebody must pay the loss," growled one creature of the Irrigation branch. "The sooner it is realized he is a failure and cannot continue the better the country will be."[50] Helping these flounderers remain, wrote J. S. Tempest, commissioner of Irrigation, would only be throwing "good money after bad." A fortune in development costs had blown away, and ranching was the only way out.[51]

It was partly this total rejection of dry belt farming, especially in the Tilley East area, that made the Interior Department so listless during the catastrophe. Since most of the lands were no longer owned by the Dominion, following the clever campaign of the Interior Department and others in settling them, Cory and company preferred to wash their hands of the whole regrettable mess. Accordingly, the Department sat on the disaster for years, like a chicken sitting on a nest of broken eggs. Its basic virtue was patience—it would wait for Alberta to do something; it would wait for more reports that should have been done a generation earlier; it would wait for negotiations over the transfer of natural resources to the provinces to end; and then the waiting would be over, and Alberta could handle it.[52]

Often the object of settlers' scorn—UFA Minister of Agriculture George Hoadley. A 2704, Provincial Archives of Alberta.

In the end, the "empire" was even better suited to sheep than cattle. Mrs. John Parkkari, senior and junior, near Alderson, 1928 c. NA 2083-26, Glenbow-Alberta Archives.

UFA Agriculture Minister George Hoadley saw the game, and at times it bothered him more than the disaster. "If they wish to turn over the whole responsibility to us," he told Premier Brownlee, "we must make them put themselves on record so that the public will know that they are trying to escape the responsibility of solving the Dry Area Problem."[53] The hoped-for confession would have another benefit which Hoadley could not bring himself to mention—it would show the public that there was a problem, a fact he himself had earlier denied. Needless to say, wait as he might, the confession was not forthcoming.

While Hoadley drummed his fingers, the ruins of Nineveh fell into the laps of stockmen, who to a remarkable degree, were not the old cattlemen, but sheepmen. On the driest tracts of the firmament, in the Tilley East country, there had been enormous sheep ranches for many years. In 1919 there were 85,000 woolies in the vicinity of Alderson, some 35,000 on the Taylor spread and 22,000 on the Knight and Watson operations alone. In the shearing season that summer, 1,400 animals were being clipped daily.[54] Ten years later, wool shipments from Alderson amounted to 160,000 pounds; in 1930, 200,000 pounds.[55]

From the big-time operations many dejected tillers got their start. When twin lambs were born, the ewes could not look after both in the large herds on the open prairie; consequently, one of them, called appropriately the "bum lamb," was given to anyone who would take it.

Farmers soon came to realize that there were several advantages to sheep over cattle. Sheep could stand much more cold, and they could paw through the snow for forage. Cattle would eat young Russian thistle, but sheep actually thrived on it. Cattle had little taste for sage, but sheep loved all varieties of it. Sheep survived better on sparse pasture, and normally six to eight could run in place of a single cow. And sheep provided two crops—lambs and wool.

One family that understood these things and shifted from farming to combined farming-sheep ranching was the Gleddies. Christopher Gleddie had come from Arendal, Norway, had married Magda Evenson of the same place and had moved to Washburn, Wisconsin, to an eight acre stump farm. In time he grew tired of dynamiting pine stumps, grubbing them out by hand and burning them. The winters were heavy and long, with so much snowfall that the livestock had to be fed in the barns till May. When Gleddie heard of free homesteads in Canada where winters were said to be mild and there were no stumps, he leapt at the chance. Travelling by train to Langevin, he filed on a homestead near the new town of Carlstadt.

Next spring, in 1910, he shipped his effects west. When he unloaded the cargo in that mad, first season for so many, the locals, if they could be called that, for they had scarcely more experience in the promised land than he, were bemused that he should bring bobsleds and storm windows to a land where snow melted as it alighted and where nature's furnaces crackled through wintertide.

Arriving before Chris had finished the new house, Magda and her three boys were temporarily settled in a nearby shack. From the moment of detraining, Magda seemed queasy, out of sorts, and soon she grew ill. When Doc Mason was unable to relieve her, Chris sent to the Hat for a doctor who speedily recognized the grim symptoms of diphtheria. It was already too late for treatment. As the life force in her ebbed, she asked to be moved to the partially finished new house, and in her first night there she died.

In the days of strict quarantines, the medical health officer directed that the burial take place the same day. A. S. Lockrem, a neighbor, fashioned a coffin of pine, but the officer would not even permit him to go to town to buy black cloth to drape over it. Other friends dug a grave, and during the solemn service newcomers, jolted from the ecstasy of possessing the new land, watched from nearby knolls. The first thing son Stein remembered was playing on the grave as if it were a sand pile.

In the fiery summer of 1918, the family cut two or three hay racks of upland hay from west of Alderson and stacked the barn to the rafters. A year to the day before the great conflagration in Alderson, a spectacular electrical storm ignited the barn. Chris plunged into the lightning-lit night in his bed clothes and released six of the horses tied in the stable. Out they tore in terror, their manes afire. One was so terribly burnt it had to be shot. As the barn went up, Chris, deeply religious, stood back and quoted Job—"The Lord giveth and the Lord taketh away. Blessed be the name of the Lord."[56]

In autumn 1920, Gleddie went into sheep ranching. He bought one hundred old sheep for $3 each, and the herd gradually multiplied. By the thirties, the family operations included four thousand ewes and one hundred rams spread over three abandoned townships.[57]

Year after year these sheepmen went through an amazing cycle which has all but disappeared. Two of three winters the woolies would stay out for the duration, in flocks of perhaps 1,400 tended by a herder. On May first, the sheepmen built a headquarters including a big shed 40 x 100 feet, housing 100–120 pens. Lambing occurred all through May but especially in the first two weeks. As

Docking tails, earmarking females and castrating males—the Gleddie spread, Stein and Christopher on left, 1940 c. PA-2987-2, Glenbow-Alberta Archives

the ewes gave birth near the shed, the lambs born at night were picked up by a watchman and brought along with the ewes to the pens. At 5:30 to 6:00 A.M. a shedman appeared to make sure the lambs were all sucking. If one had died, the sheepmen would skin it "cased," peeling it off like a glove, which they would then pull over a twin born to some other ewe. The mother of the deceased lamb would then receive the bogus offspring, smelling remarkably like her own flesh and blood. The ruse invariably worked, and after three days of nursing and lying with his stepmother, the young one would absorb enough of the proper scent that the skin of the legitimate, but dead, heir could be removed.

Lambs born in the day were placed with their mothers in pens on lamb wagons. Then they were set in shelters, housing about forty mothers and forty lambs, limited enough to ensure proper bonding.

The next big moment in the cycle was clipping—between about

June 20 and July 7. For this season the Gleddies tried to get at least ten shearers. The wool was packed in 350–400 pound bags and shipped for anything between 50¢ a pound to 4½¢. In the next two weeks the sheep were dipped to rid them of ticks and other vermin. Then they ran at large until October 1, when the lambs were cut from the flock, the best of the ewe lambs were kept, and the rest were shipped to Calgary.

The star of the operations was "Judas," the wether, a castrated lamb, who for a handful of oats would betray his own mother. Judas had a bell, and he would lead the others to the clippers, the dipping vat, and in the epitome of duplicity, to the slaughter, by starting the procession of trusting dolts up the ramp into double-decked boxcars in which they were conveyed to abattoirs. Wherever Judas went, the flock was sure to follow. It would appear that the only thing that could blunt the wether's avidity for the double-cross was filthy tobacco. Perverse sheepmen would sometimes slip him a plug, which disturbed the cold callousness of his Quisling mind and made him quite stupid.[58]

Settlers might have wished for a similar effect of a handful of snoose on the bellwethers that had led *them* into the land of Cain.

Special Areas and
Serpents

YEARS PASSED, and somehow the Gleddies always survived. Yet in the late thirties even they were forced to leave Alderson. By the time they slipped into Tilley to occupy the old CPR experimental farm, they had witnessed nearly twenty years of virtually uninterrupted evacuation. For most of the Alberta dry areas, as the twenties became the thirties, there was little sense of transition.

In spring 1933, David Elton, veteran of southern Alberta, addressed the Oddfellows at Bow Island. He said he did not fancy the word "depression," but instead called the boom the "smallest [he] ever saw."[59] In truth, what he had seen the decade before was the smallest.

Long before the Great Depression, most of the damage had been done. Farm abandonment would never be as severe as it had been in 1926. That year there were 10,400 vacant or abandoned farms comprising 2,337,715 acres—the dry areas accounting for over 62 percent of the former and almost 70 percent of the latter.[60] In 1931 there were 3,760 fewer abandonments in the province as a whole, and 3,221 fewer in the dry areas. Even by 1936, in the depths of the Depression, there were 1,102 fewer abandonments in Alberta, covering a quarter million acres less than in 1926, and in the dry areas there were 1,849 fewer abandonments embracing 375,400 fewer acres than in 1926.[61]

There are other ways to measure the Alberta calamity of the twenties. One is by standing it against the legendary evacuation of Southern Saskatchewan in the next decade. With roughly twice as many operating farms in Saskatchewan in 1936 as in Alberta in 1926, the latter had very nearly as many abandonments. In fact, the three Alberta dry belt census divisions had more abandonments in 1926 than the *five* most heavily vacated Saskatchewan census divisions in 1936.[62]

In all southern census divisions in Saskatchewan the population peaked in 1931, or possibly a year or so before, and was followed by a horrific decline by 1936. In 1931 the population of all four census divisions running across the southern tier of the province from Alberta to Manitoba, on a line just south of Swift Current and Moose Jaw, was 159,382. By 1936 this immense region had lost 14,743 persons.[63] The three Alberta dry belt census divisions, on the other hand, comprising 81,787 people at the peak in 1921, had lost 16,798 people by 1926. Thus, the Alberta region in the twenties, with three-quarters the area and half the population of its Saskatchewan counterpart in the thirties, lost two thousand more people.[64]

For two-thirds of the Alberta dry belt, the high tide of disaster occurred during the so-called "roaring twenties," a fact demanding much rethinking of the nature of that decade in the West. In the entire region from a few miles east of Lethbridge to Saskatchewan, and from the Red Deer River south to Montana, there were over *four times* the number of vacant or abandoned farms in 1926 as in 1936.[65]

Only in the other third, the most northerly portion of the strange heartland, the province between the southern shores of brackish Lake Sullivan, north of Hanna, and the Red Deer River to the south, would conditions in the thirties be somewhat worse than those in the twenties. Even for this precinct, abandonment in 1926 exceeded that in 1931, and the population loss for 1921–1926 exceeded that for the 1926–1936 period. But by 1936 this census division alone would have over 3,700 abandonments, two and a half times that in the worst pummelled census division in all Saskatchewan.[66]

This greater intensity of the problem over a longer period and a more compact area is the best explanation of the creation of the special areas in Alberta and not Saskatchewan. The first two special areas were erected in the Tilley East and the Berry Creek areas. The former, comprising nearly 2,500 square miles, was created in 1927 and placed under a special provincial board in September 1929, followed by the latter, embracing nearly 2,000 square miles in May 1932. Immediately, the boards began to implement the final solution—the securing of control of as much land in the region as possible. The means to this end included trading other real estate beyond the arid zone for mortgage company properties in the zone, and confiscation through tax recovery proceedings. In Berry Creek at the 1933 tax sale alone, some nine hundred parcels of land tumbled into the board's hands.[67] By 1935 the province controlled 80 percent of the lands in Tilley East and 70 percent in Berry Creek. As the settlers fled—3,785 people and 6,600 carloads were moved courtesy of the railroads, the province and the Dominion by March 1935—the boards were able to provide hundreds of thousands of acres for private and community grazing. The object was to convert the area into large scale, self-sufficient ranching-farming concerns.[68]

The first two special areas led to others only slightly better off—the Sullivan Lake, Neutral Hills, and Sounding Creek areas erected in 1935, and the Bow West area, in 1937. The initial commitment to curtain off these no-man's-lands was made before the

Prairie Farm Rehabilitation Administration began its fight to save much of Palliser's Triangle from an eternal dustbowl. In that struggle, memorialized by James Gray, a new breed of agricultural experts emerged, their feet more on the ground, their hearts more in the communities they served, their minds more appreciative of the powers of nature, than the circle of pundits who had announced to the world the readiness of the land for the plow. The new men included Gordon Taggart, E. S. Archibald, George Spence, L. E. Kirk, L. B. Thomson, "Ace" Palmer, and others. In large measure, their hopes were founded upon the lessons from southern Alberta and southwestern Saskatchewan in the twenties. What they accomplished with regrassing, dugouts, community pastures, new equipment, new grasshopper poison, strip farming, trash farming, and resettlement was remarkable. They even made inroads later on the drylands through the St. Mary's and South Saskatchewan Irrigation projects.[69] But that said, it should be remembered that they did not save the vile heart of the desert, nor could they in a century, without the elixir of more irrigation water than they had ever seen.

In 1940, a major study of the eight million acres consigned to the oblivion of the special areas disclosed that 80 percent of the total region contained not marginal but submarginal, brown soil. In the Tilley East area, the figure was over 88 percent; in the Berry Creek area, over 94 percent. From Alderson eighteen miles south to the South Saskatchewan, thirty-one miles east to the same river as it flows north, to ten miles north, there was not a speck of land classed better than submarginal. The same was true of the Berry Creek region. From north of Pollockville, twenty miles south to the Red Deer River, eighteen miles west to the Red Deer as it flows south, to thirty-six miles east, there were less than three sections classed as good as marginal.

As the authors explained, "submarginal" implied that "even if the land were secured without payment for its use, the returns which would be secured would be insufficient to induce the farmer to farm the land permanently." The authors added, "The conclusion that so large a part of the territory must be considered as suitable only for grazing will not surprise those familiar with this part of the province."[70] Without doubt, however, it would have surprised, even shocked the likes of W. R. Motherwell, Angus MacKay and H. W. Campbell, when at the height of the ebullient settlement period the empire of dust was thrown open.

The conclusion, of course, was too critical, too condemning; some deemed the empire hardly so unyielding, so fruitless. In the fall of 1934, a Chinese merchant in Lloydminster trundled home from the station a strange trunk filled with mysterious ingredients for the treatment of rheumatism in his countrymen. Dutifully gathered at Hilda to the south, the cargo comprised a tangle of two hundred live, snapping rattlesnakes.[71]

12   To Him That Overcometh

Charlotte Cotter and the Clique

IT WAS SUNDAY, May 12, 1929, at St. Mary's Anglican Church, Alderson. Many oldtimers were there, most of the remaining war vets of the district, called by Charlotte Cotter's repeated announcements through her contacts at the Post Office and her columns in the Hat *News,* heralding an important ceremony. The service was long in coming and would long be remembered. Mr. and Mrs. A. C. Wagner had motored down from Calgary and had brought with them a precious gift—a memorial tablet of Gothic form and Italian marble, with golden lettering and oaken base. It was to honor A. C.'s brother, Harry, slain at the Somme in 1916.

Preaching from Revelations 3-21, Reverend J. Laurie Cooper reminded the hushed and attentive listeners—"To him that overcometh will I grant to sit with me on my throne, even as I overcame and am set down with my Father on his Throne." The altar was banked with snap dragons, carnations and sweet peas, and near the tablet was a bouquet of pink roses, the gift of Harry's widow, then in Vancouver. Draped over the tablet was the Union Jack. When the unveiling was over, the congregation stood and sang lustily a verse of the national anthem.[1]

The last of the decade had been a time of memories for others too. One summer day, ten months earlier, none other than the tall figure of Charles England, the original promoter and first mayor of Carlstadt, hopped off the train, bringing greetings from his current home in Vashon, Washington. Then he snapped a few shots of his old hometown, and his heart must have sunk at what he saw.[2] It was the same feeling everyone had on visiting towns and villages in the southeast after missing the previous fifteen years. The manager of the Cooper Brothers' Circus was utterly shocked at the deterioration of Bow Island in the summer of 1927 after he had seen the new town in 1912 busting at the seams.[3]

Near the time of the great stock market crash, Chester McCorkle Coffey, perhaps the greatest photographer of the settlement of the dry areas, appeared in Alderson. Staying a few days with the Cotters who still made some effort to farm his original homestead north of town, Coffey was now an eminent photographer in his pre-Carlstadt stamping ground of Oregon. He had left Alderson in 1916 after his fill of the frigid offerings of the weather factory and had gratefully missed the ensuing decade of drought, save for the occasional visit.[4] He was in town taking photographs for the movies.

What became of his artistry this time is unknown, but he himself probably discovered the fate of his years of earlier work. Some seasons before, young Franklin Cole, son of pioneers Al and Kate Cole, had chanced upon the old Coffey place in the company of spirited cronies. They discovered piles of Coffey's precious glass negatives which had recorded every aspect of the habitation and growth of Carlstadt and of the merciless heart of the Tilley East country. At first, they picked up the strange plates gingerly, remarking a moment on the images of the past when their hometown looked new and filled with people and stores which they faintly remembered or could not quite recall. Then a bedevilment came into them. Their eyes rolling, they turned into imps and smashed the legacy to smithereens.[5]

By 1925 the town of Alderson began the last fifteen or so years of its fleeting existence, a shadow of its former self. Business was at a standstill. Even the forebearing Martin Stubbs, owner of the once proud Carlstadt Hotel, renamed the Alberta Hotel, had had enough. In the past eight years the establishment had been opened and closed like shutters blowing in the wind. One day in the terrible year of '24 he had the hotel sectioned and hauled to Gleichen. (In a similar manner, the elegant Alamo of nearby Suffield was carted to Sylvan Lake.)[6] Three or four blocks away from the crater the inn had left, the Union Bank was barely hanging on, its longtime manager O. J. Wood gone since 1921, delinquencies and irrecoverable debts mounting like distant thunder. Where four spanking new elevators and a feed mill stood west of the station in 1917, there was not a board by the mid-twenties.[7]

From the beginning of the decade and increasingly thereafter, the governance of the village fell, partly by default, into the hands of a closely knit clique. From 1922 to 1929 Howard Burton Brigham was the secretary-treasurer of the village before becoming a regular councillor in 1930 and reeve in 1931. Born in Athens, Pennsylvania, in 1879, he had served with the U.S. army in the Philippines before coming to Carlstadt in 1909. He was a barber, notary public, village auditor, secretary-treasurer of several outlying school districts and of the village school, an active church member, a general store owner, and a mean chorder on the piano at local dances.[8]

A kind and capable man, Brigham had once played semi-professional baseball, a fact which probably occasioned a parody of "Casey at the Bat" written in the early days by Charles England, featuring not Casey but "Bert" Brigham. But the fact was that Brigham had respiratory ills, some thought consumption, with his thinness and coughing, but it was really emphysema. His son, Howard Jr., recalled vividly how his father looked forward to the mystifying medicinal packages from a Chinese herbalist in Seattle.

Emphysemic Bert Brigham and family, mid-1920s. NA 4777-22, Glenbow-Alberta Archives.

The packages contained weird cigarettes which exuded the most dreadful exhalation but which somehow soothed his frequent, violent coughing spells. Sometimes Brigham would swoon from the heaving, and his wife Grace, her face screwed up in disgust, would have to light the stinking balm and waft the smoke toward him. From the same herbalist, he also procured therapeutic black balls covered in white wax, which were peeled and dropped in hot tea.[9]

Brigham's first wife had died of bronchial pneumonia in the winter of 1918, and he had married Grace, a pretty and adept miss who worked in the bank and served for a time on the village council.[10] Despite his growing malady which aged him twenty years in the next five, Brigham fathered four children.[11] He was an excellent conversationalist, and his store was the typical country meeting place for all folk. With its big Coleman lamp, it attracted the gadabouts, the town gossips, the tale-mongering sheepmen, and the odd bonafide customer.[12]

Al Cole was another oldtimer who had worn many hats. In the early days, he operated a livery, was a locator, village constable and pound keeper.[13] From 1922 to 1936 he served on the village council, several times as reeve, and he sat on the school board, seemingly for decades. He had a well in town which the council regularly rented for years, even after it had been condemned in 1920.[14] He did odd jobs hauling coal or water, taxiing people around, and census taking. An avid hunter, he ferried nimrods in his touring car through the wastes to the haunts of ducks and geese at Twelve Mile Coulee. For dry-throated libertines it was said that he could produce a bottle of spirits in any emergency.

His wife Kate was a model of class-conscious England in whose veins coursed noble blood, the result of the illicit union of a lord and his maid, her grandparents. A domestic science teacher, Kate first came to Canada to look after her brother.[15] She swore that she would never return to the homeland unless attired in finery similar to that which adorned her on emigrating.[16] The considerable returns from the season of 1911 allowed her the wish, and passage was booked, with the return trip scheduled in April on a new liner, the Titanic. Fickle fate then intervened in the guise of an unruly stallion—which kicked Al in the ribs, broke some and forced cancellation of the voyage.[17]

Frank Steed was another who presided over the fall of Alderson. Born in Indiana, he took a course at the Marion Business College and was later trained as a telegrapher. Like others of the compact, he had arrived in the exciting early days of settlement, and had long experience in local governance. From 1917 to 1920, he had the distinction of being reeve of King municipal district northwest of Alderson, without doubt the worst hit municipality in all the West in all the hard times of both the twenties and thirties. Trustee of the Alderson school district for years, he was also once secretary of the farcically named Rainy Valley school district. He was a village councillor off and on after 1923, and secretary-treasurer after 1930. An agent for Massey Harris and Imperial Oil, he ran a service station and general store.[18]

Steed had chewed tobacco back east. When he heard that spitting was frowned on out west, he promptly stopped and took up smoking, priding himself for years in making the "difficult" transition. When he and his attractive young wife left Indiana, he brought with him a most unusual memento. He had been working at a steel rolling mill in Red Key, Indiana, one day in 1904, chopping steel, when he spied a young flunkey flouting safety regulations. Dropping his gloves, he delivered an animated tongue lashing to the scatterbrain. Retrieving his gloves, he reached out, and the chopper took off his little finger and most of the next. After a doctor sewed up the ends, he appeared in tears before his shocked wife, one hand in a bandage and the other bearing the severed fingers. He put the digits in a clear ink bottle, filled it with alcohol, and took the collection west. Always the "things" were at his writing desk. Twenty years after the accident, the shrunken appendages, nails and all, fascinated his daughter Hazel who would twirl them around in the bottle as a pleasant pastime.[19] When Steed sold out in 1929, intending to head south, his wife Nellie put her foot down and refused to repatriate the fingers. In a private ceremony, Frank thereupon buried them on the homestead.[20]

After a whirlwind tour of the States, Steed's roaming spirit subsided. Less than a year later, he returned to the desolate but familiar surroundings of home, repurchased his old business and resumed his role in the administration of a precinct of the mouldering empire.[21]

Easily the most intriguing of the old guard still in town were the Cotters. Wemyss M. Cotter was the son of James Cotter, chief factor of the Hudson's Bay Company, Moose Factory, James Bay.[22] A former employee of the Bay himself and a manager of the Merchant's Bank in Barrie, Ontario, Wemyss and Dr. R. H. Mason, his wife's brother, had arrived in Carlstadt in May 1909. Playing an important part in the town's history, Cotter had been reeve at the time of the great fire in 1914, justice of the peace, official auditor for King municipality, as well as councillor, school trustee and rector warden of the Anglican Church for several years.[23]

Cotter's spouse Charlotte, who had arrived in September 1909, was the daughter of the late George John Mason, senior official of

Postmistress Charlotte Cotter in her garden, 1915. NA 4777-4, Glenbow-Alberta Archives.

the Post Office Department and was related to the late Justice Harrison. Her family were early pioneers of Toronto.[24] Well-educated and an accomplished musician (she played the organ at St. Mary's until 1935), Charlotte represented the upper crust of town life, the polite and cultured element which included at various times the Wagners, the Swanbys, the Coles, the Scollards, the Starrs, the Macmorrises, and others, most of whom participated in the elite "400 Social Club" almost until there was no social life left. Of medium height, very slim with attractive hair and curled bangs, she had a petite, rather long face, thin but not unattractive either in early adulthood or old age. She did not regularly keep up with the styles, but she invariably dressed well, and she always stood out in a crowd. By the twenties she had bad teeth, and at least to some, bad breath, but there was a neatness about her, a fancy for jewelry and paint when the occasion warranted, and penetrating eyes which some said were lovely and which all agreed took in much more than the average.

Like the Aries stereotype she resembled, born on March 31, Charlotte loved to be the centre of attraction and the animator of social events. Hating impediments, she was childless; it was even rumored through a seamstress in the know that she had induced her own miscarriages in the early years, a practice her brother Doc

Mason apparently detested. Unmindful, she craved tea parties and bridge and the company of social lions. Whenever chinooks melted the snow and the water froze into rinks, she and Wemyss would don skates and dazzle the locals with terpsichorean dervishes, twirls, figures, and stops.[25]

Charlotte was a bird fancier, and the movement of the winged community she observed in meticulous detail. In early fall she would notice when the wild canaries, thrushes, warblers and meadowlarks were lingering; in winter in the deepest freeze she would see a horned lark burrowing with its beak in the snow by the roadside; in summer she would witness the aerial display of predatory hawks, darting and diving after smaller winged prey. She applauded CPR agent George Jardine's hobby of releasing homing pigeons fresh off the train for a return flight to Calgary. She kept fancy pigeons herself, shielding them with all the possessiveness of a mother. She also appointed herself guardian of the town's Hungarian Partridges against the wiles of youthful slingshooters. The birds, for their part, seemed to sense her comforting spirit. Once a homing pigeon moved in with her fancy birds. Another time a wild duck, thirst-crazed and near exhaustion, waddled into her yard, seemingly instinctively going to her for relief from the heat and the dust.[26]

The couple's affinity for birds marked them as somewhat peculiar. Their house behind the post office on Railway Avenue was ever a source of mystery to the local ragamuffins who were never permitted entrance. The tiny place was a miniature museum with stuffed animals, much silverware, ornaments and crystal. There were several trunks, rarely if ever opened since the day they had arrived in Carlstadt, jammed with precious relics from the past. It was little wonder that children were never welcomed. Some lively lads considered themselves lucky to get into the post office, though, like Jimmy Sharp they were invariably turfed out if they delayed their exit even a moment to eye the numerous posters in the vestibule.[27] A few kindly photographs survive with children in the apparently loving arms of the Cotters, but the depictions were staged and belied the true relationship between these natural adversaries.

St. Mary's Anglican Church,
Alderson, 1915 c. NA 4777-25,
Glenbow-Alberta Archives.

A common gathering—bidding
a friend farewell at Alderson
station, 1917 c. Charlotte
Cotter, centre. NA 4777-15,
Glenbow-Alberta Archives.

Alderson buildings were either
wrecked for lumber or carted
across the plains. George
Conley heading to Scandia,
early 1920s. NA 4711-15,
Glenbow-Alberta Archives.

At Halloween, the Cotter residence was the favorite target of local hellions. Evidently Wemyss felt so afflicted by the spiteful ghouls, that he once drove great stakes into the ground and spiked them to the four corners of the outhouse. Thus fortified, the throne could withstand the onslaught of a locomotive. Another year, Wemyss apparently moved the edifice, and the pit of perdition, draped aptly with funereal black tar paper, gulled the tricksters and swallowed some up in the darkness, the stench, and the ooze.[28]

Despite the Cotters' aversion to children, no one knew more about the people of the entire district than Charlotte. She resolutely denied reading everyone's postcards in the mail room, but she probably could not help herself more than once. There were two other reasons why she knew the inhabitants better than anyone else—she was the registrar of vital statistics for the entire sub-region of the dry belt, a role which put her finger on the pulse of the community, recording its births, marriages and deaths, and investing her probing with an official air; and for roughly three decades she gathered the despatches and local rumor and happenstance, and translated them into her remarkably informative column in the weekly *Medicine Hat News*.

All through the long years of dismantlement of the town, she reported the heartache and the separation without mincing words. She knew the fathers and the mothers, the sons and the daughters; she knew where they had come from and where they had gone; she knew when their families thrived and when loved ones were swept away. By the 1930s, her column was more of a diary than a news report, for by then the population had so changed and so diminished that it must have appeared to some at least that she was speaking of ghosts, known only to herself and the clique and scant others. She brooded over the diaspora like a mother hen whose eggs had rolled away into far and barely visible corners, out into the walk where some were trampled or ferreted away by dark influences. She coveted the letters of ex-Aldersonians who had sought a better life. She reported on the colonies of settlers that had rerooted themselves—in Minot, North Dakota, where a friend told of drought year after year and probably wondered why he had moved at all; or in western

or northern Alberta where several told of a cornucopia and mar-
velled at the flowing crystal water; or in the seeming paradise of
Santa Anna, California, where the roads were all paved and food
was cheap and oranges grew.[29]

All of Alderson's lost children Charlotte Cotter loved in her own
way, appreciating their civility in writing and reciprocating regularly. However much she loved attention herself, she could be exceedingly gracious and sympathetic when necessary. And she understood better than most the many things to lament.

Dissolution

IT SEEMED THAT the furies pursued
those of faint heart who left Alderson.
The J. H. Gast family had gone to Oak
Harbor, Washington, from the New
Holland district in fall 1923. One Sunday morning the next May,
Gast poured coal oil on a smouldering kitchen fire; it exploded, igniting his clothes and burning him horribly. As he writhed in terror, flames tore through the house, trapping his four children aged
thirteen, eleven, eight and five in the attic. Their charred remains
were found in the smoky ruins, and a week later, their father died of
the searing. His wife, who had tried to smother the flames on Gast,
was the sole survivor.[30]

A few weeks later, Marie Wood, eldest daughter of Mr. and Mrs.
Owen J. Wood, formerly of Alderson, went swimming in the Old
Man River near Macleod. Her father was known to everyone in
town as the manager of the Union Bank for ten years, extending
back to the heyday of the village. Her mother Gertrude had been a
lasting part of community life, especially with the women of the
Methodist Church. While the Woods had lived more comfortably
than most and had often visited outside the province, they too had
had their share of grief and close calls. In April 1919, when
Gertrude was eight months pregnant, they buried little Margaret,
aged one and a half years, victim of the flu. Earlier, near the end of
the boom, Marie, then two and a half years old, fell through the

cover of the backyard cistern in Carlstadt. Screaming, she tumbled into four feet of water at the bottom of a sixteen foot pit. Her aunt heard and came running, saw her terror-stricken form, flailing, floundering, submerging, and she plunged in, grasped the drowning tot, and held her above the surface until help came.[31] Unharmed, Marie lived to be an exceptionally bright child. Now in the stifling heat of 1924 ten years on, she and two girl friends resolved to swim across the Old Man River at the customs house.

One girl succeeded, but Marie and the other encountered difficulty. Their cries for help were answered by Thomas Mackintosh who immediately waded into the river and succeeded in bringing one lass to shore absolutely exhausted, before diving back in for Marie. She had gone down, and not until he dived several times could he catch her body and bring it to shore. A doctor was summoned, but it was too late.[32]

The treachery of the rivers. How placid they often appeared, pure as crystal, beckoning, clean, untainted. Yet how violent they could be and how often the evil spirits of the deep, like those of the land itself, could rise up and smite the interlopers. How often they sucked the settlers, their children and their animals down, luring them into the coolness, tempting them to cross. The rivers exacted an annual toll on lives, like a tax. Many other tributes in the area would never be remitted, but as long as there were people, this one would always be paid.

Several others who had escaped the desert were treated to similar hard fate. After C. E. Cole opened a general store in Carseland and H. R. Metz began business in Cayley, and Arthur Swanby, son of Thom Swanby, was at Madden for a time, all were visited by fire.[33] In mid-depression Charles Riddock of Calgary who had superintended the moving of Alderson houses was crushed between a motor and an eleven-ton boiler he was removing from the Cooperative Dairy Plant at Calgary.[34] Harry Thurston, former residents' son, with a wife near childbirth, died in Calgary after smashing his auto into a street car. When his father George came to the city to arrange the funeral, his car was stolen.[35]

In April 1935, Andrew John McKeller, aged thirty, son of a pioneer family north near Jenner, was working far from home at the Turkey Point Relief Camp, St. Thomas, Ontario. He was in love and about to wed. Riding from camp on his bike one spring evening, scant hours before the marriage, his mind in the future, he was hit by a car and killed. Authorities were uncertain of his identity—until they discovered on the corpse a receipt for an engagement ring.[36]

Back in town, even before spring 1926 workers were tearing out the wiring and the engine of the lighting system at the Union Bank.[37] About the same time other banks all over the dry areas—at Retlaw, Travers, Enchant, Etzikom, Sunnynook—sealed their doors, and their servants slunk away, deeply regretting their folly.[38] The buildings the banks retained, hoping for some purchaser who would relieve them of the last of their burdens. In Alderson such a buyer appeared three years later—the village council.

The Union Bank was one of the finest remaining structures in town, a two-storey brick edifice with basement, good furnace, six neat rooms upstairs which could serve as cloak rooms, card rooms and a kitchen for dances. On the ground level, there was a front and back entrance and an outstanding dance floor. In front there was a convenient vestibule and the manager's old office which provided a nice anteroom.[39]

All in all, the town was delighted with the acquisition, but it had been hurried by the announcement that John L. Scott was poised to wreck the old town hall for lumber, after one more dance. Lumber was at a premium, though one could never tell by the abysmal sales at the local yards. Harry Wagner's old firm, the Finlay Company, lurched through the mid-twenties near bankruptcy. The town had threatened seizures back in 1924 unless taxes were paid, and by summer 1927, led by Al Cole, it determined to carry out the threat, extending its target to the C. F. Starr lumber yards as well.[40]

One morning in mid-August before a large crowd, H. B. Brigham auctioned off the stock of the two lumber yards and a blacksmith shop. Included in the great bargains were a few household effects, a good office safe, and an automobile.[41] The town then purchased the scales from Finlay and placed them on the east side of Broadway as its own.[42] In January 1931, what remained of the Finlay adventure from the Hat was bought, all buildings save the office were wrecked, and everything was carted to Tilley.[43]

On the eve of the town's final descent into hell, Sir Edwin Alfred Herbert Alderson died in England on December 14, 1927. He had been commander of the first Canadian Division and later the Canadian Army Corps in the Great War. It was after him, at the suggestion of Charlotte Cotter, that the town was renamed in 1915.[44] Then after two good crops in 1927 and 1928, the first since 1916, the region began another decade of drought, infestations and dust storms, no worse than what it had already seen, but terrifying and dispiriting enough. By this time the remaining farmers had been heavily into sheep ranching and trapping since the early twenties. Even that did not save the hardy Dutch settlers of the New Holland district, north of Alderson, for most of them tramped out after the disaster of 1924.[45]

Amid this dilapidation, the village was beset from another quarter—the Department of Municipal Affairs. Its itinerating Inspector H. A. Kidney pored over the books of Alderson and Suffield in early summer 1927 and spewed back a venomous report to Edmonton recommending the prompt disorganization of both villages. He wrote with all the fury a man can muster when he needs not tell those he has just heaped in abuse what he has said. Damning secretary-treasurer H. B. Brigham as "grossly careless and inefficient," Kidney reported that the financial statement for 1926 clashed with the figures on the books, that the council had not met once in the first half of the year, that the assessment had not been done, and that the CPR lots in Alderson had "never been assessed for any purpose." Then he hung Al Cole's hide out to dry—"The Reeve is a worthless sort of individual with no property qualifications, and looked upon as the village character 'who has never worked and never will.'"[46]

The report was enough for Deputy Minister W. D. Spence who set upon following his subordinate's advice. There was one technicality—the municipality of Sunny South where the town was located, was also in process of dissolution. It did not seem wise to disorganize the village first, have it fall into the decrepit hands of the municipality, then dissolve the municipality and have the Department take it over. A delay would be necessary to orchestrate the simultaneous interment of the two jurisdictions.[47]

The other factor which held up the dissolution was the alacrity with which the somnolent council sprang into action after Kidney's visit. Just two days later, Brigham assessed the fifty-six lots still owned by the CPR. Almost instantaneously the railway filed notice of appeal on the grounds that the assessment was both excessive and illegal.[48] Puzzled, Brigham sought advice from the departmental tax specialists and discovered what an earlier secretary-treasurer had learned, what Kidney should have known and what he himself might have guessed had he known anything about the railway's dealings in the West—namely, that unsold and unimproved townsite lots along the mainline owned by the CPR were exempt from taxation for *twenty years* after the date of patent, March 17, 1910![49]

Embarrassed by Kidney's faulty instruction to Brigham and faintly impressed by the latter's response which included the raid on the lumber yards for back taxes, the Department laid low and played a waiting game. It may never have discovered or cared that Al Cole indeed owned property in town. When the CPR properties finally became assessable in 1930, the railway forked over the taxes. The temporary enrichment of the town coffers prolonged the council's life a few more seasons.

Undaunted, Kidney resumed his attack that year. He reported a similar state of affairs—little or no action taken under the Tax Recovery Act by the council, the sale of village property but no trace of titles, a rental agreement between Al Cole and the council to supply water from the former's well which had been condemned by the Department of Health and the absence of several parcels of land from the roll because the owners were unknown.[50] "It has always been a mystery to me," Kidney wrote another municipal inspector a year and a half later, "as to why this place should remain an organized village. It is the most God-forsaken place in the whole south country possibly with the exception of Seven Persons. There are no improvements made with any taxes that are collected and the only reason that I can see for the continuance of the organization is to provide funds to pay a 'secretary.'"[51]

In September 1932, Kidney reported that the CPR, the principal ratepayer, wished to relinquish ownership of its lots and had offered them to the village.[52] At the same moment, the railway's superintendent of townsites offered over eighty lots and ten acres in the townsite of Suffield, including "everything" to that village for $1.[53] It was not one of the brighter moments for the corporation, but at least it was spared the groveling the Canada Land and Irrigation Company had practised for years. Fifteen days into the decade of the thirties, an official of that colossal failure admitted sardonically—"This company were [sic] . . . over optimistic when laying out the [Suffield] townsite. It should have contained about 50 lots instead of 2,000."[54]

In such circumstances, there was little motivation to do anything. In further defense of the Alderson council, it may be said that it often agonized over the morality of tax sales which created more hardship for its citizens. It was one thing to offer for sale the property of those who had disappeared, but quite another to do the same for indigents still in town. Sometimes the council simply decided not to hold such sales. Most often, nothing was realized from them anyway. Of the 137 parcels listed in the tax sale of June 1, 1931, for example, only one property was sold.[55] Other times, the council sought to exempt faithful but departed servants of the town like F. E. McDiarmid, W. G. Scollard and V. E. Starr on condition that they agree to an extended payback of arrears, but these exceptions were the very sorts of irregularities the Department condemned.[56]

By April 1934, less than three years after the 1931 census had recorded eighty-one souls in the village, the council members, secretary and auditor and their families represented all the resident prop-

A time to rest—Frank Steed
and granddaughters, Alderson,
1943. PA 2647-2, Glenbow-
Alberta Archives.

erty holders in Alderson. There were four additional tenant families
in the village, three railroad families, two led by section foremen
and one by the caretaker of the station.[57] When two vacancies occurred on council in late 1935, there was no one left to fill the gap.
Frank Steed thereupon informed the Department of Municipal Affairs that the long beleaguered council at last acceded to self-
termination.[58] By Order-in-Council, signed by new Premier William Aberhart, the village of Alderson was dissolved on January 31,
1936.[59]

The King's Visit

THE ANNIHILATION OF the United Farmers a few months earlier recalled former Premier Greenfield's prophetic vow to save the dry areas or go under with them. For fourteen years the government had struggled, grasping at straws, before being claimed by the relentless undertow. As the beaten farm ministers and MLAs passed forever from the political stage, Perren Baker, run ragged in his fight to save the schools, mindful of the day he had been carried on the shoulders of jubilant electors so long ago, accepted his fate. Glancing at the shattered south and the enlarged family farm near Foremost run now by a son, he slipped more or less permanently into the happier surroundings of city life, first in Edmonton and later Vancouver.[60]

Baker and a few others were aware of the way the disaster had marked the developing Prairies, especially Alberta, for generations to come. The dry belt had been a strange heartland, and befitting a region of such import, as it had gone, so too had the province. In the beginning, the great new breadbasket wrought from the desert demanded transportation and communication services by the score. So many railroads were planned, surveyed and even built that when the history of projected prairie lines comes to be written it will find itself excessively preoccupied with this strange region. Likewise, the height of the settlement period in the West will always focus on the region. When it succumbed, it became a bitter heartland, not merely for the anguish and personal sacrifice it exacted, but also for the way it demanded all the attention and all the resources that an economic heartland might normally expect to draw—save in this case, instead of feeding the province, it drew the lifeblood from it.

So excruciating and so importunate was the catastrophe that responses to it became etched in the landscape and in the statutes, policies and governance that the era gave to the future. It forced abiding solutions to dry farming problems, if not for the worst of areas, for their periphery and much of southwestern Alberta; for the strange heartland itself, it riveted attention for decades on the only viable remedy—irrigation. It also necessitated the revolutionary measure of debt adjustment, an entirely new relationship between creditor and debtor in the province, aspects of which, like the impairment of the personal covenant in mortgages, endured to the present. Dethroning the one-roomed schools and the municipalities, it set the scene for the large school divisions and county government. So influential was the calamity that for those who ignored it, the origins of post-1940 Alberta would always be something of a puzzle.

As for the Tilley East region, it was nearly done. If the twenties had seen the removal of most of the farmers, the thirties finished the villages. The latter years were a wailful time of death and reminders of death for the citizens of Alderson. They were seasons when a generation which had been robust and vibrant and at the pinnacle of its powers in 1910 flowed very perceptibly to the end of its allotted time, like a freshet first gushing out into the sands, then, as if losing way, meandering, dissipating, slowing, and then sinking from sight.

In 1930 an old minion of the Lord Brassey who had held large estates in Alberta and Saskatchewan in the late 1800s, John Evans, proprietor of the Brassy Arms Hotel in 1911, died.[61] T. H. Harris, an early and prosperous merchant, passed away in Vancouver at age eighty-six.[62] Ed Sobie, who in the early days was jokingly said to serve in his restaurant everything from quail on toast to nightingales' tongues, died in Vancouver.[63] Mr. and Mrs. A. D. Thompson, he the Confederate veteran, died in Virginia.[64] W. G. Scollard, a man of many social gifts and a dear friend of the Cotters and Coles, expired of a stroke in Stettler.[65]

In June 1933, one of the ruling clique, ailing H. B. Brigham, his wife and four children, moved to Medicine Hat. Confined to bed most of the time, the emaciated ex-secretary literally wasted away. One Sunday, the following April, his son Howard Jr. went to Sunday School with the presentiment that the dreadfully ill eighty or ninety pound skeleton that was his father would die that day. When the lad returned, the undertaker was at the house.[66]

Almost at the same moment, the large Brigham store on Broadway was being wrecked and hauled to Tilley.[67] Three and a half years later, thieves broke into the reassembled store, blew the strong box and escaped with $830. The explosion set fire to the building which went up in smoke, torching other structures and very nearly consuming half of Tilley.[68]

On November 16, 1935, Wemyss M. Cotter, postmaster for twenty-six years, aged sixty-four, met the number one train and took an unusually heavy load of mail to the post office. Inside the door, he collapsed and died. From Tilley, Tide Lake, Jenner, Alderson, and Suffield, his many friends motored over heavy roads to the funeral in the Hat.[69] Badly shaken, Charlotte Cotter ceased her column for a time, visited her old friends, the O. J. Woods, formerly of the Union Bank in Alderson, now in Lethbridge, and began to reorient her life around the fashionable circle in the Hat.

Charlotte had not recovered before another loss occurred which to her was only slightly less traumatic—King George V died. "[He] is mourned as the centre of the loyalties of a great Empire," she wrote in tears, "but in this hour of universal sorrow, I think of him chiefly as my beloved master and friend. . . . He will live in history as a king who led his empire in dark days, but still more as a king who came closer than any other monarch to the hearts of his subjects." At the school, Miss Madge Gleddie, daughter of Chris and Gurine Gleddie, speedily orchestrated an impressive tribute to the fallen leader. Pupils participated in readings such as "He Feared God and Served the People," "Indians Mourn the Death of the Great White Chief," and "Reminiscences in the Life of King George." After two minutes of silence, the children sang "Abide With Me," a favorite hymn of the King's.[70]

No one ever forgot the trauma of the mid-thirties in Alderson, the sense of uprooting, loss of control and direction. "It strikes me that we are all in the same boat with Christopher Columbus," wrote Charlotte Cotter, reflecting a saying of the time. "He didn't know where he was going when he started; when he got there he didn't know where he was, and when he got back he didn't know where he had been."[71] About the only certainty Aldersonians had was the sensation that their town was sinking into the desert and that the world was passing them by. It seemed that every second week in 1934 a building was moved into burgeoning Tilley with its new stores, its elevators, its multiple gasoline pumps, its ripening grain and its network of life-giving irrigation canals.[72] Scollard's large store and residence went west that year, as did A. D. Thompson's butcher shop.[73]

And that spring and summer, as ten years before, the caravans of the dispossessed rolled through town. One train of seven covered wagons, advertising "Rimbey or Bust" and bearing three families from Bracken, Saskatchewan, lurched through in the first week of June. They had left on May 18, and expected to arrive in another four or five weeks. Saskatchewan, they said, was a virtual wilderness, blown-out, burnt-out, and swarming with hoppers.[74]

A week later, after four years of drought, there was a series of meetings among the farmers of the Jenner-Empress area at which a massive exodus was discussed. W. C. Smith, Empress MLA, explained that the only area he knew big enough to accommodate all who wanted to go was the Smoky River country. Rain fell in the next couple of days, and the farmers were duped for the umpteenth time into staying and trying it again.[75]

In the meantime, landmarks in the Tilley East area continued to disappear. In a way it was just as well. Seeking shelter from the cold, horses and cattle would get into the derelict buildings and sooner or later the rump of one would close the door, and the home would become a tomb. Several animals at once were sometimes trapped this way, and unless some passer-by released them, they starved to death.[76]

Fortunately, the better buildings, at least, moved quickly. In September 1936, a few years before the death of its former owner, the large three-storey house built by Thom Swanby was taken down and the lumber carted to Gleddie's ranch. When it was gone, it was as if some bethel had been torn away, for it had been the locus of much gaiety and fellowship. It was the place that so many settlers had stayed their first night, and the place of that first memorable Christmas in 1909. It brought memories of the time at the beginning when Thom Swanby and Matt Hostland first saw Tide Lake on a map. They loaded their fishing poles and gear onto a wagon and headed north to the vast slough which dried up almost every year and which was rarely over three feet deep. It was a big joke, and the locals never forgot it.[77]

Almost the same time that Swanby's house was moved, the elegant three-storey Lockrem house began its relentless roll toward Brooks. The wheels of three wagons were needed to support the edifice. Just before it was moved, looters visited the building and stole seven windows. It was this structure that a Medicine Hat real estate promoter had emblazoned on his letterhead in the early days.[78]

The American House, completely renovated only six years before, once a way station for illegitimately pregnant city girls waiting out their terms, was wrecked and moved to Tilley in 1937. In the early forties the United Church was carted to Rolling Hills. St. Mary's Anglican Church, the repeated beneficiary of the Wagner family in England which sought expressly to maintain the temple as a shrine for slain Harry, made the familiar trip to Tilley where it survived another forty years. Like ashes on a dry sea, the holy paraphernalia—the frontlets, liddels, altar cloths and altar vase, the lectern, the alms dish and the cross—were scattered amongst the neighboring Anglican sanctuaries from whence some had come as gifts half a lifetime before.[79]

Amid this dispersal of the relics of the town, eyes were ever on the arterial routes. In 1931 the new Hat-Brooks highway made Alderson, always the midpoint, ten miles closer to each centre. But the old road ran up Railway Avenue, and the new ran north of the tracks where the first townsite had been. As a result, the traffic tended to keep on going. Frank Steed built a garage north of the station to slow it down, but of course it did nothing for the diminishing cluster of buildings across the right-of-way.[80]

It may have been Charlotte Cotter's deep need for movement and excitement that so often focused her columns on the mobile folks streaming through with their sense of purpose and direction and boldness. When F. Nordenmark crossed the desert in 1933, Charlotte ran out to speak to him. There he was, pulling a 500 pound

Queen Elizabeth and King
George at Medicine Hat, 1939.
NA 4777-23, Glenbow-Alberta
Archives.

barrel on two wheels from British Columbia to the Atlantic. He slept inside it, and at six foot two inches he just fit. The adventure stirred Charlotte.[81]

But attention in the last years was ever on the trains. The villagers remembered the Prince of Wales trip in 1928 when the prince himself alighted on the Alderson platform and strutted up and down smiling while a lackey handed out balloons and wooden whistles to the children.[82] They knew when the Royal Scot, "the crack flier and speed queen of the London, Midland and Scottish Railway" was coming five years later, and they remembered its well-lit interior, its fine upholstery, and lavishly pannelled woodwork, as the little engine with eight cars slowed down to acknowledge the crowd one evening.[83]

But the focus so often was on the transit, on the locomotives

Charlotte Cotter, near the time of the Royal "visit." NA 4777-17, Glenbow-Alberta Archives.

crossing the stage of the little town, on people passing in the night, on former residents going to an affliction. Whenever there was a significant passage, Charlotte Cotter told the people—when, for example, the body of her brother, Dr. R. H. Mason, the village's first physician, rumbled through one winter night en route from Seafield Heights in Nanaimo to the family vault in Mount Pleasant Cemetery, Toronto.[84] When Alderson reverted to the status of a flag station in 1938 and nearly thirty years of regular stops ended, it seemed to Charlotte as if another great heart had been stilled.[85]

As the dismal decade drummed itself into the past, the highlight of 1939 was to be the visit of the Royal couple in late May. The mythical two came from the east with the sun. All eyes and ears were riveted on the reports of the approach, but few recorded the details with the awe and adulation that Kate Cole etched into her diary. She used the word "thrilling" five times on five different days. Eyes abrimming, she cheered the magnificence of the King's speech in Quebec, the wonderful reception of the couple in Montreal, the Queen's "clear and ringing voice" in Ottawa. As the coach bearing the objects of their deepest affections approached the little hamlet of Alderson, Kate Cole and her friend Charlotte Cotter were positively ecstatic.[86]

For miles around, people from the scattered homesteads got up early, donned their Sunday best and headed for Alderson station. Many arrived as early as 10 A.M. and were greeted by a redcoat on the platform who directed them in the interests of security into the broiling sun below the right-of-way, near the snow fences which were still up. Within the hour, some sixty royalists, including two nursing mothers, had assembled. As the people steamed in the heat for another ninety minutes, the Royal coach chugged out of Suffield half an hour late. At last they saw the pilot train approaching, and spirits lifted. Some had been informed that their majesties were poised to appear at the rear end of the train and that the train would slow down where crowds warranted.[87]

At top speed, the pilot flew by, followed by the Royal train with the blinds drawn. The velocity was so great that one stunned observer claimed he could not even see the blue and silver of the coaches. Among the perspiring and jilted mob that day, few were as let down and bruised in soul as the two aging ladies, Kate Cole and Charlotte Cotter. Summoning all her reserve and all her monarchist sympathies, Charlotte spoke for the two—"Well that is that, and God bless them anyway."[88]

Down the track the train roared, like a car blaring through a windswept cemetery, its crosses down, its tombstones strewn about. Guests aboard from king and queen to chefs and valets knew they were passing through bad country, the worst of the prairie, and if they could not bear to look upon it, it was because their minds were necessarily on destinations of significance. It is doubtful if any sensed that embedded in the bleakness and disarray of the moonscape around them was the profoundest tragedy imaginable.

EPILOGUE   *The Ruins of the Empire*

P OOR ALDERSON, POOR NINEVEH.
Everywhere for an infinity the
empire lay in the dust. I might have been at Winnifred, Whitla or
Pakowki to the south, at Tripola or Steveville near the Red Deer
River, at Bow City or Retlaw to the west, at Scapa or Spondin
north of Hanna. It was all the same—there was nothing left. A
score of other towns were wisps of what they had been—Richdale,
Stanmore, Chinook, and Sibbald on the Hanna-Oyen roadbed;
Wardlow, Cessford, Pollockville, and Sunnynook on the unfinished
Hanna-Hat line; Skiff, Nemiskam, Orion and Manyberries on the
Lethbridge-Weyburn line; Grassy Lake, Purple Springs, and Seven
Persons on the Crow's Nest line; Bowell and Suffield on the CPR
mainline.

Some sixty years after the ebbtide of the mid-twenties and almost
fifty after the King's passage, however much the wand of irrigation

All that remains—the foundations of the England and England Block—looking south across the heart of Broadway. Photo by the author.

had transformed parts of the desert around Bow Island and south of the Hat; however much the crusty, alkaline prairie was now bespeckled with hundreds of wells drawing up the riches of gas and oil from the monstrous formations below; however much hubs like Medicine Hat, Brooks, and Swift Current had grown proud—nothing could ever wipe away the great sorrow that had befallen so vast a kingdom. Untold grief had visited drylanders here, as it always would on the most arid reaches.

And what of Alderson, this one-time agate in the sand? In 1941 a mountie appeared in the Bingville area to the northeast. It was not quite an oasis in the desert, but it was a pocket of better land, graced with a little more rain. There he addressed the leather-hided settlers, the toughest in the history of the West, those who had survived a generation of departure and the Great Depression, who had ground a living from the hard land, and who were still in place. Under orders from the federal government, by arrangement with Alberta, he bade them to decamp within thirty days. The Department of National Defense had chosen their homeland as the most desolate block in the country—a perfect wasteland for the noxious effluvia of the new Suffield Chemical Warfare Base. Those who resisted were expropriated.

Meanwhile Alderson lived on, after a fashion. Decrepit and ailing, the broken community passed through the 1940s with a post office, a store, and a school. Shortly after 1950 all three were sealed. Sometime later the vacant station went. In the late seventies, a band of hooligans descended on the empty town at Halloween and fired the sole remaining major structure, the decaying Woollven store. It had been the first and the last. . . .

The fiery sun was fast sinking as I stood at the south end of town, gazing at the wreck hanging from the crosspiece of Railway Avenue and anchored on the post of Broadway. Everything was down, except a few boards of Al Cole's once spacious livery and a nearby small shack the size of a railway section house, several blocks south of the tracks.

The dwelling was a dung heap of dilapidation—doors open, windows out, birds in the attic, droppings on the walls, manure on the floors—muck, vermin and sand in a sea of flotsam and filth. Beneath these dusty leavings, the planking was dry-rotted, wowed, and near the centre, broken through, exposing a dark cellar of unknown contents, a death trap for range cattle.

In the dusk I returned pensively, up the west side of Broadway that had burned in the simmering summer of 1919, past the rubble of brick where the Union Bank had been before the town bought it as a community hall in the latter days, past an old rusty Ford ditched in an in-filled basement, past a lone half-dead poplar, its bare arms outstretched and hooked, the roost of ferruginous hawks.

From the right-of-way, I saw faintly the headstones of the graveyard to the east. I shook my head at the whole receding spectacle, thought a moment again of Carlstadt, "Star of the Prairie," and saw before me the most God-forsaken place in all the south country.

It was now dark. The hot southwester had come up again, and it blew into the night.

Alderson, Alberta
May 26, 1984

APPENDIX

THE APPENDIX provides the statistical and cartographic background to the arguments of the book. The census division maps (figures 1 and 2) show the areas to which broad settlement and abandonment figures apply, though Alberta divisions fall more neatly into the dry belt than Saskatchewan ones. The special areas map (figure 3) reveals the spread of these strange jurisdictions from the dry belt core east of Tilley. The annual average wheat yields chart (figure 4) emphasizes the magnitude of the 1915–16 crops, especially for the drylands, and the consistently poorer harvests of these areas following that date. One aspect of the strange heartland thesis is graphically depicted in the school divisions map (figure 5).

Population tables 1 to 6 demonstrate the growth and decline of the dry belt and the greater devastation of Alberta. Township population losses (tables 2 and 5), however, are a more accurate measure of evacuation than gross census division tallies. Precipitation tables 7 to 9 show the striking deficiency and variability of rainfall at Medicine Hat, features further intensified in Alderson-Suffield. Combined with temperatures table 10, these figures depict the tenor of the seasons for four decades. Tables 11 to 13 allow for a detailed subregional study of wheat yields and grain marketed, while tables 14 and 15 add the element of grain prices. Finally, dry belt bank statistics (table 16) disclose the involvement of Union and Royal branches in the funding of the empire.

FIGURE 1
Alberta Dry Belt
Census Divisions 1,
3 and 5 (1921–
1936).

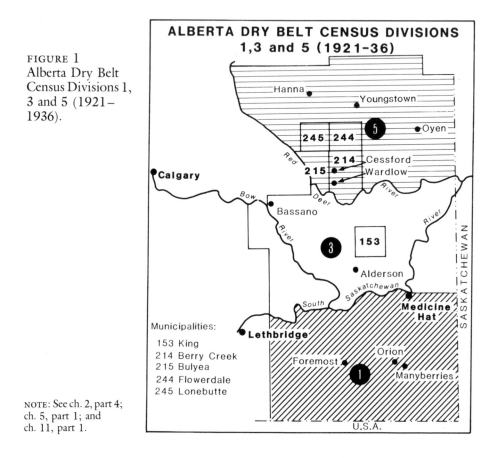

ALBERTA DRY BELT CENSUS DIVISIONS
1,3 and 5 (1921-36)

NOTE: See ch. 2, part 4;
ch. 5, part 1; and
ch. 11, part 1.

TABLE 1   Alberta Dry Belt Population

	1906	1911	1916	1921	1926	1931	1936
Alberta	185,195	374,295	496,442	588,454	607,599	731,605	772,782
Census Division 1	7,765	24,738	29,927	30,664	25,624	28,849	29,699
Census Division 3	745	9,330	13,266	17,404	12,125	15,066	14,742
Census Division 5	283	13,170	24,500	33,719	27,240	26,651	21,359

NOTE: See ch. 2, part 4; ch. 5, part 1; and ch. 11, part 1.

SOURCE: Canada, *Census of the Prairie Provinces, 1936* (Ottawa: King's Printer, 1938), pp. 848, 853, 858.

TABLE 2   Alberta Dry Belt Rural Townships Showing Heaviest
Population Losses, 1921–1926*

Percentage Loss	Census Division 1 (no. townships: 209)	Census Division 3 (no. townships: 206)	Census Division 5 (no. townships: 221)	Totals (no. townships: 636)
25–34 percent	18	13	36	67
35–44 percent	26	16	23	65
45–54 percent	22	25	18	65
55–64 percent	16	23	16	55
65–74 percent	11	10	14	35
75–84 percent	4	14	2	20
85–100 percent	4	19	5	28
	101	120	114	335**

NOTES: See ch. 7, part 1; and ch. 11, part 1.

*   One township comprises 36 sections or 23,040 acres.

**   The 335 townships with at least 25 percent population loss represent 53 percent of all rural townships in the three census divisions. The 101 Division 1 townships lost 4,544 people; the 120 Division 3 townships lost 5,233 people; and the 114 Division 5 townships lost 5,636 people—a total depletion of 15,413 persons.

SOURCE: Canada, *Census of the Prairie Provinces, 1936* (Ottawa: King's Printer, 1938), pp. 848–61.

TABLE 3:   Alberta Dry Belt Vacant or Abandoned Farms, 1926–1936

	1926 total farms vacant or abandoned		1931 total farms vacant or abandoned		1936 total farms vacant or abandoned	
	No.	*Acres*	*No.*	*Acres*	*No.*	*Acres*
Alberta	10,400	2,337,715	6,640	1,409,619	9,298	2,081,351
Census Division 1	1,336	317,167	402	109,036	289	73,080
Census Division 3	2,352	586,988	531	160,386	616	159,770
Census Division 5	2,772	700,606	2,306	522,746	3,706	996,511

NOTES: See ch. 11, parts 1 and 3.

The greatest number of vacant or abandoned farms for all Alberta (17 census divisions) for the three censuses was 3,706 in Census Division 5, 1936. This division also led the province in 1926 and 1931.

SOURCE: Canada, *Census of Prairie Provinces, 1926* (Ottawa: King's Printer, 1931), p. 702; Canada, *Seventh Census of Canada, 1931*, Vol. 8 (Ottawa: King's Printer, 1931), p. 695; Canada, *Census of the Prairie Provinces, 1936* (Ottawa: King's Printer, 1938), p. 1174.

FIGURE 2
Southwestern
Saskatchewan Census
Divisions 4 and 8 (1921–
1936).

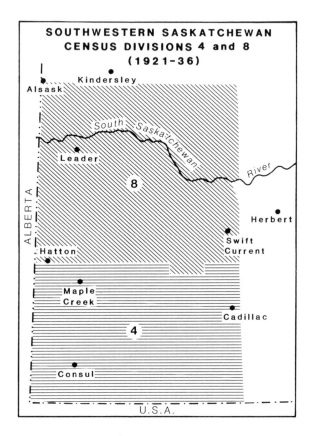

**SOUTHWESTERN SASKATCHEWAN
CENSUS DIVISIONS 4 and 8
(1921–36)**

Kindersley

Alsask

South Saskatchewan River

Leader

8

Herbert

Swift
Current

Hatton

ALBERTA

Maple
Creek

Cadillac

4

Consul

U.S.A.

NOTE: See ch. 2, part 4; ch. 5,
part 1; and ch. 11, part 1.

TABLE 4:   Southwest Saskatchewan Population, 1906–1936

	1906	1911	1916	1921	1926	1931	1936
Saskatchewan	257,763	492,432	647,835	757,510	820,738	921,785	931,547
Census Division 4	2,908	10,497	21,121	23,198	24,740	28,126	25,806
Census Division 8	2,717	17,569	37,120	45,667	44,470	49,361	45,690

NOTES: See ch. 2, part 4; ch. 5, part 1; and ch. 11, part 1.

These census divisions comprise a smaller area than that considered by the Saskatchewan *Royal Commission of Inquiry into Farming Conditions* (1921), p. 34.

SOURCE: Canada, *Census of the Prairie Provinces, 1936* (Ottawa: King's Printer, 1938), pp. 380, 388, 400.

TABLE 5: Southwest Saskatchewan Rural Townships Showing Heaviest Population Losses, 1921–1926*

Percentage Loss	Census Division 4 *(no. townships: 209)*	Census Division 8 *(no. townships: 262)*	totals *(no. townships: 471)*
10–14 percent	13	26	39
15–24 percent	15	34	49
25–34 percent	17	23	40
35–44 percent	9	14	23
45–54 percent	11	5	16
55–64 percent	5	4	9
65–74 percent	4	5	9
75–84 percent	1	2	3
85–100 percent	1	1	2
	76	114	190**

NOTES: See ch. 11, part 1.

* One township comprises 36 sections or 23,040 acres.

** The 190 townships with at least 10 percent population loss represent 40 percent of all rural townships in the two census divisions. The 76 Division 4 townships lost 1,919 people; the 114 Division 8 townships lost 4,530 people—a total depletion of 6,449 persons.

SOURCE: Canada, *Census of the Prairie Provinces, 1936* (Ottawa: King's Printer, 1938), pp. 388–91, 400–404.

TABLE 6: Southwest Saskatchewan Vacant or Abandoned Farms, 1926–1936

	1926 total farms vacant or abandoned		1931 total farms vacant or abandoned		1936 total farms vacant or abandoned	
	No.	*Acres*	*No.*	*Acres*	*No.*	*Acres*
Saskatchewan	4,907	1,020,217	5,183	1,024,211	11,222	2,486,253
Census Division 4	491	115,542	251	54,930	626	143,214
Census Division 8	916	212,091	462	97,624	732	171,918

NOTES: See ch. 11, parts 1 and 3.

The greatest number of vacant or abandoned farms for all Saskatchewan (17 census divisions) for the three censuses was Census Division 7, immediately east of Division 8, 1936. Division 8 led the province in 1926.

SOURCE: Canada, *Census of Prairie Provinces, 1926* (Ottawa: King's Printer, 1931), p. 422; Canada, *Seventh Census of Canada, 1931,* Vol. 8 (Ottawa: King's Printer, 1936), p. 627; Canada, *Census of the Prairie Provinces, 1936* (Ottawa: King's Printer, 1938), p. 722.

TABLE 7:   Annual Precipitation in Inches for Southern Alberta and Southwestern Saskatchewan, 1890–1938

	Calgary	Lethbridge	Medicine Hat	Swift Current
1890	14.33		7.79	17.50
1891	10.45		9.70	24.55
1892	7.91		7.81	20.30
1893	11.05		9.08	14.54
1894	11.71		10.09	9.66
1895	15.11		11.39	12.33
1896	16.06		18.18	14.11
1897	20.58		17.25	16.24
1898	15.58		15.90	15.25
1899	26.15		22.28	19.39
1900	17.57		22.05	14.61
1901	22.21		20.08	18.58
1902	34.57	27.92	13.68	17.64
1903	22.78	14.81	9.90	18.38
1904	11.89	11.40	9.70	12.84
1905	14.32	13.78	8.99	15.68
1906	16.24	22.48	11.62	19.02
1907	14.96	15.50	6.96	13.22
1908	17.92	14.94	9.67	12.26
1909	15.72	10.32	9.80	19.28
1910	11.91	7.90	6.45	11.22
1911	18.78	21.31	16.04	14.14
1912	21.41	13.21	9.78	14.64
1913	17.06	14.17	12.65	12.62
1914	17.81	16.52	12.17	12.48
1915	18.36	17.27	16.13	14.27
1916	13.91	24.57	17.90	23.98
1917	11.54	12.03	13.42	11.92
1918	9.11	7.63	10.20	12.22
1919	12.20	12.27	7.66	12.33
1920	14.45	14.05	10.74	11.56
1921	13.49	12.76	12.95	14.93
1922	10.63	12.34	11.54	14.28
1923	23.01	16.40	13.64	16.39
1924	24.30	16.00	9.86	16.73
1925	18.06	18.75	14.61	14.33
1926	24.39	16.19	11.90	15.88
1927	29.83	23.85	25.28	23.13
1928	16.65	18.08	7.64	11.77
1929	13.44	19.71	8.17	14.86

Table 7—*Continued*

	Calgary	Lethbridge	Medicine Hat	Swift Current
1930	14.48	12.34	13.23	13.55
1931	11.83	11.42	9.96	11.87
1932	21.03	19.24	16.81	19.04
1933	12.97	19.18	15.11	17.89
1934	14.03	15.28	13.05	11.46
1935	17.83	11.30	12.50	17.35
1936	9.77	12.74	9.63	11.80
1937	19.49	16.30	9.80	8.31
1938	16.73	15.70	17.61	14.91
AVERAGE	16.63	15.67	12.64	15.21

NOTE: See ch. 1, part 3; ch. 2, parts 1 and 3; ch. 5, part 1; ch. 7, part 2; ch. 8, part 3; and ch. 11, part 1.

SOURCES: Alberta, *Annual Reports of the Department of Agriculture;* Lethbridge Research Station; Environment Canada, Atmospheric Environment Services, Calgary, Winnipeg.

TABLE 8:   Crop Growing Season Precipitation in Inches, Jenner, Suffield and Medicine Hat, Alberta

	April	May	June	July	August	Total for Season
Jenner, 9 year average	0.88	1.78	2.43	1.96	1.51	8.56
Suffield, 10 year average	0.45	1.13	1.48	2.28	1.02	6.36
Medicine Hat, 41 year average	0.70	1.68	2.57	1.80	1.34	8.09

NOTES: See ch. 1, part 3; ch. 2, parts 1 and 3; ch. 5, part 1; ch. 7, part 2; ch. 8, part 3; and ch. 11, part 1.

Figures end at December 31, 1923, and cover the entire period that statistics were kept at each station.

SOURCE: Tilley East Commission, 1926, p. 17.

TABLE 9:   Monthly Precipitation in Inches, Suffield, Alberta, 1913–1923

Year	Jan.	Feb.	Mar.	Apr.	May	June	July	Aug.	Sept.	Oct.	Nov.	Dec.
1913	...	...	...	...	...	...	...	...	0.35	0.03	0.05	0.30
1914	0.60	0.30	0.55	0.02	0.12	1.15	0.37	0.74	0.65	1.31	0.40	0.75
1915	0.37	1.00	0.20	0.01	0.81	3.68	3.22	0.95	2.11	0.83	...	0.53
1916	0.55	0.33	0.43	0.06	4.07	2.60	7.20	1.77	1.18	0.77	0.25	0.70
1917	0.20	0.45	0.30	0.59	0.23	0.93	1.57	1.73	0.92	1.01	0.30	1.20
1918	0.95	0.55	0.52	0.20	0.23	0.77	1.16	0.58	0.22	0.12	0.48	0.40
1919	...	0.10	0.30	0.81	...	0.23	1.91	1.14	...	0.32	0.45	0.30
1920	1.09	0.08	0.34	0.78	1.03	1.01	2.92	0.07	0.10	0.80	...	0.65
1921	T.	0.20	0.90	0.80	2.00	0.65	1.15	0.86	1.37	0.28	0.93	T.
1922	0.60	0.35	0.30	0.98	1.08	0.95	0.85	0.71	0.96	0.18	0.19	0.15
1923	0.15	1.03	0.15	0.26	0.64	2.87	2.45	1.62	0.00	0.60	0.00	...
Sums	4.51	4.39	3.99	4.51	10.21	14.84	22.80	10.17	7.86	6.25	3.05	4.98
Means	0.50	0.44	0.40	0.45	1.13	1.48	2.28	1.02	0.79	0.57	0.34	0.50

NOTES: See ch. 2, parts 1 and 3; ch. 5, part 1; ch. 7, part 2; ch. 8, part 3; and ch. 11, part 1.
   ...—Not recorded.
   T.—Traces.

SOURCE: B. Russell and W. H. Snelson, *Report on Southern Alberta Drought Area* (Ottawa: Department of the Interior, December 1924), appendix.

TABLE 10: Mean Daily Maximum Temperature in Degrees Celsius, Medicine Hat, 1901–1940

Year	Jan.	Feb.	Mar.	Apr.	May	June	July	Aug.	Sept.	Oct.	Nov.	Dec.	Annual
1901	− 3.9	− 4.1	7.7	15.7	22.1	18.7	26.7	28.8	15.8	19.0	6.0	2.6	12.9
1902	− 0.2	− 3.7	6.2	14.8	20.7	19.9	25.4	28.3	22.4	16.9	1.8	− 5.5	12.3
1903	− 1.2	− 2.2	− 0.9	14.6	18.5	25.7	25.8	24.2	19.1	18.4	1.4	4.2	12.3
1904	− 2.1	−12.2	− 3.7	15.3	19.9	24.3	30.2	27.3	22.3	17.1	12.3	0.3	12.6
1905	− 6.9	− 3.9	11.7	15.7	18.2	22.2	27.6	29.4	22.8	12.2	9.2	1.5	13.3
1906	− 2.2	3.7	5.6	19.0	17.1	22.7	29.6	27.6	23.3	16.2	3.1	− 4.4	13.4
1907	−17.3	− 1.9	2.5	9.5	15.8	23.1	26.4	25.7	20.4	18.9	8.9	2.1	11.2
1908	3.6	− 0.9	4.1	16.9	21.6	22.7	30.1	NR	23.4	11.1	7.7	0.3	NR
1909	− 7.2	− 4.4	6.2	9.2	18.4	23.6	26.8	29.7	25.5	14.7	1.7	− 5.6	11.6
1910	− 0.4	− 5.7	14.4	20.8	21.5	26.8	29.1	23.4	19.6	16.7	NR	NR	NR
MEAN	− 3.8	− 3.5	5.4	15.2	19.4	23.0	27.8	27.2	21.5	16.1	5.8	− 0.5	12.8
1911	NR	− 5.2	9.8	11.8	19.9	27.1	26.4	24.7	18.8	13.2	− 0.4	− 1.7	NR
1912	− 6.8	0.1	− 0.7	17.1	20.9	28.3	26.4	26.4	17.9	14.1	9.4	4.7	13.2
1913	− 8.5	− 2.7	1.3	18.3	20.6	28.0	29.3	29.1	24.8	12.3	8.8	3.6	13.7
1914	− 2.6	− 6.8	7.9	16.2	22.4	25.9	33.9	29.2	22.8	14.4	8.3	− 5.9	13.8
1915	− 4.3	− 1.7	4.2	21.8	21.1	21.7	25.4	31.6	18.8	17.1	5.7	1.8	13.6
1916	−18.5	− 2.8	6.6	16.3	18.2	23.1	28.5	26.5	21.4	12.1	6.2	− 7.1	10.9
1917	− 5.7	− 9.1	1.9	11.3	22.7	24.3	33.3	29.0	21.8	11.7	13.9	− 9.6	12.1
1918	− 7.1	− 3.4	7.6	16.6	20.6	28.7	29.3	27.8	23.2	18.1	7.1	1.8	14.2
1919	5.8	− 4.0	0.0	16.8	23.2	28.9	30.0	29.6	22.9	8.9	− 0.6	− 3.5	13.2
1920	− 6.9	− 0.5	3.0	7.9	19.7	25.0	31.1	29.9	23.6	15.2	6.6	0.5	12.9
MEAN	− 6.1	− 3.6	4.2	15.4	20.9	26.1	29.4	28.4	21.6	13.7	6.5	− 1.5	12.9

1921	0.3	1.9	3.6	12.9	20.1	28.8	30.2	28.6	18.7	18.5	1.2	− 1.6	13.6
1922	− 3.9	−10.0	4.0	11.8	20.1	28.1	29.1	29.3	23.9	16.8	6.7	− 6.6	12.4
1923	− 1.9	− 3.3	3.3	15.0	22.4	26.3	29.3	27.8	24.2	15.1	9.8	0.2	14.0
1924	− 6.2	4.8	4.7	13.5	22.8	23.9	30.7	25.1	21.9	15.8	1.9	− 9.7	12.4
1925	− 5.2	− 3.0	3.2	14.8	22.2	25.7	29.0	26.6	17.4	8.3	6.6	2.3	12.3
1926	0.5	2.8	9.1	16.8	21.7	25.3	31.1	25.4	13.8	14.7	2.7	− 3.7	13.4
1927	− 4.5	− 3.7	5.2	11.8	14.3	23.9	27.3	25.4	19.3	16.3	− 2.1	−12.0	10.1
1928	− 1.7	2.3	8.1	11.8	25.6	21.4	27.0	25.7	21.7	11.7	9.0	2.7	13.8
1929	−10.6	− 7.4	7.7	10.8	18.7	24.7	31.7	30.9	18.9	16.8	6.4	− 3.9	12.1
1930	−11.3	5.5	6.6	17.3	19.8	24.0	30.6	29.6	20.6	10.7	6.1	5.1	13.7
MEAN	− 4.5	− 1.0	5.6	13.7	20.8	25.2	29.6	27.4	20.0	14.5	4.8	− 2.7	12.8
1931	6.2	8.2	5.7	15.2	20.4	25.3	27.7	28.0	19.7	15.9	1.2	− 0.5	14.4
1932	− 6.4	− 3.3	− 2.7	14.3	19.7	23.6	27.6	26.6	20.4	9.9	3.3	− 2.8	10.9
1933	− 1.1	− 3.9	5.8	10.3	17.6	26.7	29.2	27.5	19.3	11.3	6.4	− 8.3	11.7
1934	2.7	3.6	4.7	16.8	23.6	21.8	28.5	27.3	15.1	15.6	7.1	− 3.9	13.6
1935	− 9.3	0.4	− 0.8	8.0	15.8	22.1	29.0	25.6	22.0	13.0	− 1.6	1.4	10.5
1936	− 9.1	−21.1	2.6	10.7	24.1	24.8	33.6	27.4	20.2	14.7	7.1	− 4.6	10.9
1937	−15.2	− 8.9	2.8	14.7	20.3	25.2	29.7	26.8	21.6	15.1	1.6	− 2.6	10.9
1938	− 0.3	− 8.9	4.7	12.6	17.5	24.2	28.4	25.7	26.7	16.8	2.8	− 0.6	12.5
1939	− 0.1	−11.0	2.6	14.3	21.4	19.2	29.6	28.8	20.9	11.7	13.8	4.6	13.0
1940	−10.9	− 6.2	1.6	8.2	21.8	23.5	27.4	29.8	24.0	16.2	− 3.4	1.3	11.1
MEAN	− 4.4	− 5.1	2.7	12.5	20.2	23.6	29.1	27.4	21.0	14.0	3.8	− 1.6	11.9

NOTES: See ch. 1, part 3; ch. 2, parts 1 and 3; ch. 5, part 1; ch. 7, part 2; ch. 8, part 3; and ch. 11, part 1.

NR—No Record.

SOURCE: Environment Canada, Atmospheric Environment Services, Calgary.

FIGURE 3
Alberta Special Areas,
1938

NOTE: See ch. 11, part 3.

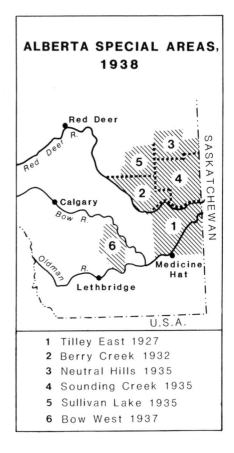

**ALBERTA SPECIAL AREAS,
1938**

1 Tilley East 1927
2 Berry Creek 1932
3 Neutral Hills 1935
4 Sounding Creek 1935
5 Sullivan Lake 1935
6 Bow West 1937

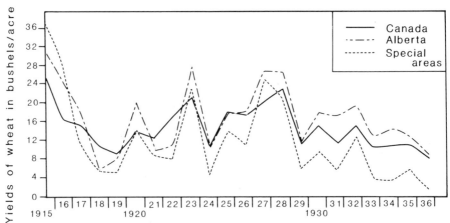

FIGURE 4   Annual Average Wheat Yields for Canada, Alberta and Special Areas,
1915–1936

NOTE: See ch. 5, part 1; and ch. 11, part 3.

TABLE 11   Alberta Dry Belt Wheat Yields, 1910–1921

District	Average Size of Farms Acres (1921)	Average Cultivated Acres (1921)	Wheat Yield/Acre											
			1910	1911	1912	1913	1914	1915	1916	1917	1918	1919	1920	1921
Enchant	530	337	—	20	21	18	4	42	30	14	6	nil	7	2
Hanna	747	469	—	22	15	16	8	29	23	8	2	4	10	5
Jenner	1200	860	—	24	22	23	8	44	34	9	6	4	12	6
Lethbridge	655	402	—	20	19	16	5	33	31	13	5	nil	5	6
Macleod	948	585	4	24	16	13	6	31	24	13	4	nil	4	2
Medicine Hat	1252	769	nil	15	12	11	3	41	33	7	1	nil	5	3
Youngstown	1173	673	—	—	17	23	8	26	23	11	5	2	10	8

NOTE: See ch. 5, parts 1 and 2; ch. 6, parts 1 and 2; and ch. 7, part 2.

SOURCE: Arthur Woolley to Secretary, Survey Board for Southern Alberta, Feb. 15, 1922, Table XVIII, 69.289 f43b, PAA.

TABLE 12   Grain Marketed in Thousands of Bushels from Southern Alberta, 1915–1921

	1915–16	1916–17	1917–18	1918–19	1919–20	1920–21	To Nov. 1921	TOTAL
Veteran	2,007	1,649	816	140	306	1,386	885	7,189
Jenner	2,120	1,918	720	332	421	1,188	533	7,232
Medicine Hat to Brooks	2,255	1,688	318	239	669	474	253	5,896
Medicine Hat to Walsh	1,318	1,493	789	97	113	562	306	4,678
Medicine Hat to Burdett	3,611	3,993	1,088	185	80	720	271	9,948
Lethbridge to Grassy Lake	2,513	3,081	1,506	496	585	2,403	653	11,237
Lethbridge to Champion	5,596	4,986	3,651	1,236	62	2,322	294	18,147
Wilson to Coutts	3,217	3,120	1,445	185	96	1,682	1,114	10,859
Stirling to Manyberries	2,675	2,477	930	163	116	1,248	546	8,155
Stirling to Spring Coulee	1,830	2,103	1,124	385	369	1,434	616	7,861
Suffield to Lomond	3,863	3,154	1,633	326	78	1,124	193	10,371
Macleod	4,244	3,197	2,318	707	136	1,264	264	12,180
Youngstown	5,886	4,208	1,821	652	913	3,208	837	17,525
TOTAL	41,135	37,067	18,159	5,143	3,944	19,015	6,765	131,228

NOTE: See ch. 5, parts 1 and 2; ch. 6, parts 1 and 2; and ch. 7, part 2.

SOURCE: Arthur Woolley to Secretary, Survey Board for Southern Alberta, Feb. 15, 1922, Table xxi, 69.289 f43b, PAA.

TABLE 13   Grain Marketed in Thousands of Bushels from Medicine Hat to Brooks, Alberta, 1915–1921

	1915–16	1916–17	1917–18	1918–19	1919–20	1920–21	to Nov. 1921
Southesk	33	12	5	5	4	6	3
Cassils	26	14	10	10	3	85	40
Brooks	309	161	42	40	52	80	42
Tilley	77	29	8	10	17	25	21
Alderson	679	428	72	14	9	79	40
Suffield	450	233	71	18	23	91	41
Bowell	58	43	35	8	12	40	12
Redcliff	313	298	19	17	21	15	6
Medicine Hat	310	470	56	117	528	53	48
TOTAL	2,255	1,688	318	239	669	474	253

NOTE: See ch. 5, parts 1 and 2; ch. 6, parts 1 and 2; and ch. 7, part 2.

SOURCE: Arthur Woolley to Secretary, Survey Board for Southern Alberta, Feb. 15, 1922, Table XXI, 69.289 f43b, PAA.

TABLE 14   Average Price of Wheat Per Bushel, Hanna, 1913–1940

NO. 1 NORTHERN

Year	Price $		Year	Price $
1913	0.71		1927	1.28
1914	1.14		1928	1.05
1915	0.95		1929	1.06
1916	1.87		1930	0.46
1917	2.02		1931	0.41
1918	2.06		1932	0.36
1919	1.99		1933	0.49
1920	1.81		1934	0.63
1921	1.11		1935	0.66
1922	0.91		1936	1.06
1923	0.88		1937	1.13
1924	1.50		1938	0.43
1925	1.33		1939	0.58
1926	1.28		1940	0.55

NOTES: See ch. 6, part 2; and ch. 9, parts 1 to 4.

Winnipeg cash closing, basis in store Fort William, less freight rate of 18.6¢ a bushel.

SOURCE: M. C. Urquhart and K. A. Buckley, *Historical Statistics of Canada* (Toronto: Macmillan, 1965), pp. 345, 359.

TABLE 15   Average Price of Wheat Per Bushel—Hanna

No. 2 Northern

Crop Year	Price $		Crop Year	Price $
1920–21	1.78		1928–29	1.02
1921–22	1.06		1929–30	1.03
1922–23	0.89		1930–31	0.43
1923–24	0.88		1931–32	0.37
1924–25	1.45		1932–33	0.34
1925–26	1.28		1933–34	0.44
1926–27	1.23		1934–35	0.60
1927–28	1.22		1935–36	0.64

NOTES: See ch. 6, part 2; and ch. 9, parts 1 to 4.

Fort William price less freight rate of 18.6¢ a bushel.

SOURCE: A. Stewart and W. D. Porter, *Land Use Classification in the Special Areas of Alberta* (Dominion Department of Agriculture, 1942), p. 73.

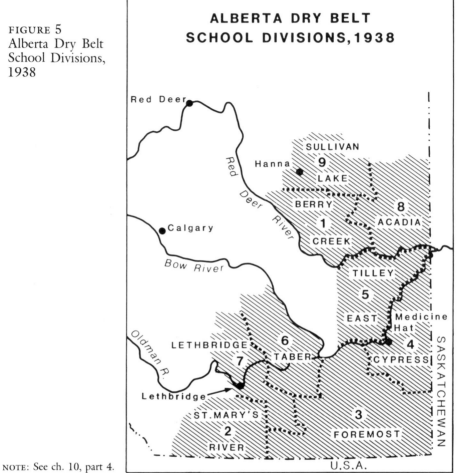

FIGURE 5
Alberta Dry Belt
School Divisions,
1938

NOTE: See ch. 10, part 4.

TABLE 16   Alberta Dry Belt Bank Statistics, 1915–1926

	Deposits	Advances	Deficits	Debts Written Off
1915	1,392,604	2,307,908	915,304	
1916	2,947,913	2,474,977	+472,936	
1917	5,213,653	2,594,009	+2,619,644	
1918	4,010,956	2,960,876	+1,050,080	
1919	3,591,753	4,406,187	814,434	
1920	3,590,920	5,680,292	2,089,372	160,011
1921	3,478,278	4,330,870	852,592	172,738
1922	3,183,280	4,238,817	1,055,537	171,488
1923	3,162,926	4,450,932	1,288,006	391,491
1924	3,378,652	3,988,851	610,198	654,587
1925	2,890,103	3,394,292	504,189	772,621
1926	3,897,915	3,215,234	+682,681	951,367

NOTES: See ch. 9, part 2.

Figures from Union branches at Empress, Cereal, Chinook, Sunnynook, Hanna, Medicine Hat, Irvine, Lethbridge, Cluny, Sedalia, Bassano, Etzikom, Foremost, Bow Island, Consort and Brooks; Royal branches at Patricia, Duchess, Craigmyle, Medicine Hat, Lethbridge and Gleichen; Trader's branch at Consort.

SOURCE: Annual Accounts Reports, Royal Bank Archives, Calgary.

ABBREVIATIONS

ARA   Alberta Annual Report of the Department of Agriculture
ARE   Alberta Annual Report of the Department of Education
BCSD   Berry Creek School Division Papers
DMA   Deputy Minister of Agriculture Papers (Saskatchewan)
GAA   Glenbow-Alberta Archives
HH   *The Hanna Herald*
LH   *The Lethbridge Daily Herald*
MHN   *Medicine Hat News*
PAA   Provincial Archives of Alberta
PAC   Public Archives of Canada
SAB   Saskatchewan Archives Board
SH   Scrapbook Hansard (Alberta)
UAA   University of Alberta Archives

NOTES

1 The Wiles of the Desert

1. J. W. Morrow, *Early History of the Medicine Hat Country* (Medicine Hat: *Medicine Hat News*, 1923), pp. 12–13. As Ernest Hodgson notes, Morrow's description derived partly from Victor Hugo's tale of a similar sad end.
2. Irene M. Spry, *The Papers of the Palliser Expedition, 1857–1860* (Toronto: Champlain Society, 1968), pp. 9, 18, 414. Note also Henry Youle Hind, *North-West Territory, Report on the Assiniboine and Saskatchewan Exploring Expedition* (Toronto: J. Lovell, 1859), p. 31.
3. *Report of the Commissioner of the North-West Mounted Police*, 1874, pp. 15, 21, 28, 41–42, 46, 50.
4. David H. Breen, *The Canadian Prairie West and the Ranching Frontier, 1874–1924* (Toronto: University of Toronto Press, 1983), p. 43.
5. Ibid., p. 92.
6. Keith Stotyn, "An 'Act' of Western Pressure—The Creation of a Canadian Irrigation Policy," paper presented to Medicine Hat Triangle Palliser Conference, May 1986, *passim.*
7. Breen, *The Canadian Prairie West*, pp. 71–76.
8. Canada, Department of the Interior, *Annual Report for 1896*, p. 33.
9. Stotyn, "An 'Act' of Western Pressure," p. 4.
10. Canada, Department of the Interior, *Annual Report for 1896*, pp. 32–35; ibid., *Annual Report for 1894*, pp. 27–28.
11. Ibid., *Annual Report for 1894*, p. xvii.
12. A. M. Burgess to T. White, Jan. 9, 1887, RG 15, Vol. 159, no. 141376, PAC.
13. Canada, *Journals of the House of Commons*, 1876, p. 20.
14. Canada, *Sessional Papers 1880–81*, Vol. 14, pp. 15, 17.
15. W. A. Waiser, "A Willing Scapegoat: John Macoun and the Route of the CPR," *Prairie Forum* 10 (Spring 1985): 65–81.
16. Canada, *Journals of the House of Commons, 1907*, appendix 4, p. 1.
17. Canadian Pacific Railway, *The Canadian Pacific Railway Company's Experimental Farms* (Winnipeg: Free Press, 1884), pp. 10, 13–15.

18. Doug Owram, *Promise of Eden: The Canadian Expansionist Movement and the Idea of the West* (Toronto: University of Toronto Press, 1980), p. 219.

19. "The Settler's Paradise," *Macleod Gazette*, Feb. 29, 1888, p. 4.

20. Gerald Friesen, *The Canadian Prairies: A History* (Toronto: University of Toronto Press, 1984), p. 250–52.

21. An Admirer of Manitoba, letter to the Editor, "Crops in the North-West," *The Toronto Mail*, Aug. 6, 1887, p. 7.

22. J. A. Kirk, "Northwest Crops," *The Times*, Sept. 10, 1887.

23. "Don't Want Settlers," *The Times*, Mar. 1, 1888.

24. "Our True Immigration Policy," *The Times*, Feb. 5, 1891.

25. "To Intending Emigrants," *The Times*, Jan. 28, 1892.

26. "The Outlook for Crops," *The Times*, Apr. 6, 1893.

27. See Howard Palmer, "Patterns of Immigration and Ethnic Settlement in Alberta: 1880–1920," in Howard and Tamara Palmer, eds., *Peoples of Alberta: Portraits of Cultural Diversity* (Saskatoon: Western Producer Prairie Books, 1985), p. 5.

28. "The Exceptional Year," *MHN*, July 22, 1897.

29. Environment Canada, Atmospheric Services.

30. *MHN*, May 8, 1902.

2   The Planning of Nineveh

1. See D. J. Hall, *Clifford Sifton, Vol. 1: The Young Napoleon, 1861–1900* (Vancouver: University of British Columbia Press, 1981), pp. 25–126; "Everything in Canada[']s Favor," in Canada, *Canada, The Granary of the World* (Ottawa: Department of the Interior, 1903); Frank Oliver, editorial, "The Deputy Minister," *Edmonton Bulletin*, Dec. 17, 1896, 74-169-510, Pearce Papers, UAA.

2. Frank Oliver, editorial, "Reserved Lands," *Edmonton Bulletin*, July 27, 1896, 9/2/5/1/15, Pearce Papers, UAA.

3. David H. Breen, *The Canadian Prairie West and the Ranching Frontier, 1874–1924* (Toronto: University of Toronto Press, 1983), pp. 40, 111–13, 139, 150.

4. Canada, *Canada West: The Last Best West* (Ottawa: Minister of the Interior, 1910), p. 17.

5. Kingman Nott Robins, *The Province of Alberta* (Rochester, N.Y., 1910), pp. 13, 17, 23, 25, 28–30, 38–39.

6. Elliott Flower, "The Great Weather Factory," *MHN*, Feb. 25, 1909, p. 5.

7. "Did Not Know of Kipling," *MHN*, Sept. 17, 1908, p. 10.

8. Medicine Hat Board of Trade, *Hot Stuff*, 1907.

9. "The Medicine Hat Weather Joke," *MHN*, Jan. 9, 1909, p. 7.

10. "Obituary," *MHN*, Sept. 7, 1911; "The Death of John T. Hall," *MHN*, Sept. 14, 1911.

11. Quoted in *High River Times*, Nov. 21, 1907, p. 1.

12. "Advertising the Hat," *MHN*, Dec. 23, 1909, p. 1.
13. "Finlay Bridge Opened By Premier Rutherford," *MHN*, May 21, 1908, p. 1.
14. "Wonder City of Canada," *Calgary Herald*, Oct. 4, 1907, p. 1.
15. Medicine Hat News, *Kipling Visited Medicine Hat*, Oct. 1907.
16. "The Crops," *MHN*, Mar. 2, 1905.
17. "Our Spring Weather," *MHN*, Mar. 2, 1905.
18. Medicine Hat Board of Trade, *Medicine Hat*, 1908, p. 9.
19. "The Crops," *MHN*, June 9, 1904.
20. Medicine Hat Board of Trade, *Medicine Hat*, p. 10.
21. "Dry Farming Congress," *MHN*, Nov. 18, 1909, p. 5.
22. Ora Williams, "Soil Culture," *MHN*, Apr. 8, 1909, pp. 6–7.
23. W. M. Martin to R. Fenerty, Jan. 31, 1919, DMA xxii.ii, SAB.
24. W. C. Palmer, "Ten Commandments of the Dry Farmer," *Carlstadt Progress*, May 2, 1912.
25. Lomond Book Committee, *History of Lomond and District* (Lethbridge: Southern Printing, 1966), p. 97.
26. ARA 1910, p. 95.
27. "Summer Rains Are Not Needed," *MHN*, Sept. 16, 1909, p. 9.
28. "Alberta Swept Everything Before It at the Dry Farming Congress," *MHN*, Oct. 19, 1911, p. 1.
29. "Hon. S. Fisher at Lethbridge," *MHN*, Aug. 26, 1909, p. 5.
30. J. D. "Taber Will Double Wheat Yield," *Calgary Herald*, July 23, 1908, p. 1.
31. H. Jeffs, *Homes and Careers in Canada* (London: James Clarke & Co., 1914), p. 136.
32. "The Warm Chinook in Sunny Alberta," *MHN*, Mar. 19, 1908, p. 6, Richard A. Haste, reprinted from *Canada West Magazine*.
33. "Big Mass of Men Fight in Struggle for Land," *LH*, Sept. 10, 1909, p. 1.
34. "Obtained a Most Valuable Homestead," *MHN*, Dec. 15, 1909, p. 3.
35. "High Prices for Medicine Hat Land," *MHN*, May 26, 1910, p. 1.
36. "Another Homestead Rush," *The Financial Post of Canada*, Jan. 15, 1910, p. 4; Alyce Butterwick, ed., *Shortgrass Country: A History of Foremost and Nemiskam* (Foremost Historical Society, 1975), p. 5.
37. Butterwick, *Shortgrass Country*, pp. 6–13.
38. Canada, Department of the Interior, *Annual Report for 1910*, p. 26.
39. Ibid., *Annual Report for 1911*, p. 38; "The Rush Is On," *MHN*, June 2, 1910, p. 1.
40. *Canada Census* 1911, pp. 376–77. See also Howard and Tamara Palmer, eds., *Peoples of Alberta—Portraits of Cultural Diversity* (Saskatoon: Western Producer Prairie Books, 1985), p. xiv.
41. "Medicine Hat's Growth in 1909," *MHN*, Dec. 30, 1909, p. 1.
42. "Hat Leads Canada By Big Margin in Building Increase," *MHN*, Jan. 25, 1912.
43. "More Steel Was Laid in Alberta During 1912 Than in All Other Provinces of Canada Together," *MHN*, Apr. 10, 1913, p. 3.

44. "Medicine Hat Is Talked of Most of All," *MHN*, Mar. 6, 1913, p. 12.

45. F. M. Ginther to James McDonald, Mar. 3, 1913, box 20, f 2, Ginther Papers, Medicine Hat Archives. See also table 1 in the appendix.

46. "Builders of Medicine Hat, F. M. Ginther," *The Medicine Hat Manufacturer*, n.d., p. 7, Ginther Inventory, Ginther Papers, Medicine Hat Archives.

47. "Realty Organization That Is Headed by Man of Experience Who Has Always Believed in Hat," *MHN*, Feb. 15, 1913, Ginther Inventory, Ginther Papers, Medicine Hat Archives.

48. Environment Canada, Atmospheric Services.

49. *We Sell the Earth* (Medicine Hat: F. M. Ginther Land Co., 1912), pp. 21–22, box 23, f 9, Ginther Papers, Medicine Hat Archives.

50. *Sunny Southern Alberta* (Medicine Hat: F. M. Ginther Land Co.), p. 6, box 20, f 9, Ginther Papers, Medicine Hat Archives.

51. "Realty Organization . . ."

52. "What Is Medicine Hat's Industrial Backing?" *MHN*, Nov. 13, 1913, p. 2.

53. Ginther to McDonald, Mar. 3, 1913.

54. F. M. Ginther to A. McGillivary, Aug. 25, 1913, box 20, f 2, Ginther Papers, Medicine Hat Archives.

55. F. M. Ginther to John Greenlees, Mar. 3, 1913, box 20, f 2, Ginther Papers, Medicine Hat Archives.

56. F. M. Ginther to William Essery, Sept. 9, 1913, box 20, f 2, Ginther Papers, Medicine Hat Archives.

57. F. M. Ginther to Editor, Oct. 29, 1913, box 20, f 8, Ginther Papers, Medicine Hat Archives.

3 Glimpses of the Shortfall

1. Chester B. Beaty, *The Landscapes of Southern Alberta: A Regional Geomorphology* (Lethbridge, Alta.: University of Lethbridge Production Services, 1975), pp. 63–66.

2. Alberta, *Annual Reports of the Department of Agriculture;* Alberta Climate clippings file, "Weather Extremes Reports," GAA; Canada, Atmospheric Environment Services; Canada, *Temperature and Precipitation: 1941–1970 Prairie Provinces* (Department of the Environment: Atmospheric Environment Services, 1972), p. 40, *et passim;* Lethbridge Research Station.

3. Nels Anderson interview, May 24, 1984, Brooks, Alberta.

4. Alix Board of Trade, *Alix: The Centre of Alberta, The Garden of the West* (Alix: Alix Free Press, 1911); see also Calvin Goss, "The Valley of the Bow," *The Brooks Banner*, Dec. 1, 1910.

5. *Winnifred, Our Trails, Trials and Memories* (Maleb: 1965), p. 52.

6. Mary Steigel, "The Tony Steigel Sr. Family," in Richmound Historical Society, *Richmound Heritage* (Altona: Friesen, 1978), p. 37.

7. "The Details of Tragic Death of Man and Wife Suffocated in a Dugout," *MHN*, Mar. 9, 1911, p. 1.

8. "Three Settlers Frozen to Death," *MHN*, Feb. 9, 1911, p. 1.

9. Augustus S. McLean interview, Nov. 20, 1957, by Una MacLean, MacLean papers, GAA; Helen D. Howe, *Seventy-Five Years Along the Red Deer River* (Altona: Friesen, 1971), p. 125.

10. Lomond Book Committee, *History of Lomond and District* (Lethbridge: Southern Printing, 1966), p. 162.

11. John Julius Martin, *The Prairie Hub* (Strathmore: *The Strathmore Standard*, 1967), p. 170; S. Evangeline Warren, *Seventy South Alberta Years* (Ilfracombe: Stockwell, 1960), pp. 97–99.

12. Martin, *The Prairie Hub*, pp. 140, 170.

13. R. S. Tribe, "Just One Man's Life in the Canadian West," 1963, 1965, pp. 39–40, GAA.

14. Mary Elizabeth (Hart) Mohl, "The Hart Family Story," in Book Club Committee, *Roads to Rose Lynn* (Intercollegiate Press, 1978), pp. 114–15.

15. Charles Seefeldt interview, Nov. 20, 1957, Cessford, by Una MacLean, Una MacLean papers, GAA.

16. "Prairie Fire Sweeps by Hanna," *HH*, Jan. 3, 1913, p. 1.

17. "Emmanual Hagel Homestead," in Schuler History Committee, *Saga of Schuler Stalwarts* (Schuler: 1973), p. 56.

18. Thelma Dennis, "Rural Housing in Alberta, 1880–1920," paper presented to Rural Conference, Victoria, B.C., Feb. 1984; Paul Voisey, "A Mix-Up Over Mixed Farming: The Curious History of the Agricultural Diversification Movement in a Single Crop Area of Southern Alberta," in David C. Jones and Ian MacPherson, eds., *Building Beyond the Homestead* (Calgary: University of Calgary Press, 1985), p. 192.

19. Tribe, "Just One Man's Life . . .," p. 38.

20. *Winnifred, Our Trails, Trials and Memories*, p. 62.

21. Bindloss Pioneer Committee, *Golden Memories, 1912–1963* (Bindloss Pioneer Committee, 1963), p. 65.

22. Tribe, "Just One Man's Life . . .," pp. 38–40.

23. *Roads to Rose Lynn*, p. 127.

24. Pendant d'Oreille Lutheran Church Women, *Prairie Footprints* (Val Printing, 1970), pp. 79, 184.

25. *Golden Memories*, p. 65.

26. "Killed at Bow Island," *MHN*, June 9, 1910, p. 1.

27. *History of Lomond and District*, p. 85.

28. Neil Rutherford interview, May 2, 1984, Bowell, Alberta.

29. "Homesteader Killed Instantly When At the Bottom of His Well," *MHN*, Mar. 6, 1913, p. 1.

30. Nels Anderson interview.

31. E. L. Landorph, "Western Railroads and Their Water Supplies," in *More and Better Water For our Farms and Rural Communities*, Report of Conference at Lethbridge, June 22, 1917, RG 15, Vol. 1280, f 586849, PAC.

32. *The Carlstadt News*, Oct. 31, 1912.

4   Carlstadt, Star of the Prairie

1. "Seven Persons, Alberta," *MHN*, Mar. 9, 1911.
2. "Grassy Lake," *MHN*, Dec. 23, 1909, p. 5.
3. William Raisbeck to John Perrie, Aug. 1, 1916, f 1170b, 74.174, PAA; "Grassy Lake Is To Have A Newspaper," *LH*, Sept. 16, 1909, p. 3.
4. *Prairie Census* 1936, p. 835.
5. William Raisbeck to Minister of Municipal Affairs, June 4, 1912, f 1170c, 74.174, PAA.
6. Deputy Minister to Raisbeck, June 28, 1912, f 1170c, 74.174, PAA.
7. "Rapid Growth," *The Financial Post of Canada*, Jan. 8, 1910, p. 19.
8. "Suffield's New Hotel," *MHN*, Oct. 20, 1910.
9. "Suffield," *MHN*, Dec. 1, 1910, p. 1.
10. "The Real Estate Business," *Carlstadt Progress*, Feb. 29, 1912.
11. Nels Anderson interview.
12. "Carlstadt," *MHN*, Sept. 23, 1909, p. 8.
13. Ibid., Sept. 2, 1909, p. 7.
14. Ibid., Sept. 23, 1909, p. 8.
15. Bertha (Swanby) Hostland interview, Jan. 3, 1985, Calgary, Alberta.
16. Ibid.
17. "Carlstadt," *MHN*, Jan. 6, 1910, p. 11.
18. "Carlstadt," *The Times*, Feb. 15, 1910.
19. Ibid., Mar. 29, 1910.
20. Ibid., May 3, 1910.
21. CPR land sales records, Carlstadt, Vols. 51, 70, CPR papers, GAA.
22. "Introductory," *Carlstadt Progress*, Dec. 28, 1911.
23. "Climate and Resources," *Carlstadt Progress*, Feb. 22, 1912.
24. "The Real Estate Business."
25. "Carlstadt," *Carlstadt Progress*, Feb. 29, 1912.
26. Editorial, *Carlstadt Progress*, Mar. 7, 1912.
27. "The Real Estate Business."
28. "Introductory."
29. Kalgos, "Valley o[f] The Bow," *Carlstadt Progress*, June 13, 1912.
30. "Wheat Is Driving the Cattle Out," *Calgary Daily Herald*, Aug. 10, 1909, pp. 1, 4.
31. Kalgos, "The Rancher's Lament," *Carlstadt Progress*, July 18, 1912.
32. "A New Editor at the Helm," *The Carlstadt News*, Aug. 1, 1912.
33. A. J. Stevens to Minister of Public Works, Jan. 29, 1911, f 1211c, 74.174, PAA.
34. *Prairie Census* 1936, p. 856; Nels Anderson interview.
35. S. F. McEwen to Department of Municipal Affairs, Mar. 12, 1912, f 1211c, 74.174, PAA.
36. Certificate of title, OD125, Nov. 1, 1910, Land Titles Office, Calgary.
37. Ibid., SV100, May 30, 1913.
38. "As We See It," *The Carlstadt News*, Dec. 19, 1912.
39. "The Carlstadt News Advertisers' Directory," *The Carlstadt News*, June 26,

1913; "Busy Burg Business Directory," *The Carlstadt News,* Sept. 5, 1912; *The Carlstadt News,* Feb. 25, 1914.

40. F. J. Conn, diary, Feb. 14, Apr. 7, Oct. 31, Nov. 12, 1913, GAA.

41. "The Centres of the Medicine Hat District: Carlstadt," *The Times,* Feb. 28, 1911, p. 29; "Carlstadt," *The Times,* April 11, 1911.

42. *Canada Census* 1921, pp. 524.

43. Ibid., pp. 738–39.

44. Nels Anderson interview.

45. "Chinatown Charred," *The Carlstadt News,* Oct. 10, 1912.

46. "Local and General," *The Carlstadt News,* Nov. 14, 1912.

47. "City and Country," *The Carlstadt News,* Nov. 5, 1914.

48. "Carlstadt Loses Leading Citizen," *MHN,* June 11, 1914, p. 8; "H. R. Bean Taken by Death, Sunday," *The Carlstadt News,* June 11, 1914.

49. Village minutes, May 10, 1911; Jan. 18, 1912, 74.503, PAA.

50. Minister of Municipal Affairs Order 10928, Oct. 21, 1912; village minutes, Oct. 11, 1912, 74.503, PAA.

51. Alberta (Wagner) Pinsen interview, Nov. 10, 1984, Duncan, B.C. by phone. Mrs. Pinsen is Bert's daughter.

52. C. England to C. R. Mitchell, Dec. 16, 1910; JP 849, C. H. Wagner, 69.210, PAA.

53. Village minutes, Aug. 15, 1913.

54. Ibid., Dec. 27, 1913.

55. "Dedication of a New Church at Carlstadt," *Occasional Paper of the Qu'Appelle Church Quarterly,* no. 114 (Spring 1914): 22–24.

56. Village minutes, Mar. 2, 1914.

57. Ibid., Mar. 16, 1914.

58. "Farmer's Hotel Burns to Ground," *The Carlstadt News,* June 25, 1914.

59. "Council Meets," *The Carlstadt News,* June 25, 1914.

60. Village minutes, June 29, 1914.

61. "Whole Block Wiped Out in Mid-Night Fire," *The Carlstadt News,* Aug. 13, 1914; "Carlstadt Had $20,000 Blaze," *MHN,* Aug. 13, 1914, p. 8.

62. D. L. Hogan to H. E. Hume, Feb. 4, 1933, RG 15, 2005, PAC.

63. "Carlstadt's New Name," *MHN,* May 27, 1915, p. 1; "Alderson Is New Name of Carlstadt," *MHN,* June 24, 1915, p. 2; "Alderson," *MHN,* Dec. 22, 1927, p. 7. Following an unconfirmed report that German residents of Prussia, Saskatchewan, had named a boulevard "Lusitania" to commemorate the sinking of the big liner, the Army and Navy Veterans' Association of Regina sent a delegation to the outpost to demand that it change the insulting title of the town and the Teutonic names of its streets including, "Prussia," "Hanover," "Wilhelm," and "Kaiser." The visit was "entirely successful," and soon "Prussia" became "Leader," Saskatchewan. ("Veterans Sending a Delegation to Prussia," *Regina Leader Post,* Sept. 14, 1917, p. 10; "Veterans Visit to Prussia, Sask. Most Successful," *Regina Leader Post,* Sept 19, 1917, p. 10.)

64. "Farewell to Mr. & Mrs. Wagner," *The Carlstadt News,* Dec. 24, 1914.

65. Alberta (Wagner) Pinsen interview.
66. Lieut. C. H. Wagner letter to Editor W. D. MacKay, "Harry Wagner Writes," *The Alderson News*, June 15, 1916.
67. "Alderson," *MHN*, Nov. 30, 1916, p. 7.

5   Motoring on the Boulevard of Sunnynook

1. "He Lived a Noble Life and Died For Us," *HH*, May 3, 1917, p. 1.
2. "More Local Men Mentioned in the Casualty Lists," *HH*, May 24, 1917, p. 1.
3. "Four Brothers Lay Down Their Lives," *HH*, Jan. 8, 1919, p. 1.
4. "Etzikom," *MHN*, Dec. 7, 1916, p. 8.
5. "The Triumph of German," *HH*, Nov. 9, 1916.
6. Edna D. Norton, "The Mother's Story," *The Alderson News*, Mar. 8, 1917.
7. "Agriculture and Conscription," *HH*, Aug. 9, 1917, from *The Farmer's Advocate*.
8. "Farmers Protest Against Draft," *HH*, May 9, 1918, p. 1.
9. Alberta Provincial Police, *Annual Report, 1919*, p. 18.
10. C. W. Peterson, *Wake Up, Canada! Reflections on Vital National Issues* (Toronto: Macmillan, 1919), p. 1.
11. Canada, *Debates of the House of Commons*, 1912–13, Vol. cviii, pp. 2149–55.
12. Saskatchewan, *Royal Commission of Inquiry into Farming Conditions* (Regina: King's Printer, 1921), p. 34. See also fig. 2, and table 4 in the appendix.
13. *Canada Census 1936*, pp. 840–67; *Prairie Census* 1916, pp. 288–90. Number of farms calculated include all of Bow River, Lethbridge, Macleod, and Medicine Hat districts; one-quarter of Red Deer and Battle River districts; and one-third of Calgary East district. See also fig. 1 and table 1 in the appendix.
14. *Prairie Census* 1916, pp. 292–95.
15. Ibid., pp. 288–90, 292.
16. Ibid., p. 292; Saskatchewan, *Royal Commission of Inquiry into Farming Conditions*, p. 34.
17. "Saskatchewan's Big Year," (1915), DMA vi.i, part 11, SAB.
18. "Bountiful Southern Alberta," *The Agricultural Gazette of Canada*, 2 (Dec. 1915): 1139, quoting E. F. Hutchings in *The Monetary Times*. See also tables 11–14 in the appendix.
19. "Wonderful Crops Seen By Hatters," *MHN*, Aug. 26, 1915, p. 2.
20. R. Huisman, Jr., letter to editor, "Communication," *The Alderson News*, Apr. 13, 1916. See also table 13 in the appendix.
21. Environment Canada, Atmospheric Services. See also table 10 in the appendix.
22. Nels Anderson interview.
23. *Golden Jubilee Empress 1914–1964*, [Empress, Alta. 1964], pp. 6, 16; "Busy Empress," *MHN*, May 7, 1914, p. 8; *Prairie Census* 1936, p. 856.
24. A. D. Fidler to John Perrie, Jan. 15, 1917, f 1061b, 74.174, PAA.
25. Ira Lapp interview, Dec. 21, 1984, Brooks, Alberta.

26. Alyce Butterwick, ed., *Shortgrass Country: A History of Foremost and Nemiskam* (Foremost Historical Society, 1975), pp. 92–93.
27. "Pokawki," *[sic]*, *MHN*, Nov. 4, 1915, p. 8.
28. Arthur Woolley to Secretary, Survey Board for Southern Alberta, Feb. 15, 1922, Table XXI.
29. Wilfrid Eggleston, *While I Still Remember* (Toronto: Ryerson Press, 1968), pp. 9–10.
30. Ibid., pp. 15–17.
31. ARA 1916, p. 165.
32. "Pre-War Days Are Quickly Resumed," *HH*, Oct. 9, 1919, p. 1.
33. "Returned Soldiers Welcomed at Clivale," *HH*, Oct. 9, 1919, p. 1.
34. "Burfield," *HH*, May 1, 1919, p. 8.
35. "Fraserton Plowing Bee," *HH*, May 15, 1919, p. 8.
36. "New CPR Lines on the Prairies," *Calgary News Telegram*, Jan. 25, 1913, Glenbow Railways clipping file, GAA; "New Branch CPR Running North from Medicine Hat," *MHN*, Mar. 18, 1920, p. 3.
37. W. Pearce to Mr. Dennis, Aug. 2, 1912, 9/2/6/3/21, Pearce Papers, UAA.
38. W. Pearce to W. A. James, July 1913, [n.d.], Pearce Papers 74-169-332.1, UAA.
39. "Canadian Pacific Will Run Line Along Red Deer," *HH*, Mar. 13, 1919, p. 1.
40. "South Country Has Good Claim for Hanna-Medicine Hat Line," *HH*, Apr. 4, 1918, p. 1.
41. "Steel Is Going Down on Hanna-Hat Route," *HH*, Feb. 20, 1919, p. 1.
42. "Sunnynook," *HH*, Apr. 24, 1919, p. 6.
43. Ibid., May 29, 1919, p. 8.
44. Ibid., July 17, 1919, p. 6; ibid., Sept. 18, 1919, p. 8; "Rose Lynn," *HH*, Sept. 18, 1919, p. 8.
45. "Konowall," *HH*, Jan. 8, 1920, p. 6.
46. "Hammers Humming in Hanna," *HH*, Nov. 18, 1920, p. 1.
47. "Business Directory of Hanna, 1920," *HH*, Mar. 4, 1920, p. 2; *Prairie Census* 1936, p. 816.
48. "Hanna-Hat RR and Its Towns Are Booming," *HH*, Dec. 23, 1920, p. 1.
49. "Cessford Throbs with Strength of Age and Enthusiasm of Youth," *HH*, Feb. 3, 1921, p. 4; "Has Great Faith in Town and District," *HH*, Feb. 3, 1921, p. 4.
50. "Pollockville Forging to the Front," *HH*, Dec. 23, 1920, p. 1; "Putting Pollockville and Hanna-Hat Line on Map," *HH*, Jan. 27, 1921, pp. 4–5.
51. "Carolside Special Section," *HH*, Feb. 12, 1920, p. 6.
52. "Washee Washee!!" *HH*, Jan. 20, 1921, p. 2; "The White Restaurant," *HH*, Jan. 20, 1921, p. 2.

6   In the Thrill Zone of the On Rushing Calamity

1. "Sunnynook Is Everything Its Radiant Name Would Indicate," *HH*, Jan. 20, 1921, p. 2.

2. W.J. Winning, Cessford, Alberta, paraphrased testimony before Southern Alberta Survey, Dec. 16, 1921, Hanna hearing, f 43c, 69.289, PAA.

3. "Tax Sale," *HH,* Sept. 1, 1921, p. 3.

4. "Tax Sale," *HH,* Oct. 13, 1921, p. 6.

5. "UFA Locals Asked to Co-Operate in Distribution of Relief to Settlers in Drought Area South of Hanna," *HH,* Mar. 4, 1920, p. 1.

6. "Seed Grain Needed in Flowerdale M.D. Outlook Is Very Bad," *HH,* Mar. 25, 1920, p. 1.

7. ARA 1919, p. 10; "Hatton," *MHN,* Feb. 19, 1920, p. 8.

8. "Trying to Run . . .," *The Carlstadt News,* Dec. 31, 1914.

9. "Personal," *The Alderson News,* Dec. 20, 1917.

10. Arthur Woolley to Secretary, Survey Board for Southern Alberta, Feb. 15, 1922, Table XXI, confidential, f 43b, 69.289, PAA. See also tables 12 and 13 in the appendix.

11. "Alderson," *MHN,* Apr. 20, 1916, p. 7.

12. Editorial, *The Alderson News,* July 4, 1918.

13. Ibid., July 25, 1918; "It Has Come," *The Alderson News,* July 18, 1918.

14. Inga (Carlson) Parkkari interview, Dec. 29, 1984, Calgary, Alberta.

15. Burials on the Carlstadt Circuit, in possession of author.

16. "Alderson," *MHN,* July 16, 1919, p. 3.

17. Inga (Carlson) Parkkari interview.

18. "Alderson Is Swept By Disastrous Fire, Loss About $75,000," *MHN,* Aug. 25, 1919, p. 1; "People of Alderson Have Good Idea of What Real War Is Like," *MHN,* Aug. 27, 1919, p. 1.

19. "John Goehring Meets Death in Drowning," *The Alderson News,* Aug. 16, 1917.

20. Inga (Carlson) Parkkari interview.

21. George A. Steele to Deputy Minister of Municipal Affairs, Dec. 13, 1920, f 1211b, 74.174, PAA.

22. "Alderson," *MHN,* Nov. 20, 1919, p. 7.

23. Lillian Ost, *Seven Persons, One Hundred Sixty Acres and a Dream* (Medicine Hat: Seven Persons Historical Society, 1981 c), p. 17.

24. "Fire Does $125,000 Damage at Sunnynook—Beaver Lumber," *HH,* Apr. 21, 1921, p. 1.

25. "Hatton," *MHN,* Apr. 21, 1921, p. 8.

26. Greg Buekert interview, Jan. 4, 1985, Medicine Hat, Alberta.

27. M. C. Urquhart and K. A. Buckley, *Historical Statistics of Canada* (Toronto: Macmillan, 1965), pp. 345, 359.

28. R. M. Graham to Board of Trade, Toronto, Jan. 31, 1924, RG 17, Vol. 3279, f 559-1 (1), PAC.

29. A. G. Vasseur to Minister of the Interior, Feb. 25, 1922, RG 15, Vol. 1147, f 4650480, PAC.

30. W. Cawdron, Nobleford, Alberta, paraphrased testimony to Southern Alberta Survey Board, Dec. 1, 1921, Lethbridge hearing, f 43c, 69.289, PAA.

31. George Coutts, Pandora, Alberta, paraphrased testimony to Southern Alberta Survey Board, Dec. 16, 1921, Hanna hearing, f 43c, 69.289, PAA.

32. A. Stewart and W. D. Porter, *Land Use Classification in the Special Areas of Alberta* (Dominion Department of Agriculture, 1942), pp. 36, 61.

33. Environment Canada, Atmospheric Environment Services, Calgary, Winnipeg. See also table 7 in the appendix.

34. B. Russell and W. H. Snelson, *Report on Southern Alberta Drought Area* (Department of the Interior, 1924), appendix. Tilley East Commission, 1926, p. 17. See also tables 8 and 9 in the appendix.

35. Environment Canada, Atmospheric Environment Services, Calgary, Alberta. See also table 10 in the appendix.

36. Woolley to Secretary, Feb. 15, 1922, Table XVIII. See also table 11 in the appendix.

37. Stewart and Porter, *Land Use Classification* . . ., p. 43. See also fig. 4 in the appendix.

38. Helen D. Howe, ed., *Seventy-Five Years Along the Red Deer River* (Calgary: Friesen, 1971), pp. 152–53.

39. Arthur Ion, diary, Aug. 19, 1919.

40. Pendant d'Oreille Lutheran Church Women, *Prairie Footprints* (Val Printing, 1970), p. 96; ARA 1920, p. 35.

41. H. E. R. Davies, Enchant, Alberta, paraphrased testimony to Southern Alberta Survey Board, Dec. 8, 1921, Enchant hearing, f 43c, 69.289, PAA.

42. Wilhelm Kowalewski to honourable Sir, June 25, 1921, DMA xxiii.i, SAB.

43. ARA 1920, p. 35; Report of Committee Appointed to Investigate Farming Conditions in Southwestern Saskatchewan and Southern Alberta, Calgary, Aug. 14, 1921, f 42, 69.289, PAA.

44. "Gophers As Bad As Drought," *The Farmer's Advocate and Home Journal*, Aug. 6, 1919, p. 1263.

45. "Gopher Killing Contest," *MHN*, Aug. 5, 1915, p. 7.

46. *Prairie Footprints*, p. 71.

47. Arthur Ion, diary, Nov. 18, Dec. 3, 1926.

48. Bow Island Lion's Club Book Committee, *Silver Sage: Bow Island 1900–1920* (1972), p. 311; *Winnifred, Our Trails, Trials and Memories*, p. 21; "Winnifred," *MHN*, Jan. 13, 1926, p. 8.

49. William R. Babington to William Harvey, Managing Director, The Standard Trusts Company, Winnipeg, Dec. 19, 1920, DMA xxii.ii, SAB.

50. G. W. Hess, Flowerdale municipality, paraphrased testimony to Southern Alberta Survey Board, Youngstown hearing, Dec. 15, 1921, f 43c, 69.289, PAA.

51. Mrs. Edward Body to UFWA Calgary, Sept. 15, 1921, f 5a, 69.289, PAA.

52. John M. Kramer to Premier of Saskatchewan, Dec. 13, 1919, M4 19 (3), SAB.

53. Mrs. Reinhard Frerichs to Premier Greenfield, Sept. 16, 1921, f 5a, 69.289, PAA.

54. Canadian Red Cross, Alberta Division, "Report of the Survey Made by the Alberta Red Cross of Conditions in Crop Failure Districts, Sept. 13–24, 1921," p. 7, RCF #437, PAA.

55. Alberta Provincial Police, *Annual Report, 1924*, PAA.

56. Rex vs. William F. Hilsabeck, murder, 1924, Hanna Supreme Court Criminal Files, PAA.

57. Sheriff to Deputy Attorney General, June 23, 1924, Hanna Supreme Court Criminal Files, PAA.

58. P. Pelletier to Sheriff, Judicial district of Hanna, Sept. 18, 1924, Hanna Supreme Court Criminal Files, PAA. For the relationship of conditions to insanity generally, see Provincial Police Commissioner to J. E. Brownlee, May 25, 1925, 79.287, f 10e, PAA; Tilley East Drought Area Investigation, minutes of Cavendish meeting, Mar. 24, 1926, RG 89, Vol. 7, f 5120, PAC.

59. "Hatton Farmer Found Guilty Manslaughter in Maple Creek Trial"; "Sentences Inhuman Father Seven Years Imprisonment on Manslaughter Charge," *MHN*, June 4, 1925, pp. 2–3.

60. "Insane Mother Kills Two Children and Self," *The Carlstadt News*, Oct. 17, 1912; "'Insane'—Coroner's Verdict," *The Carlstadt News*, Oct. 24, 1912.

7   The Sorcerer and the Clouds

1. John Glambeck, "With the UFA Locals in the Dry Belt," *The Western Independent*, Dec. 17, 1919, p. 2.

2. William F. Rabbitt, "What Farmers in the South Are Determined to Do," *The Western Independent*, Dec. 17, 1919, p. 9. Italics in the original.

3. "No Exodus from Southern Alberta," *MHN*, Nov. 2, 1922, p. 6.

4. C. W. Peterson, "The Dryland Pioneer," *The Farm and Ranch Review*, Aug. 20, 1921, p. 7.

5. *Prairie Census* 1936, pp. 848–61.

6. "Farmers Will Fight to the Death," *The Morning Albertan*, Feb. 16, 1921, p. 3.

7. Robert Gardiner biography (1921), box 5, f 64, Walter Norman Smith papers, GAA.

8. Biographies: UFA Members, Alberta Legislative Assembly (1921), box 5, f 64; Alyce Butterwick, ed., *Shortgrass Country* (Calgary: Foremost Historical Society, 1975), pp. 136–37.

9. Butterwick, ed., *Shortgrass Country*, p. 137.

10. Biographies: UFA Members.

11. Butterwick, ed., *Shortgrass Country*, p. 137.

12. "Salvating [sic] the Drought Areas," *The Farm and Ranch Review*, Nov. 20, 1921, p. 5.

13. *Canadian Annual Review*, 1921, pp. 516–17.

14. Seed Grain fodder and Relief Advances, 1876–1926, RG 15, 2005, PAC; Certified copy of a Report of the Committee of the Privy Council, approved

by His Excellency the Governor General on July 27, 1918, PC 1873, RG 17, Vol. 1310, f 262395, PAC; July 29, 1919, PC 1575, RG 17, Vol. 1346, f 267939, PAC.

15. H. R. Earl to Deputy Minister of Municipal Affairs, Oct. 20, 1920, DMA xxiii.i, SAB.

16. Assistant publicity commissioner to Hon. Mr. Hoadley, June 20, 1922, f 5a, 69.289, PAA.

17. Bow Island Lion's Club Book Committee, *Silver Sage: Bow Island 1900-1920* (1972), p. 305.

18. "Over Five Million Dollars Outstanding for Seed Grain Premier Tells Legislature," *Edmonton Bulletin,* Feb. 17, 1923, SH.

19. "Government Paternalism Towards South Country Was Criticized by Leader of the Opposition," *Edmonton Journal,* Mar. 22, 1922, SH.

20. "Relief Plan for South Is Before House," *Edmonton Bulletin,* Mar. 25, 1922, SH.

21. "Provincial Accounts Show Nearly Two Million Deficit; Four Million in Two Years," *Edmonton Bulletin,* Mar. 1, 1923, SH.

22. *Royal Commission on Dominion Provincial Relations,* Province of Alberta, Comparative Statistics of Public Finance, appendix J., p. 8.

23. "Lid Is Closed by Alberta Government on Guarantees, Seed Grain or Relief Doles," *Edmonton Bulletin,* Feb. 14, 1923, SH.

24. J. Melrose to F. H. Auld, Oct. 20, 1920, DMA xxiii.i, SAB.

25. H. R. Earl to Deputy Minister of Municipal Affairs, Oct. 20, 1920, DMA xxiii.i, SAB; C. Lindholm, Iddesleigh, paraphrased testimony to Southern Alberta Survey Board, Dec. 21, 1921, Jenner hearing, f 43c, 69.289, PAA.

26. M. O'Reilly to Premier, June 18, 1922, f 34, 69.289, PAA.

27. J. R. Johnson to Herbert Greenfield [July 1922], f 34, 69.289, PAA.

28. J. R. Johnson to Mr. Higginbotham, Jan. 2, 1923, f 5b, 69.289, PAA.

29. Alex Johnston and Andy A. den Otter, *Lethbridge: A Centennial History* (Lethbridge: City of Lethbridge and The Whoop-Up Country Chapter, Historical Society of Alberta, 1985), pp. 81–82. For early irrigation projects in the Lethbridge-Cardston area see Andy A. den Otter, *Civilizing the West: The Galts and the Development of Western Canada* (Edmonton: University of Alberta Press, 1982), chs. 8, 9.

30. "Dominion Government to Drain Sullivan Lake," *HH,* Apr. 24, 1919, p. 1.

31. E. T. Drake to M. Halladay, Jan. 21, 1920 in "Report Made on Sullivan Lake Scheme," *HH,* Feb. 12, 1920, p. 1.

32. B. Russell and W. H. Snelson, *Report on Southern Alberta Drought Area* (Interior Department: Dec. 17, 1924), p. 13.

33. Rev. J. W. Morrow, Medicine Hat, testimony to Southern Alberta Survey Board, Nov. 29, 1921, Medicine Hat hearing, f 43c, 69.289, PAA.

34. "C.P.R. Contract Farmers Going to South America Unless C.P.R. Accedes to All Their Demands," *Morning Albertan,* Feb. 28, 1924, p. 3.

35. S. G. Porter to D. H. Hays, Dec. 22, 1930, box 24, f 290, CPR papers, GAA.

36. "Salvage Colonization Government Idea on Lethbridge Northern," *Edmonton Journal*, Apr. 7, 1925, SH.

37. Alberta, *Report of the Commission Appointed to Report on the Lethbridge Northern and Other Irrigation Districts in Alberta*, Oct. 1930; V. Meek, et al., "Canada Land and Irrigation Project," 1925, f 474, 69.289, PAA.

38. E. E. Noble, Chinook, Alberta, paraphrased testimony to Southern Alberta Survey Board, Dec. 15, 1921, Youngstown hearing, f 43c, 69.289, PAA.

39. H. C. Ficht, Lomond, Alberta, paraphrased testimony to Southern Alberta Survey Board, Dec. 8, 1921, Enchant hearing, f 43c, 69.289, PAA.

40. "Sudden Death of F. S. Ratliff During Night," *MHN*, Mar. 25, 1926, p. 4.

41. "History and Methods of Hatfield, 'The Rainmaker,'" *MHN*, Feb. 10, 1921, p. 5, from *Wide World Magazine*.

42. Agreement between Charles M. Hatfield and the United Agricultural Association of Medicine Hat, Jan. 12, 1921, DMA xxiii.i, SAB.

43. F. H. Auld to W. C. Gibbard, July 25, 1921, DMA xxiii.i, SAB.

44. Tilley East Commission, 1926, p. 17. See also table 8 in the appendix.

45. "Experts to Produce Satisfactory Rainfall," *MHN*, Feb. 17, 1921, p. 3.

46. "Rainmaker Proposes to Prove Beyond Doubt Rain Follows His Operations," *MHN*, Apr. 28, 1921, p. 6.

47. "No Need to Worry About Lack of Rainfall While Operations of Hatfield Are in Progress," *MHN*, May 12, 1921, p. 3.

48. "Winnifred," *MHN*, May 12, 1921, p. 8.

49. Ibid., May 5, 1921, p. 8.

50. Ibid., May 26, 1921, p. 7.

51. F. W. Gershaw, *Saamis: The Medicine Hat* (Medicine Hat: Val Marshall, [1967]), p. 164.

52. Russell and Snelson, *Report on Southern Alberta Drought Area*, appendix. See also table 9 in the appendix.

53. "Predicts Bumper Crop in Areas North of City," *MHN*, June 28, 1921, p. 3.

54. Russell and Snelson, *Report on Southern Alberta Drought Area*, appendix; Environment Canada, Atmospheric Services. See also tables 9 and 10 in the appendix.

55. F. H. Auld to W. C. Gibbard, July 25, 1921.

56. W. C. Gibbard to F. H. Auld, July 7, 1921, DMA xxiii.i., SAB.

57. "Winnifred," *MHN*, Aug. 11, 1921, p. 8.

58. "Alderson," *MHN*, Aug. 25, 1921, p. 8.

59. "Is Still Medicine Hatfield," *MHN*, Aug. 11, 1921, p. 6.

8 It Does Not Matter How You Farm It

1. Tom Nesmith, "Visions of Eden: Scientific Agriculture and Rural Life at Ontario Agricultural College," unpublished paper, draft, ch. 3, p. 139.

2. John A. Widtsoe, *Dry-Farming: A System of Agriculture* (New York: Macmillan, 1911, 1920), pp. 408–11; E. B. Ingles, "Some Aspects of Dry-Land Ag-

riculture in the Canadian Prairies to 1925," (M.A. thesis, University of Calgary, 1973), p. 12, 28.

3. H. W. Campbell, "Summer Soil Culture," *MHN,* July 22, 1909, p. 8.
4. Professor W. C. Palmer, "Ten Commandments of the Dry Farmer," *Carlstadt Progress,* May 2, 1912. See also Widtsoe, *Dry-Farming;* William MacDonald, *Dry Farming: Its Principles and Practice* (New York: Century, 1911); Thomas Shaw, *Dry-Land Farming* (St. Paul: Pioneer Co., 1911); E. R. Parsons, *Parsons on Dry Farming* (Aberdeen: The Dakota Farmer, 1913).
5. "Summer Rains Are Not Needed," *MHN,* Sept. 16, 1909, p. 9.
6. Reported in R. Fenerty to W. M. Martin, Dec. 15, 1918, DMA xxii.ii, SAB.
7. F. H. Auld to R. Fenerty, Jan. 10, 1919, attached, DMA xxii.ii, SAB.
8. F. H. Auld to R. F. Beckwith, Sept. 20, 1918, DMA xxii.ii, SAB.
9. J. Murray, "The Why and How of Summer Fallowing," address at Western Canadian Irrigation Association Convention, Lethbridge, July 1920, DMA xxiii.i, SAB.
10. W. M. Martin to R. Fenerty, Jan. 10, 1919, attached.
11. Ibid.
12. Alberta, *Report of the Survey Board for Southern Alberta* (Edmonton, Jan. 1922), p. 18.
13. Murray, "The Why and How of Summer Fallowing."
14. R. Fenerty to F. H. Auld, Dec. 15, 1918, DMA xxii.ii, SAB.
15. Mr. Earle, testimony to Southern Alberta Survey Board, Nov. 29, 1921, Medicine Hat hearing, f 43c, 69.289, PAA.
16. James Gray, *Men Against the Desert* (Saskatoon: Western Producer Prairie Books, 1978), p. 74.
17. Bracken, "Soil Drifting," address to Western Canadian Irrigation Association Convention, Lethbridge, July 1920, DMA xxiii.i, SAB. See John Kendle, *John Bracken: A Political Biography* (Toronto: University of Toronto Press, 1979), pp. 23–24.
18. P. M. Abel, "Soil Drifting," *Grain Growers' Guide,* July 28, 1920, p. 9.
19. Medicine Hat Board of Trade, *Medicine Hat,* 1908, p. 10; "Baraca," *HH,* July 3, 1919, p. 10; M. O'Reilly, paraphrased testimony to Southern Alberta Survey Board, Dec. 16, 1921, Hanna hearing, f 43c, 69.289, PAA.
20. E. C. Chilcott, "Dry Farming in the Great Plains Region of the United States," in John Bracken, *Dry Farming in Western Canada* (Winnipeg: Grain Growers' Guide, 1921), p. 301.
21. See for example Professor W. C. Palmer, "Ten Commandments."
22. P. M. Abel, "Some 1922 Summerfallows," *Grain Growers' Guide,* Aug. 23, 1922, p. 7.
23. Lewis J. Harvey to C. M. Hamilton, July 19, 1920, DMA xxiii.i, SAB.
24. John Stewart, paraphrased testimony to Southern Alberta Survey Board, Dec. 1, 1921, Lethbridge hearing, f 43c, 69.289, PAA.
25. G. Harrad to Greenfield, Sept. 20, 1921, f 5a, 69.289, PAA.
26. T. Lannan to Minister of Agriculture, June 29, 1921, DMA xxiii.i, SAB.

27. "Dry Farming Practices and How to Remove Them," *HH*, Aug. 29, 1918, p. 5.

28. J. Bracken, "The Management of Drifting Soils," *Farmer's Advocate and Home Journal*, Jan. 21, 1920, p. 79.

29. C. McConkey, "Winter Rye on the Prairies," *The Farm and Ranch Review*, Aug. 20, 1921, p. 13.

30. F. H. Auld to Henry Lewis, Aug. 9, 1921, DMA xxiii.i, SAB.

31. J. R. Johnson to Herbert Greenfield, [July 1922], f 34, 69.289, PAA.

32. P. H. Tolley, paraphrased testimony to Southern Alberta Survey Board, Dec. 13, 1921, Macleod hearing, f 43c, 69.289, PAA.

33. K. H. Walker and A.E. Palmer, "Grain and Hay Production and Social Service Suggestions," n.d., 1944 c., Lethbridge Experimental Farm Archives.

34. W. H.Walker to Deputy Minister, Feb. 8, 1921, DMA xxiii.i, SAB.

35. T. Lannan to Minister of Agriculture, June 29, 1921.

36. F. H. Auld to Thomas Rennie, Dec. 3, 1920, DMA xxiii.i, SAB.

37. Advertisement, "The Advantage of Mixed Farming," *The Farm and Ranch Review*, Nov. 5, 1921, p. 4.

38. F. H. Auld to Thomas Rennie, Dec. 3, 1920.

39. J. R. Johnson to H. Greenfield [July 1922].

40. Peter W. Harder to F. H. Auld, Aug. 4, 1920, DMA xxiii.i, SAB.

41. Mr. McDaniel, testimony to Southern Alberta Survey Board, Nov. 29, 1921, Medicine Hat hearing, f 43c, 69.289, PAA.

42. Paul Voisey, "A Mix-Up over Mixed Farming: The Curious History of the Agricultural Diversification Movement in a Single Crop Area of Southern Alberta," pp. 16–28, presented to Rural History Conference, Victoria, B.C., Feb. 1984.

43. Mr. Earle, testimony to Southern Alberta Survey Board; Duncan McCuaig, written report to Southern Alberta Commission [1921 or 1922], f 43a, 69.289, PAA.

44. Lewis J. Harvey to C.M. Hamilton, July 19, 1920.

45. R. Hansen to F. H. Auld, June 28, 1921, DMA xxiii.i, SAB.

46. Report of the Illustration Stations for Alberta, 1924.

47. Ibid., 1926.

48. F. H. Auld to J. J. Keeler, July 27, 1921, DMA xxiii.i, SAB.

49. S. E. Greenway, "Much Abandoned Land Seen on Central Alberta Tour," *Free Press Prairie Farmer*, Aug. 18, 1926, p. 8.

50. "Scientific Research in Agriculture," *The Farm and Ranch Review*, Apr. 5, 1922, p. 8.

51. C. W. Peterson, "The Problem of the Sub-Humid Districts, *The Farm and Ranch Review*, June 20, 1923, p. 5.

52. Alex Johnston, *To Serve Agriculture: The Lethbridge Research Station, 1906–1976* (Canada Department of Agriculture, 1978), p. 22; Paul Voisey, "Forging the Western Tradition: Pioneer Approaches to Settlement and Agriculture in Southern Alberta Communities" (Ph.D. thesis, University of Toronto, 1983), pp. 280–85.

9 The Blowing Sands of Financial Ruin

1. E. G. Gordon, letter to editor, "Who Shall Inherit Alberta," *LH*, Sept. 4, 1924, p. 10.
2. J. K. Atkinson to Attorney General, Oct. 13, 1921, f 51, 69.289, PAA.
3. Jacob Schellenberg to Premier Martin, Aug. 3, 1921, M4 I9 (4), SAB.
4. R. N. Mangles, Youngstown, Alberta, testimony to Southern Alberta Survey Board, Dec. 15, 1921, Youngstown hearing, f 43c, PAA.
5. Mrs. F. A. Moir, to H. Greenfield, Jan. 2, 1922, f 5a, 69.289, PAA.
6. R. E. Newton, Retlaw, Alberta, paraphrased testimony to Southern Alberta Survey Board, Dec. 8, 1921, Enchant hearing, f 43c, 69.289, PAA.
7. W. A. Day, Macleod, Alberta, paraphrased testimony to Southern Alberta Survey Board, Dec. 13, 1921, Macleod hearing, f 43c, 69.289, PAA.
8. Tilley East Commission, 1926, pp. 3–9.
9. "Official Report of the Conference between Members of the Government of Saskatchewan and Representatives of Organizations with Respect to the Existing Financial Situation in the Province of Saskatchewan," Nov. 11, 1921, DMA xxiii.i, SAB.
10. Martin to Jacob Schellenberg, Aug. 7, 1921, p. 7613, Martin papers, SAB.
11. Martin to J. S. Carr, Feb. 11, 1922, p. 7877, Martin papers, SAB.
12. Auld to David Stenhouse, Apr. 18, 1922, DMA xxiii.i, SAB.
13. Mangles, testimony.
14. Report of the Commissioner on Banking and Credit with Respect to the Industry of Agriculture in the Province of Alberta, Nov. 1922, *passim*, box 4, f 42, W. N. Smith papers, GAA.
15. Ibid., pp. 6–8, 10–12, 26–29, 43.
16. Select Standing Committee on Banking and Commerce, *Journals of the House of Commons*, 1923, p. 311.
17. T. D. Regehr, "Bankers and Farmers in Western Canada, 1900–1939," in John E. Foster, ed., *The Developing West* (Edmonton: University of Alberta Press, 1983), p. 308.
18. Report of the Commissioner on Banking . . ., pp. 10–12.
19. Annual Accounts Reports, Royal Bank Archives, Calgary, Alberta. See also table 16, in the appendix.
20. "Too Many Foreclosures," *Edmonton Journal*, Mar. 16, 1922, SH.
21. Tilley East Commission, p. 17.
22. William R. Babington to William Harvey, Managing Director, The Standard Trusts Company, Winnipeg, Dec. 19, 1920, DMA xxii.ii, SAB.
23. List of Foreclosures [1922], f 8, 69.289, PAA.
24. Ginther Inventory, Ginther papers, Medicine Hat Archives.
25. Personal Covenant in Mortgages, unsigned memo 1927 c., f 582, 69.289, PAA.
26. E. C. Pardee to H. Greenfield, Nov. 23, 1923; Pardee to Greenfield, Sept. 21, 1925, f 79, 69.289, PAA; "Mortgage Loans Official Answers Attorney General," *Edmonton Bulletin*, Mar. 18, 1924, SH; Lethbridge Board of Trade to J. E. Brownlee, Dec. 10, 1926, f 582, 69.289, PAA.

27. E. C. Pardee to H. Greenfield, Nov. 23, 1923, f 79, 29.289, PAA.
28. Ibid.
29. Bob White interview, Mar. 19, 1985, Brooks, Alberta.
30. Ibid.
31. "Pioneer Albertan E. J. Fream, Dies"; "Outstanding Builder of Farm Movement," *The Western Farm Leader,* May 19, 1950, clipping; Hon. J. E. Brownlee, "Another Member of the Old Brigade Passes: A Tribute," May 19, 1950, clipping.
32. E. J. Fream to J. E. Brownlee, June 21, 1923, including a report on Fream's visit to Regina, f D11, 67.287, PAA. Just who copied whom is a point of some dispute. See "Drought Relief Act Replaced By New Ruling," *Edmonton Journal,* Apr. 16, 1923, SH.
33. Fream to Brownlee, June 21, 1923; Fream to Brownlee, Dec. 10, 1924, f D11, 69.289, PAA.
34. Fream to Brownlee, Dec. 10, 1924.
35. G. J. Keys to E. J. Fream, Mar. 6, 1925, f D11, 69.287, PAA.
36. Fream to Associated Mortgage Investors, Mar. 14, 1925, f D11, 69.287, PAA.
37. "Longer Period to Redeem Property Taken for Taxes," *Edmonton Bulletin,* Feb. 28, 1924, SH.
38. Seed Grain, Fodder and Relief Advances, 1876–1926, RG 15, 2005, PAC.
39. James C. Thompson, provincial auditor, to J. E. Brownlee, June 8, 1926, f 82b, 69.289, PAA.
40. Ibid.; Henry Brace, "Crime Report," Confidential, Aug. 17, 1926; Statement of H. J. Cardell, Aug. 14, 1926, f 82b, 69.289, PAA.
41. "Mortgage Men Claim Restrictive Law is Keeping Money Out," *Edmonton Journal,* Mar. 24, 1924, SH.
42. C. W. Bowman, memo, May 22, 1925, including Peterson's "A Rational Land Credit System for Western Canada," RG 17, Vol. 3279, f 559-1 (1), PAC.

10   Glory, Glory to Alberta

1. "Woolchester," *MHN,* Feb. 19, 1925, p. 8.
2. Jim Sharp interview, Jan. 5, 1985, Medicine Hat.
3. ARE 1921, pp. 38, 45.
4. ARE 1922, pp. 43, 45.
5. Ibid., p. 44.
6. ARE 1921, p. 93.
7. Jim Devaleriola, teacher biography, June 1978, in possession of the author.
8. ARE 1915, p. 133.
9. Alberta, *School Buildings in Rural and Village School Districts* (Edmonton: King's Printer, 1916), p. 8.
10. Lyman school board minutes, Sept. 25, 1926, box 8, f 43, BCSD, GAA.

11. Ibid., Feb. 4, 1927; Mar. 29, 1930.
12. ARE 1922, p. 30.
13. E. B. Swindlehurst, *Alberta's Schools of Agriculture, A Brief History* (Edmonton: Queen's Printer, 1964), pp. 78–82.
14. ARE 1923, pp. 52, 79.
15. ARE 1923, p. 72.
16. ARE 1921, p. 57; ARE 1922, p. 60.
17. Creole Belle school board minutes, Apr. 7, 1919; May 3, 1919; Aug. 23, 1919; Nov. 1, 1919; Nov. 14, 1919; Nov. 26, 1919; Dec. 8, 1919; May 29, 1920, box 4, f 15, BCSD, GAA.
18. Ibid., May 1, 1921.
19. Bow Island Lion's Club Book Committee, *Silver Sage: Bow Island, 1900–1920* (1972), pp. 175–76.
20. E. J. Fream to Dr. F. W. Gershaw, Nov. 24, 1926, RG 89, Vol. 7, file 5120, PAC.
21. M. C. Urquhart and K. A. H. Buckley, *Historical Statistics of Canada* (Toronto: Macmillan, 1965), p. 221.
22. ARE 1922, p. 60; ARE 1923, p. 71.
23. Forcina school board minutes, May 12, 1920—June 25, 1921, box 5, f 22, BCSD, GAA.
24. Charlie McLay to L. A. Thurber, Jan. 27, 1930, box 5, f 22, BCSD, GAA.
25. Arlington school board minutes, Jan. 20, 1923, box 1, f 1, BCSD, GAA; Brown school board minutes, Feb. 9, 1923, box 2, f 9, BCSD, GAA; Jennings school board minutes, Feb. 10, 1919, box 6, f 3, BCSD, GAA.
26. D. C. McEacherne to C. F. Patterson, Mar. 10, 1925, Keystone, box 6, f 33, BCSD, GAA.
27. J. F. Boyce, to L. E. Helmer, Dec. 26, 1927, Britannia, box 2, f 7, BCSD, GAA.
28. *Alberta Gazette,* May 19, 1923, pp. 668–71.
29. Cessford school board minutes, Feb. 9, 1923, box 3, f 10, BCSD, GAA.
30. Connorsville school board minutes, Jan. 14, 1922, box 3, f 13, BCSD, GAA.
31. Arlington school board minutes, Feb. 24, 1927, box 1, f 1, BCSD, GAA.
32. Ibid., Jan. 13, 1928; Feb. 13, 1928; Jan. 14, 1929.
33. Connorsville school board minutes, Mar. 20, 1923; Jan. 22, 1927, box 3, f 13, BCSD, GAA.
34. Creole Belle school board minutes, July 5, 1919, box 4, f 13; Homestead Coulee school board minutes, Apr. 16, 1928, box 6, f 27, BCSD, GAA.
35. Crocus Plains school board minutes, Oct. 7, 1922, box 4, f 17, BCSD, GAA.
36. ARE 1923, p. 72; ARE 1924, p. 72.
37. Perren Baker, "Minister of Education—Hopes and Disappointments," in Alyce Butterwick, ed., *Shortgrass Country* (Calgary: Foremost Historical Society, 1975), pp. 171–74; Baker, "Statement of the Minister of Education in Withdrawing the School Bill of 1930," Perren Baker papers, GAA; L. J. Wilson, "Perren Baker and Alberta's School Reorganization," *Canadian Journal of Education* 2 (1977): 25–36.

38. R. Burton to T. E. Heaton, June 22, 1933, Stanmore, box 2, f 5, BCSD, GAA.

39. "Young People More Self Reliant," *Calgary Herald,* Apr. 16, 1951; "Dr. Thurber Honored at Joint Banquet," *Red Deer Advocate,* June, 1952; "Dr. Lindsay Thurber Dies in Nova Scotia," *Red Deer Advocate,* July 16, 1963, clippings, GAA.

40. ARE 1931, p. 10; *Report of the Legislative Committee on Rural Education* (Edmonton: King's Printer, 1935), p. 20.

41. ARE 1934, p. 56.

42. Mrs. W. H. Greenslade to Thurber, Aug. 21, 1934, box 1, f 2, BCSD, GAA.

43. Rolly Jardine interview, Feb. 18, 1985, Lethbridge, Alberta.

44. ARE 1935, p. 67.

45. Mrs. Fred Galarneau to Thurber, Sept. 6, 1934, box 1, f 2, BCSD, GAA.

46. J. F. Steinbach to Thurber, Dec. 29, 1934, box 1, f 2, BCSD, GAA.

47. Mrs. George L. Williams to Thurber, Apr. 11, 1934, box 1, f 2, BCSD, GAA.

48. T. E. Heaton to T. E. Robinson, Jan. 19, 1934, box 1, f 2, BCSD, GAA.

49. Mrs. J. F. Steinbach to Thurber, Apr. 5, 1934, box 1, f 2, BCSD, GAA.

50. Mrs. Clarissa Dunford to Thurber, Sept. 17, 1934, box 1, f 2, BCSD, GAA; T. E. Heaton to Dunford, Sept. 20, 1934, box 1, f 2, BCSD, GAA.

51. M. Givens to Thurber, Aug. 13, 1935, box 1, f 2, BCSD, GAA.

52. L. Larson to Thurber, Nov. 24, 1934, box 1, f 2, BCSD, GAA; Larson to Thurber, May 4, 1935, box 1, f 2, BCSD, GAA.

53. Edward Kloepper to T. E. Heaton, Nov. 2, 1934, box 1, f 2, BCSD, GAA.

54. N. W. Dornan to Thurber, June 24, 1935, box 1, f 2, BCSD, GAA.

55. Tom J. Tompkins to Thurber, Sept. n.d., 1935; Thurber to Tompkins, Sept. 28, 1935, box 1, f 2, BCSD, GAA.

56. Tompkins to Thurber, Oct. 23, 1935, box 1, f 2, BCSD, GAA.

57. Phyllis Dove to T. E. Heaton, Sept. 12, 1934, box 1, f 2, BCSD, GAA.

58. George Spinks to Thurber, Dec. 24, 1934, box 1, f 2, BCSD, GAA.

59. F. Elwood Finigan to T. E. Heaton, Nov. 27, 1934, box 1, f 2, BCSD, GAA.

60. Mrs. E. C. H. Owen to Thurber, July 17, 1935, box 1, f 2, BCSD, GAA.

61. A. G. Kingcott to Thurber, Jan. 17, 1935, box 1, f 2, BCSD, GAA.

62. F. Blackmore to Heaton, May 1, 1935, box 1, f 2, BCSD, GAA.

63. Alvi Carlson to Thurber, Feb. 19, 1935, box 1, f 2, BCSD, GAA.

64. Cecil Stringer to Thurber, May 6, 1935, box 1, f 2, BCSD, GAA.

65. Mrs. Philip Joseph to Thurber, Mar. 12, 1935, box 1, f 2, BCSD, GAA; Thurber to Joseph, Mar. 20, 1935, box 1, f 2, BCSD, GAA. Snards is a pseudonym.

66. R. H. Imes to Thurber, Aug. 17, 1935, box 1, f 2, BCSD, GAA.

67. Square Deal Citizens' Protest, Sept. 6, 1934, box 1, f 2, BCSD, GAA.

68. Mrs. Henning Anderson to Thurber, July 29, 1935, box 1, f 2, BCSD, GAA.

69. A. G. Kingcott to Thurber, Aug. 6, 1935, box 1, f 2, BCSD, GAA.

70. Mrs. W. H. Greenslade to Thurber, Aug. 21, 1934, box 1, f 2, BCSD, GAA.

71. Rev. Chris Burnett to Thurber, Nov. 19, 1934, box 1, f 2, BCSD, GAA; Burnett to Thurber, Dec. 21, 1934, box 1, f 2, BCSD, GAA.

72. T. E. Heaton to P. P. Solberg, Oct. 19, 1935, box 1, f 2, BCSD, GAA; Solberg to Heaton, Oct. 28, 1935, box 1, f 2, BCSD, GAA; Heaton to Solberg, Oct. 29, 1935, box 1, f 2, BCSD, GAA.

73. Kenneth Chadwick to Heaton, Aug. 23, 1934, box 1, f 2, BCSD, GAA; Heaton to Chadwick, Aug. 29, 1934, box 1, f 2, BCSD, GAA.

74. G. A. Thibault to Thurber, Sept. 1, 1932, box 4, f 22, BCSD, GAA; Thibault to Thurber, Sept. 21, 1932, box 4, f 22, BCSD, GAA.

75. J. T. Ross to Heaton, Sept. 11, 1933, box 1, f 4, BCSD, GAA.

76. Edward Kloepper to Heaton, Oct. 19, 1935, box 1, f 3, BCSD, GAA.

77. T. E. Heaton to Kloepper, Oct. 25, 1935, box 1, f 3, BCSD, GAA.

78. T. E. Heaton to A. G. Kingcott, Jan. 22, 1935, box 1, f 3, BCSD, GAA.

79. ARE 1935, p. 76. See also fig. 5 in the appendix.

11   Desolate Places to Be Buried In

1. "Cruel Blow to Our City Girls," *MHN*, June 3, 1909.

2. Lomond Book Committee, *History of Lomond and District* (Lethbridge: Southern Printing, 1966), p. 99.

3. James M. Roebuck to Premier Greenfield, July 6, 1922, f 5a, 69.289, PAA.

4. Thomas Lannan to Bureau of Agriculture, July 15, 1921, DMA, xxiii.i, SAB.

5. Peter W. Harder to Department of Information, July 17, 1921, DMA, xxiii.i, SAB.

6. Flora Culp Peterson, *Life and She* (Boston: Christopher Publishing House, 1960), pp. 69–71.

7. HGC, Alta., "Will Quit the Dry Belt," *The Nor'-West Farmer*, Feb. 21, 1921, p. 166.

8. "Heaviest Rains in Years Poured Down on Medicine Hat District Last Thursday," *MHN*, June 7, 1923, p. 6.

9. "The Retlaw Farmers," *MHN*, Aug. 7, 1924, p. 4.

10. "Alderson," *MHN*, Sept. 6, 1923, p. 8.

11. "Bow Island," *MHN*, Sept. 3, 1923, p. 8.

12. "Alderson," *MHN*, Feb. 14, 1924, p. 5.

13. "Winnifred," *MHN*, May 15, 1924, p. 8.

14. Ibid., July 17, 1924, p. 7; G. J. Warmink to Herbert Greenfield, July 23, 1924, f 34, 69.289, PAA.

15. "Winnifred," *MHN*, Sept. 4, 1924, p. 8.

16. Ibid., Sept. 25, 1924, p. 7.

17. "Farmers Driven out of Bow Island Area By the Hundreds Thru Drought," *MHN*, July 31, 1924, p. 1.

18. "Bow Island Has Bad Fire," *LH*, Sept. 16, 1924, p. 1.

19. Harold G. Long of the *Lethbridge Herald*, "Living Off The Land," *MHN*, Oct. 31, 1924, p. 5.

20. Ibid., Nov. 6, 1924, p. 5.

21. "Nateby," *HH*, Oct. 2, 1924, p. 1.

22. "Winnifred," *MHN*, Apr. 30, 1925, p. 8.

23. Ibid., May 14, 1925, p. 8.
24. "Forty-Six Hours Rainfall Over Whole of District," *MHN*, June 11, 1925, p. 1.
25. "Winnifred," *MHN*, July 16, 1925, p. 8; July 23, 1925, p. 8.
26. "Bow Island," *MHN*, May 6, 1926, p. 8; May 27, 1926, p. 7.
27. "Winnifred," *MHN*, July 15, 1926, p. 8.
28. "Hail Damages Large Saskatchewan Area," *Free Press Prairie Farmer*, July 21, 1926, p. 6.
29. "Crop Conditions Very Good in South Alberta District," *Free Press Prairie Farmer*, July 21, 1926, p. 9.
30. S. E. Greenway, "Much Abandoned Land Seen on Central Alberta Tour," *Free Press Prairie Farmer*, Aug. 18, 1926, p. 8.
31. "Bow Island," *LH*, July 31, 1924, p. 10.
32. "Winnifred," *MHN*, Oct. 23, 1924, p. 8.
33. "Retlaw," *MHN*, Apr. 22, 1926, p. 8.
34. Calculated from *Prairie Census* 1936, pp. 388–91, 400–4. See also table 5 in the appendix.
35. Ibid., pp. 369, 372–73.
36. Calculated from *Prairie Census* 1936, pp. 848–61. See also table 2 in the appendix.
37. B. Russell and W. H. Snelson, *Report on Southern Alberta Drought Area* (Ottawa: Department of the Interior, Dec. 17, 1924), p. 6.
38. Tilley East Commission, 1926, p. 17.
39. A. K. Buckham to R. G. Reid, July 22, 1922, f 5b, 69.289, PAA.
40. Matt O'Reilly to Hon. Premier, Aug. 2, 1922, f 5b, 69.289, PAA.
41. James Murray, Report of Inspection of Retlaw, Enchant, Travers and Lomond Districts, Sept. 15–19, f 5b, 69.289, PAA.
42. Tilley Historical Society, *Tilley Trails and Tales* (Calgary: Friesen, 1980), p. 164.
43. "Alderson," *MHN*, Jan. 8, 1925, p. 8; R. S. Tribe, "Just One Man's Life in the Canadian West," 1963, 1965, p. 50.
44. "Crop Conditions Very Good in South Alberta Districts, *Free Press Prairie Farmer*, July 21, 1926, p. 9.
45. Harold G. Long, "Living Off the Land," *MHN*, Oct. 31, 1924, p. 5.
46. Tribe, "Just One Man's Life . . .," p. 45.
47. *Canada Census* 1921, pp. 338–39; *Prairie Census* 1926, pp. 527, 612.
48. David H. Breen, *The Canadian Prairie West and the Ranching Frontier, 1874–1924* (Toronto: University of Toronto Press, 1983), pp. 231–35.
49. E. Douglas Hardwick to W. W. Cory, May 10, 1922, Box 11, f 84, Western Stock Growers' Association papers, GAA.
50. D. J. Jennings to Commissioner of Irrigation, Dec. 20, 1924, RG 89, Vol. 7, f 5120, PAC.
51. J. S. Tempest to Director, Water Power and Reclamation, Department of the Interior, Dec. 23, 1924, RG 89, Vol. 7, f 5120, PAC.

52. Acting Commissioner to Mr. Cory, Mar. 20, 1926, RG 89, Vol. 7, f 5120, PAC.
53. G. Hoadley to Premier, July 4, 1927, f 354, 69.289, PAA.
54. "Alderson," *MHN,* July 16, 1919, p. 3.
55. "Alderson," *MHN,* July 24, 1930, p. 7.
56. Andy Gleddie, "Gleddie Family History," in *The Gleddie Family* (n.d.), pp. 17–19, 24–25; Stein Gleddie, "Stein's Story," in *The Gleddie Family,* p. 34.
57. Andy Gleddie, "Gleddie Family History," p. 25; Tryg Gleddie interview, Jan. 4, 1985, Tilley, Alberta.
58. Tryg Gleddie interview.
59. "Bow Island," *MHN,* Apr. 6, 1933, p. 7. I thank Gerry Varty for pointing out this line.
60. *Prairie Census* 1926, p. 702. See also table 3 in the appendix.
61. Ibid., 1936, p. 1174.
62. Ibid., p. 722; ibid., p. 702.
63. Ibid., 1936, pp. 367–69.
64. Ibid., pp. 848, 853, 858. See also tables 1 and 4 in the appendix.
65. Ibid., pp. 722; ibid., 1926, p. 702.
66. Ibid., 1936, pp. 722, 1174.
67. L. E. Helmer, 1934 Report re Berry Creek Area, f 61, 73.307, PAA.
68. H. A. Craig to F. S. Grisdale, Mar. 20, 1935, f 61, 73.307, PAA.
69. James Gray, *Men Against the Desert* (Saskatoon: Western Producer Prairie Books, 1978).
70. A. Stewart and W. D. Porter, *Land Use Classification in the Special Areas of Alberta* (Dominion Department of Agriculture, Feb. 1942), pp. 15, 35, fig. 3.
71. "Alderson," *MHN,* Oct. 18, 1934, p. 7.

12 To Him that Overcometh
1. "Alderson," *MHN,* Apr. 10, 1929, p. 7; May 2, 1929, p. 7; May 16, 1929, p. 8.
2. "Alderson," *MHN,* Aug. 2, 1928, p. 7.
3. "Bow Island," *MHN,* Aug. 25, 1927, p. 7.
4. "Birthday of Chester McCorkle Coffey," *Oregonian,* Jan. 15, 1933, sec. 1, p. 11; "Alderson," *MHN,* Oct. 24, 1929, p. 8.
5. Frank Cole interview, Feb. 19, 1985, Lethbridge, Alberta.
6. Nels Anderson interview.
7. Rolly Jardine interview, Feb. 19, 1984, Lethbridge, Alberta.
8. "Alderson," *MHN,* Apr. 26, 1934, p. 7; May 3, 1934, p. 7; Village minutes, *passim,* 74.503, PAA.
9. Howard Brigham, Jr. interview, Jan. 2, 1985, by phone from Medicine Hat, Alberta.
10. Village minutes, Jan. 3, 1924, 74.503, PAA; photo in possession of author.
11. Photos in possession of author.

12. Len Toole, tape, Sept. 1984, in possession of author.
13. Village minutes, May 30, 1911; Frank Cole interview.
14. Village minutes, Dec. 6, 1920.
15. Frank Cole interview.
16. May Carlson interview, Dec. 26, 1984, Calgary, Alberta.
17. Frank Cole interview.
18. Hazel (Steed) Carlson interview, Dec. 21, 1984, Brooks, Alberta; "Application of Secretary-Treasurer for Approval of Minister," June 12, 1930, f 1211a, PAA.
19. Hazel Carlson interview.
20. Ibid.; "Alderson," *MHN*, Jan. 17, 1929, p. 7; Jan. 24, 1929, p. 7.
21. "Alderson," *MHN*, Oct. 17, 1929, p. 7.
22. Ibid., Jan. 31, 1935, p. 7.
23. Ibid., Sept. 17, 1936, p. 4; "Alderson Postmaster Buried in City," *MHN*, in Mrs. Kate Cole's photo album.
24. "Alderson," *MHN*, Sept. 17, 1936, p. 4; Jan. 7, 1932, p. 8.
25. Hazel Carlson interview.
26. "Alderson," *MHN*, Aug. 20, 1936, p. 8; July 23, 1936, p. 8; Feb. 20, 1936, p. 7; Oct. 31, 1936, p. 8; Hazel Carlson interview.
27. Jim Sharp interview, Jan. 5, 1985, Medicine Hat, Alberta.
28. Frank Cole interview; Hazel Carlson interview.
29. "Alderson," *MHN*, May 23, 1923, p. 5; Feb. 16, 1928, p. 7; Mar. 15, 1928, p. 7; July 5, 1928, p. 7; May 3, 1928, p. 7.
30. Ibid., May 29, 1924, p. 8.
31. Burials on the Carlstadt Circuit; Births on the Carlstadt Circuit in possession of the author; "Carlstadt Child Has Narrow Escape," *MHN*, May 14, 1914, p. 3.
32. "Alderson," *MHN*, July 17, 1924, p. 8.
33. Ibid., Nov. 1, 1928, p. 7; Apr. 13, 1939, p. 9; Dec. 8, 1938, p. 8; H. R. Metz interview, Mar. 1, 1985, Calgary, Alberta.
34. "Alderson," *MHN*, June 13, 1935, p. 6.
35. Ibid., Feb. 19, 1941, p. 1.
36. Ibid., May 10, 1935, p. 6.
37. Ibid., Mar. 4, 1926, p. 8.
38. A. Jaycock to W. D. Spence, Apr. 30, 1926, f 111b, 74.174, PAA; Annual Accounts Reports, Royal Bank Archives, Calgary.
39. "Alderson," *MHN*, Mar. 14, 1929, p. 7.
40. Village minutes, Oct. 20, 1924; July 11, 1927.
41. "Alderson," *MHN*, Aug. 18, 1927, p. 8.
42. Village minutes, Sept. 8, 1927.
43. "Alderson," *MHN*, Jan. 15, 1931, p. 8.
44. Ibid., Dec. 22, 1927, p. 7.
45. Ibid., Jan. 8, 1925, p. 8.
46. H. A. Kidney to Deputy Minister, July 3, 1927, f 1211a, 74.174, PAA.
47. Deputy Minister to H. A. Kidney, Aug. 6, 1927, f 1211a, 74.174, PAA.

48. H. B. Brigham to Deputy Minister, July 11, 1927, notice enclosed, f 1211a, 74.174, PAA.

49. Chief Assessor to H. B. Brigham, July 14, 1927, f 1211a, 74.174, PAA.

50. H. A. Kidney to Deputy Minister, Sept. 5, 1930, f 1211a, 74.174, PAA.

51. H. A. Kidney to Joseph Renshaw, Apr. 26, 1932, f 1211a, 74.174, PAA.

52. H. A. Kidney, Inspector's Report, Sept. 14, 1932, f 952, 74.174, PAA.

53. James Duff to Secretary-Treasurer, Suffield, Sept. 2, 1932, f 1231a, 74.174, PAA.

54. J. W. McLane to R. English, Jan. 15, 1930, f 1231a, 74.174, PAA.

55. F. L. Steed to Deputy Minister, Apr. 22, 1932, f 1211a, 74.174, PAA.

56. Village minutes, June 8, 1932.

57. Acting Deputy Minister to William Hewlett, Apr. 21, 1934, f 1211a, 74.174, PAA.

58. Joseph Renshaw to Mr. Soutter, Jan. 11, 1936, f 952, 74.174, PAA.

59. Village minutes, copy, Jan. 31, 1936.

60. Alyce Butterwick, ed., *Shortgrass Country* (Foremost Historical Society, 1975), p. 137.

61. "Alderson," *MHN,* Dec. 4, 1930, p. 7.

62. Ibid., Mar. 28, 1935, p. 7.

63. Ibid., Feb. 13, 1935, p. 7.

64. Ibid., May 23, 1928, p. 7; Aug. 18, 1932, p. 8.

65. Ibid., Nov. 5, 1936, p. 8.

66. Howard Brigham, Jr. interview; "Alderson," *MHN,* Apr. 26, 1934, p. 7.

67. "Alderson," *MHN,* Apr. 12, 1934, p. 8.

68. "Tilley," *MHN,* Nov. 18, 1937, p. 8.

69. "Postmaster at Alderson Dies," *MHN,* Nov. 18, 1935, p. 5; "Alderson," *MHN,* Nov. 28, 1935, p. 8.

70. "Alderson," *MHN,* Jan. 9, 1936, p. 7.

71. Ibid., May 14, 1936, p. 8.

72. Ibid., Sept. 6, 1934, p. 7.

73. Ibid., Oct. 11, 1934, p. 7; June 21, 1934, p. 7.

74. Ibid., June 7, 1934, p. 7.

75. Ibid., June 21, 1932, p. 7.

76. Dale Cox interview, Mar. 19, 1985, Vauxhall, Alberta.

77. Orland Carlson interview, Dec. 27, 1984, Calgary, Alberta.

78. "Alderson," *MHN,* Aug. 13, 1936, p. 8; Carol Poynton interview, Mar. 19, 1985, Vauxhall, Alberta.

79. Memo, Mar. 19, 1948, f 74, Medicine Hat, Anglican Church Archives, special collections, University of Calgary.

80. "Alderson," *MHN,* June 18, 1931, p. 8.

81. Ibid., June 15, 1933, p. 7.

82. Hazel Carlson interview.

83. "Alderson," *MHN,* Nov. 2, 1933, p. 7.

84. Ibid., Jan. 7, 1932, p. 8.

85. Ibid., Feb. 9, 1938, p. 7.

86. Kate Cole, diary, May 17–26, 1939.
87. "Irvine," *MHN,* June 1, 1939, p. 9.
88. "Alderson," *MHN,* June 1, 1939, p. 9; Hazel Carlson interview, Dec. 21, 1984.

COMMENT ON SOURCES

SCHOLARS HAVE SHOWN little interest in the prairie dry belt disaster centred in southeastern Alberta in the 1920s. No other full length studies exist. The two most valuable works have long been Jean Burnet's *Next Year Country: A Study of Rural Social Organization in Alberta* (1951; 1978) and James Gray's *Men Against the Desert* (1967). The first focuses on the Hanna area in the mid-1940s and models what sociology can do for history; the second concentrates on the struggle of agricultural scientists in the 1930s, and is likely Gray's finest work. The lore of a litterateur is offered in Wallace Stegner's evocation of southwestern Saskatchewan, *Wolf Willow* (1955; 1977); that of an anthropologist is etched in John Bennett's study of the same parts, *Northern Plainsmen* (1969). The former employs fiction as well as nonfiction and extends over a century, however, and both are international, either in scope or application. The Frontiers of Settlement Series, especially W. A. Mackintosh's *Economic Problems of the Prairie Provinces* (1935), is pertinent, but dwells on the general dislocation of the Great Depression. Of the Political Economy Series, G. E. Britnell's *The Wheat Economy* (1939) comments briefly about the 1920s, regarding mostly Saskatchewan. Summaries of the dry belt crisis also appear in Vernon Fowke's *The National Policy and the Wheat Economy* (1957) and Gerald Friesen's *The Canadian Prairies: A History* (1984).

Several books develop various contexts of dry belt history. The geological background is nicely crafted in Chester B. Beaty's *The Landscapes of Southern Alberta: A Regional Geomorphology* (1975). *Southern Alberta: A Regional Perspective* (1972), edited by Frank J. Jankunis, presents several geographical insights. *Peoples of Alberta: Portraits of Cultural Diversity* (1985), edited by Howard and Tamara Palmer, offers the ethnic dimension. *Civilizing the West: The Galts and the Development of Western Canada*

(1982) by Andy A. den Otter adds the early investment and irrigation history. The changing image of the West is well documented in Doug Owram's *Promise of Eden: The Canadian Expansionist Movement and the Idea of the West* (1980) and in David H. Breen's *The Canadian Prairie West and the Ranching Frontier 1874–1924* (1983) which also highlights the relationship between ranchers and sodbusters. Complementing the latter is Don C. McGowan's *Grassland Settlers: The Swift Current Region During the Era of the Ranching Frontier* (1975). The settlement process is covered technically in Chester Martin's *"Dominion Lands" Policy* (1938) and more interestingly in Pierre Berton's *The Promised Land: Settling the West 1896–1914* (1984), though D. J. Hall's *Clifford Sifton*, 2 vols. (1981; 1985) is the fullest account of Sifton's career. A strong depiction of the Prairies during the Great War is John Thompson's *The Harvests of War* (1978). And a penetrating new synthesis of Alberta rural development is Paul Voisey's *Vulcan: The Making of a Prairie Community* (1987).

Three significant American books with varying relevance to the prairie dry belt are: Paul Bonnifield's *The Dustbowl* (1979), Donald Worster's *Dustbowl* (1979), and Douglas Hurt's *Dustbowl* (1981).

The best history of the region's cities is *Lethbridge: A Centennial History* (1985) by Alex Johnston and Andy A. den Otter. Several fine local histories exist—*Shortgrass Country* (1975), *Prairie Footprints* (1970), *The Forgotten Corner* [1981 c.], *Golden Memories* (1963), *Silver Sage: Bow Island 1900–1920* (1972), *Seven Persons: One Hundred Sixty Acres and a Dream* [1981 c.], *Winnifred, Our Trails, Trials and Memories* (1965), *History of Lomond and District* (1966), *Richmound Heritage* (1978), *Roads to Rose Lynn* (1978), *Saga of Schuler Stalwarts* (1973), *Dinosaurs to Defence* [1986 c.], and *Tilley Trails and Tales* (1980)—to name a few I found most helpful. While these works are better on the homesteading period than the abandonment, some were completed after most settlers had left. As such they are remarkable creations that illustrate better than other sources the direction of the diaspora.

No history of Alderson has ever been written. The village minutes have survived, along with correspondence with the Department of Municipal Affairs, the CPR townsite records, and the Land Titles certificates.

Local newspapers, headed by the *Carlstadt Progress* (later *The Carlstadt News* and *The Alderson News*), *The Medicine Hat News, The Lethbridge Herald* and *The Hanna Herald,* are indispensable to an understanding of the rise and fall of the drylands. Unfortunately, these and other local news rags available at the Legislature Library, and the city press (also better on the settlement period than on the exodus) are unindexed. The scrapbook

Hansard of the legislative sessions in Edmonton is indexed, however, and highly informative.

There are several archival sources relevant to a study of the dryland disaster. The best single repository is the Provincial Archives of Alberta. In the premiers' papers there are eight major files on the calamity in the twenties and several others on the continuation in the thirties. Created on an *ad hoc* basis, the former illuminate the government involvement in the Southern Alberta Survey, the seed grain relief, the Debt Adjustment Act, the Tilley East area, and the movement of settlers outward. Valuable submissions on relief and debt adjustment also exist in the attorney general's papers. Particularly worthwhile are the Department of Municipal Affairs papers which cover the disintegration of municipalities and villages. More than with any other issue during the United Farmer regime, the records of virtually every department are permeated with the calamity.

Relevant holdings of the Saskatchewan Archives Board are slimmer, partly because the problem was less severe in the twenties than in Alberta and partly because the rest of southern Saskatchewan was much harder hit during the Depression than the southwest. Uncharacteristic of Saskatchewan archives, a badly filmed and chaotically formatted relief file exists in Regina, covering the twenties. The papers of Minister of Agriculture W. R. Motherwell, Premier W. M. Martin, and especially Deputy Minister of Agriculture F. H. Auld, are nonetheless very enlightening.

Leaner are the holdings of the Public Archives of Canada. At the highest echelons, the priority of the pre-1930 crisis is reflected in the lack of *any* relevant files in the Borden, Meighen or King papers. Department of Agriculture records are largely limited to fodder and seed grain relief while the Interior Department papers stress water resources in the area, grazing matters and resettlement policy. Federal authorities viewed the crisis within the context of prairie difficulties generally, and since most of the land was no longer held by the Interior Department, they considered the problem to be provincial.

The limitation of federal documents regarding the crisis may have been accentuated by the internal organization of the two relevant departments. The main divisions of the Agriculture Department were the dairy and cold storage branch, the seed, livestock, animal health, entomological and experimental farm branches. Except in a slowly evolving experimental sense, such priorities left little room for the problems of cereal production. To a lesser degree, the same was true of the Interior Department which divided into Dominion lands, parks, forestry, reclamation and water power branches. Inherently the timber and grazing subdivision of the lands branch reveals more about ranching than farming, and the reclamation branch says more about irrigation than dryland agriculture.

The several commissions—the Better Farming Commission, the Southern Alberta Survey, the Banking Commission, the Interior Department Report on the Drought Area, and the Tilley East Commission are all illuminating.

Several caches relating to irrigation exist, including the CPR, the Canada Land and Irrigation Company and the Lethbridge Northern, at the Glenbow-Alberta Archives, the William Pearce papers at the University of Alberta Archives, and the Water Resources Branch papers at the Provincial Archives of Alberta and the Public Archives of Canada.

There are several other pertinent collections including the Walter Norman Smith, Una MacLean, Lorne Proudfoot, O. S. Longman, and the Special Areas Board papers at the Glenbow and the Ginther papers at the Medicine Hat Archives.

In sum, the historical sources for a study of the strange heartland of the dry belt are rich and varied, but concentrated where one might expect—in Alberta. There, appropriately, the fullness of the record is commensurate with the reach of the calamity.